To Karen —
Bridge those gaps!

Lynne Lancaster

Advance Praise for The M-Factor

"*The M-Factor* is a must-read for anyone who wants to understand the new Millennial generation that is now running our brave new high-tech world. David Stillman and Lynne Lancaster have written a masterful book on ways to bridge the disconnect between the older generations and the brilliant operatives who have moved into the workplace. It's a great guidebook to the current economic situation and provides smart, real-life solutions."

—Helen Thomas, White House correspondent,
Hearst Newspapers

"Young people ARE transforming the workforce and overall it's for the better, as their culture is the new culture of work. Read this thoroughly enjoyable and well-researched book to understand how to make it happen for your organization."

—Don Tapscott, author of *Growing Up Digital*
and *Grown Up Digital*

"With thoroughly engaging examples and exceptional writing, Lancaster and Stillman move beyond the often-cartoonish characterizations of the kids who grew up in the '80s and '90s and bring to life how their quirks and their strengths will impact the way we work in the '10s and '20s. Their keen insights, vivid storytelling, and practical advice make this a not-to-be-missed book. If you lead and work with Millennials—and very soon that will be all of us—you must take the time to absorb and enjoy *The M-Factor*."

—Jim Kouzes, dean's executive professor of leadership,
Leavey School of Business, Santa Clara University, and
coauthor of the bestseller, *The Leadership Challenge*

"A witty and insightful read that shatters the simplistic and degrading label of the 'entitled generation' and offers a new lens that shows the positive attributes of this next generation. *The M-Factor* provides strategic advice and helps avoid potential misunderstandings of Millennials in the workplace. A must-read for anyone who thinks 'yo—dude' is not the way they want to open the next client meeting."

—Alyson Schafer, parenting expert and author of
Honey, I Wrecked the Kids

"Understanding the Millennials is no longer an option; it's a business necessity. Whether you hire and manage Millennials or are a Millennial yourself, *The M-Factor* will shed much-needed light on the workplace's most promising—and misunderstood—generation."

—Richard Davis, chairman, president, and
chief executive officer of U.S. Bancorp

"Lancaster and Stillman have a laser-eye on the future of talent. Don't just pick up this book and read it! Pick it up, study it, identify your generational blind spots, laugh out loud, and put these no-fail concepts to work . . . in your career, in your home, and in your life."

—Harvey Mackay, author of the *New York Times* #1 bestseller
Swim With The Sharks Without Being Eaten Alive

"Millennials are a rapidly growing part of the nation's workforce and one day soon will be leading our businesses and nonprofits. This readable, informative, thought-provoking book sets the stage for understanding and working well with these new colleagues. Put *The M-Factor* on your reading list."

—David J. Skorton, president, Cornell University

"*The M-Factor* teaches readers the most important lesson they'll need for the workplace of tomorrow: how to turn the Millennials' great expectations into even greater results."

—Brian A. Gallagher, president and chief executive officer,
United Way Worldwide

the M-factor

Also by Lynne C. Lancaster and David Stillman

When Generations Collide

the M-factor

How the **MILLENNIAL GENERATION**
is Rocking the Workplace

Lynne C. Lancaster and David Stillman

HARPER
BUSINESS

An Imprint of HarperCollins*Publishers*
www.harpercollins.com

HarperCollins books may be purchased for educational, business, or sales promotional use. For information, please write: Special Markets Department, HarperCollins Publishers, 10 East 53rd Street, New York, NY 10022.

Designed by Nicola Ferguson

Library of Congress Cataloging-in-Publication Data

Lancaster, Lynne C.
   The M-factor : how the millennial generation is rocking the workplace / by Lynne C. Lancaster, David Stillman
      p. cm.
   Includes bibliographical references and index.
   ISBN 978-0-06-176931-3
   1. Personal management. 2. Young adults—Employment.
3. Generation Y. I. Stillman, David. II. Title.
   HF5549.L2825 2010
   658.30084'2—dc22
   2009043808

11 12 13 14   OV/RRD   10 9 8 7 6 5

To Sharon, Ellie, Jonah, and Sadie Stillman

and

Allan, Danny, Aliza, Hannah, and Bradley Grosh

contents

part three: managing day-to-day

part four: we're all in this together

part one

here come the millennials

one

MILLENNIAL NATION

"I have a wireless router in my trunk. Why don't I go get it?" the fresh-faced intern asked helpfully.

David yanked his head out from under the desk. He had been fiddling with his Internet connection for forty-five minutes while the new summer intern watched politely. Never mind that David had a crick in his neck, a pain in his knee, and had knocked his head on the keyboard tray. Now he didn't even know how to respond.

"Would that help us?" he asked plaintively, blinking dust out of his eyes.

The intern pondered her answer. She did not want to offend her new boss, a Gen Xer who obviously took pride in his technical know-how. On the other hand, if she let him continue grappling lamely with all those wires this could take forever, and she really wanted to make progress on her first day.

She spoke loudly and slowly as if English was David's second

How a Whole New Generation Is Colliding, Clashing, and Clicking with Traditionalists, Boomers, and Generation Xers

language: "Well, if I go get it we don't have to waste time trying to hard-wire everything and both computers can just log onto the network through my router."

David stared at her feeling English *was* his second language. He brushed himself off and there was an uncomfortable silence.

She jumped in supportively: "Don't worry; I don't need it back right now. I have, you know, another one at home."

She gave David an encouraging nod and bounded out of his office. As soon as the intern had disappeared, Baby Boomer Lynne poked her head into David's office grinning happily. After years of feeling like a dinosaur while David tormented her with the latest and greatest technologies, it was finally Lynne's turn to watch David squirm. Her enjoyment was all too brief; the intern was back in a flash. Before either boss could say a word, she dove under the desk, reconfigured the system, leaped back up, and was eagerly awaiting her next assignment. It was 8:45 a.m.

Her name was Debra. And while interns were not exactly new to BridgeWorks, this one seemed alien. What was different? She was a Millennial—our first one.

It was a landmark day at BridgeWorks as we welcomed a new generation to the team. We could only speculate if a company specializing in generational differences could be caught off guard by a single Millennial, what was happening in the rest of the business world?

We see them on the street, in the malls, in school, in our living rooms, and at times in our faces. We watch as they text message, surf the Internet, microwave a snack, listen to iTunes, and download a favorite TV show all at the same time. We wonder if the Millennials can truly do it all and if they'll actually do it a little better than we did. Amidst our musing, it seldom occurs to us that the same people who glared at us across the dinner table will soon be staring at us across the conference table.

The leading edge of the Millennial generation, born between

1982 and 2000, began showing up in part-time jobs in the late nineties, and not only has it made its presence known, this generation will continue being a force to reckon with over the next decade and beyond. As Millennials join Generation Xers (born 1965–81), Baby Boomers (born 1946–64), and Traditionalists (born prior to 1946), the question becomes, will corporate America make the same mistake it made when Generation X showed up on the job?

In the late 1980s and early nineties, when Gen X entered the workforce, companies were blindsided. Employers never expected Xers to behave differently from Baby Boomers or that they would have their own unique expectations about the workplace. From dress codes to rewards programs, Xers railed against doing things the way they had always been done, and companies struggled to adapt. Years later many companies are *still* trying to figure out Generation X.

Flash forward and it's déjà vu all over again as the Millennials make their debut. A whole new generation has arrived in the workplace and surprise, surprise—"the way it's always been done" is getting ready for more renovation.

The Millennials—sometimes called Generation Y, GenNext, the Google Generation, the Echo Boom, or even the Tech Generation—are 76 million strong and compose the fastest-growing segment of workers today. (In fact, this generation is still increasing due to immigration and will likely surpass the 80-million-member Baby Boom generation in size in the 2010 census.) Millennials had barely kicked off their careers when employers started scratching their heads and asking, "Who *are* these people?" Suddenly they seemed to be shaking up everything from how the Internet gets used at work to whether or not Mom and Dad are invited to orientation.

IDENTIFYING THE M-FACTOR

Since writing our first book, *When Generations Collide* (HarperCollins, 2002), we have been traveling the country, speaking and working with organizations on how best to bridge generation gaps. This exposure has allowed us to stay on top of the best and next practices in recruiting, retaining, managing, training, and engaging the generations, and also to spot costly new gaps on the horizon. If there is one large looming gap that we have watched organizations slowly recognize, it's the arrival of the Millennial generation. While they haven't been in the business world very long, they are already challenging the status quo. In fact, in our national survey, when Traditionalists, Baby Boomers, and Generation Xers were asked to name the toughest generation to work with, they all named the Millennials.

The more we explored who the Millennials are and what makes them tick, the more we became convinced that the best way to describe them is through seven key trends that shaped them and accompany them into the workplace. These seven trends make up what we call the "M-Factor." Over time the M-Factor will alter the way all of us work, but in the process, it will create collisions and spawn divisions as the generations bump up against each other vying to find the best way of doing things. The outcome will be a negotiated settlement based on what works. That's how change happens.

We have titled the seven trends that make up the M-Factor: Parenting, Entitlement, Meaning, Great Expectations, The Need for Speed, Social Networking, and Collaboration. While what constitutes these trends is described in detail in the ensuing chapters, each can be explained briefly as follows:

Parenting. Millennials are their parents' greatest protégés and proudest creations. As Millennials enter college and then work, rather than cut the cord, Mom and Dad are buying an extension. From orientation to the first review, Millennials aren't just keeping their folks in the loop; they're taking them along for the ride. Stand back corporate America! When you hire a Millennial you get three for the price of one—here come Mom and Dad!

Entitlement. Raised during the self-esteem movement with plenty of praise, and emerging as teens thinking they can accomplish whatever they want to in life, Millennials see themselves as a desirable commodity often worthy of special treatment when they enter the job market. They have a lot to offer but they also expect a lot, from perks to promotions. How will we set realistic standards that motivate Millennials without undermining the other generations?

Meaning. The American Dream is shifting from "having a job" to having a job that means something. Millennials want to earn a good living while doing work that has value, whether this means contributing to a company, country, cause, or community. As the economy expands, the pressure is on for organizations to connect the dots for Millennials as to how their role fits with the larger mission and how they can find meaning in their work from day one.

Great Expectations. Millennials are showing up on the job with high expectations for fulfillment and success. Unfortunately, the job experience often isn't what they hoped it would be and they change jobs looking for the right match. Traditionalists, Boomers, and Xers are caught off guard also when their expectations for Millennials go unmet. From how to dress for success to how to communicate in a meeting, employers are finding Millennials' skills sometimes miss the mark. The expectation gap between Millennials and the other generations must be bridged if everyone is to succeed.

The Need for Speed. This is a generation that has scarcely known a world without a personal computer. Since early childhood, most have been able to access information, entertainment, or other people at the push of a button. How will the arrival of a new generation of multitaskers change the ways work gets done? When is faster not necessarily better? And how will the workplace handle the speed at which Millennials expect to learn, grow, interact, and advance?

Social Networking. Access to information at lightning speed has taught Millennials to communicate in new ways. They post, chat, link, and IM passionately about politics, religion, pop culture, and life with people they've never met face-to-face. Yet these people are part of the powerful networks through which Millennials operate their lives. Not only is this generation reinventing modes of communication, they are redefining the parameters of personal and consumer relationships. They will be a tremendous force for revamping the ways we gather information, disseminate it, and learn from it, but only if the other generations are assured this can be done in a responsible way.

Collaboration. In school and at home, Millennials have been given the floor to express their opinions. It shouldn't surprise employers that Millennials are going to show up on the job and expect to have a voice. Giving orders is out; candid conversations and give-and-take negotiations are in. The trend goes further as Millennials are pushing for new forms of leadership and decision-making based on collaboration. They have highly developed skills for cooperation and they will bring these to the table, but how will the other generations react to this new way of relating?

As you can see from these brief descriptions, the trends at play as the Millennials enter the workforce are provocative and will challenge the ways many of us do things. While the workplace felt seismic shifts when Gen X came on the scene, we predict those won't hold a candle to what Traditionalists, Boomers, and Xers will experience learning to work with the Millennial generation. At the same time, Millennials will be tested as they are faced with learning to adapt to and thrive in well-established work cultures. Our goal is to frame and explain these trends with the attitude that no one is right or wrong, they're just different. And in these differences lie tremendous opportunities.

GETTING OUR ARMS AROUND THE MILLENNIALS

When the topic of generational differences comes up, it's easy to refer to the gap between "Pet Rocks" and "Pop Rocks." While popular cultural icons play into every generation's identity, we don't plan to chronicle the death of the rotary dial phone. But we do believe that each generation has been shaped by the events and conditions they experienced during their formative years. While some of these are personal, others are experienced broadly by an entire population, such as the Great Depression or the Vietnam War. To get to the heart of the Millennial generation, we needed to explore the forces that influenced them, identify how they see the world, and predict how this will affect their approach to work.

When we pitched a book on the Millennials back in 2005 we were told, "Nobody's interested in them yet." But we didn't let it drop. We've been collecting data, opinions, case studies, and analyses on them ever since. While our research for this book is Millennial-centric it is by no means limited to only what Millennials think and do. With each push to learn something new about Millennials, we studied and surveyed how our findings reflected or conflicted with the attitudes of Traditionalists, Boomers, and Xers. At the same time, we also paid attention to how attitudes changed over the course of an economic downturn. Findings in our book represent viewpoints collected during boom times and also during the decline of 2008–09.

How did we do that? In three ways...

1. Case studies and stories. Because we give keynote presentations and workshops as well as consult and conduct trainer certification programs, we have the opportunity to interview 300 to 500 people from all the generations in various organizations each year. We ask them similar questions. Where do generational conflicts arise in your organization? How do you identify the issues and measure the costs? What kinds of solutions have you devised to bridge the gaps? Our clients range literally from MTV to the IRS and every type of business from Fortune 500 companies to start-ups, educational institutions, health care, and the public sector—so we get a broad perspective. Sometimes the responses are anecdotal, where we might be interviewing recruiters about how the generations differ in the ways they approach the hiring process. Other times they are quite strategic. We might put questions to a corporate HR executive who has measurement tools and numerical targets to help him or her identify what's going on. Either way, we always learn something. Many of our clients generously agreed to allow us to include their examples in this book, but even when they aren't mentioned by name their insights are reflected throughout.

2. Capturing the voice of the Millennials. When we started our business in 1997, leading edge Millennials were just starting to think about that first part-time job. As our business grew and we did more and more interviews, we began hearing *about* the Millennials, but we seldom heard *from* the Millennials. They may have moved up from mowing lawns, but they weren't in positions of authority quite yet. The past few years we've been interviewing Millennials in earnest. When it came time to write this book we asked, how can we go deeper?

The magic for us as a Boomer and an Xer who have been friends and business partners for over a decade is that we feel comfortable butting heads about how we see the world. Since our job here was to better understand the Millennials, we thought, "What better way than to hire one?" We knew this had to be a magical relationship, so we tapped our former intern, Debra Fiterman—now an accomplished participant in the corporate world—to join us. She was charged with capturing the voice of her generation by spearheading a project we dubbed "Millennials on Record" (MOR). The idea was to tap a cross section of Millennials from around the country for in-depth, one-on-one interviews and take a deeper dive into how they see the world of work. Our MORs have provided input on everything from their search for meaning, to their career goals, to how they view the other generations.

Once we captured their voices, we could pull our whole team in to discuss, debate, and debunk ideas about the Millennials and all the generations with which they interact. When our CEO Allan Grosh (Traditionalist), program director Nancy Peterson (Cusper), associate Kel Gratke (Gen Xer), and sales representative and speaker Seth Mattison (Millennial) weighed in and added their perspectives, we knew we had found the right path. Our initial target for the MOR interviews was fifty Millennials, and we've since passed that goal. Not all of them were allowed by their companies to use their names, but their voices are heard in every chapter loud and clear.

3. Putting the numbers behind the ideas. The hardest part of writing about these issues is attempting to quantify generational attitudes. Is there a way to measure how perceptions differ between generations that can shed light on how we manage? We also needed to be careful to ask ourselves whether a particular finding is generational. Lots of factors shape who a person becomes, including gender, birth order, ethnicity, socioeconomic level, geographic location, and country of origin, not to mention individual personalities. For this book we sought out a skilled research partner, the Institute for Corporate Productivity (i4cp), the world's largest vendor-free network of corporations focused on improving workforce productivity (www.i4cp.com). Together we created a comprehensive survey about the generations with a special focus on the Millennials. The survey was designed during the fall of 2008 and conducted during the first quarter of 2009. Over 1,600 individuals responded to our rather lengthy series of questions, and hundreds of them still had energy at the end to write stories about their generational experiences.

Our survey contained a representative sampling of all four generations, across all regions of the United States, with 20 percent of responses coming from outside the United States. We had a mix of ethnicities and our respondents represented a wide variety of industries as well as the public sector and education. The results of the survey are sprinkled throughout. Since it's clunky to refer to the "BridgeWorks/i4cp Survey" every time we quote a finding, we simply call it the "M-Factor survey."

OUR POINT OF VIEW

We've spent well over a decade immersed in studying the generations, and we still see them as individuals with unique dreams and
goals. At the same time we see large social trends that shape and often explain them. As we mentioned earlier, our attitude has always
been that no generation is right or wrong, they're just different. Our
job is to get at the root of the differences and try to offer perspective,
information, and solutions. We understand many of you just want to
be able to look at the trends emerging around you and make sense
of them. Others of you have pressing business concerns you need to
address. Still others are parents of Millennials curious to understand
what makes them tick and what the future holds for them. Or, you
might be a Millennial yourself, interested in gaining perspective on
your own generation or learning how to get along with the others you'll encounter at work. Whatever your motivation, we hope
we've found the right balance of explaining why the generations see
things as they do and what you can do to bridge the gaps.

OCCUPATIONAL HAZARDS

As cultural translators and fans of the generations, we'd like to avoid
the pitfalls we've observed in other writings about Millennials. It's
too easy to go negative and sound a warning cry about the troubling
generation looming on the horizon. The negativity trap is appealing, but it's a big waste of time. New people are always coming into
the workplace and shaking up the way things get done. Along the
way, processes are re-tooled, new inventions are discovered, and
sometimes the status quo is preserved because against all odds, it still
works. That's not to say there won't be challenges. Some Boomer
and Xer authors have written negative books about the Millennials
filled with dire warnings and gloomy prophecies about this next
generation. Some Millennials have published books heralding the

arrival of their generation as saviors who will show the rest of the generations how things ought to be done, taking on a cocky "out with the old, in with the new" attitude. Millennials have lots to offer and they are bound to dazzle at times, but in the end they're going to be just as great and just as flawed as the rest of us. Ultimately, no one generation can do much of anything alone. Those who thrive during the coming sea change—as a huge population of Millennials moves in and millions of Boomers begin to move out— will be the ones who keep learning, stay flexible, and maintain a sense of humor.

A lot of negatives are being hurled at the Millennials right now. They're spoiled brats who have had everything handed to them; they're overprotected kids who don't want to grow up; they're tyrants who have plenty of opinions about the workplace but don't know the first thing about getting the job done. Sigh. It's painful to be the new generation on the block. The Xers can tell you this firsthand. When they came on the scene they were called grungy, tattooed slackers who job-hopped, had no work ethic, lacked loyalty, and would be the first generation that wouldn't do as well as their parents. Yet they rose above, put their own stamp on the workplace, and went on to launch or run some of the most successful businesses in history.

When a generation is new, they threaten us because we don't know them yet. In fact, our M–Factor survey found that 20 percent of Xers actually *dread* the Millennials' entrance into the workplace. The best antidote is to open your mind and take this opportunity to learn about the trends shaping this energizing new generation. Get familiar with the roadblocks and conflicts you can expect. Find some solutions. You might be in for a bumpy ride, but then it might just be the ride of a lifetime.

Ready or not, here they come!

part two

the transition from
life to worklife

two

PARENTING

"Thank you so much for calling," Jan lied. "Uh, huh...OK...will do. Bye now." She hung up the phone looking appalled. Standing in the doorway was her Xer colleague Kevin.

"You will not believe who that was!" Jan announced as her jaw slowly returned to its natural position. "In my eighteen years as an HR executive, I have never!"

"What?"

"Remember Rachel from last week? You know...the new hire who received a poor evaluation from her boss and is now on probation?"

"Sure. The one who wears the iPod."

"Well, guess who just called me to talk more about it? Her mother!"

Now Kevin's jaw dropped.

"Apparently she wants to talk to Rachel's boss and discuss how

Connected Via the
Cordless Umbilical

she can coach her daughter to do better," Jan imitated. "What has happened to kids today? When I was Rachel's age, we were told to sink or swim. If I made a mistake, my parents didn't ride in on a white horse and rescue me."

"What did your parents do?" asked Kevin.

"They let me figure it out!" replied Jan, frustrated. "You can't believe how some of these parents step in to *defend* their kids."

"I would have killed my parents," Kevin commented as he headed back to his office.

Jan let out a sigh and was shuffling papers around when she received another phone call. This one cheered her up. It was her daughter, Zoë.

"Sweetie, it's great to hear from you! Your first week on the new job—how's orientation going?"

"It's a little slow," replied Zoë.

"Well remember," Jan jumped in, "that's what the recruiter told us at the job fair. But hang in there; he said it picks up on day four when you go on the plant tours."

"I'm not worried about it," Zoë answered, "but, I do have a problem."

"Uh-oh, what's wrong?"

"Well, they want us to go online and make elections for all our benefits. I looked at the Web site but there are just so many choices. You're in HR, Mom. If I give you my user name and password can you just log on and set me up with all the right options?"

A couple hours later, with the assignment completed, Jan bumped into Kevin on the way to get coffee.

"Hey," he said smiling, "I can't stop thinking about that mom you told me about."

Jan just shook her head. "I can't believe I'm saying this, but I think I AM that mom!"

Work with a Millennial and sooner or later you'll find yourself working with their folks, too. Parents today are more involved in their adult kids' lives than ever before, and the umbilical cord that connects them is stretching all the way to the office. You might find yourself fielding a call from someone's dad wondering why Junior didn't get the promotion, being grilled by an employee's mother at the company picnic—yes, parents are included in these now, too—or explaining to a Millennial co-worker why it's not OK for his parents to proofread his report. In our M-Factor survey, nearly 40 percent of all respondents said they have witnessed a parent getting involved in an employee's career in a way that seemed out of line. The question is what's out of line?

MILLENNIALS ON RECORD

"I would consider my parents to be two of my best friends. They are definitely who I look to for all of my advice. When I was trying to figure out all the benefits at my job, what should I opt out of, how much should I put in my stock purchase plan...for all those questions, I asked them. Our HR department has been saying that in general the younger people will say they need to call their parents before making a decision on an offer to accept a job. It's great to have these close relationships because they've been where we are before and have made the mistakes so we can learn from them."

— *Ashley Strub, age 24, allergy consultant, ALK-Abelló*

Mom and Dad have been on the job from colic to college and are now headed for the company. As Millennials navigate perhaps the trickiest transition of their lives, it's only natural they would want their most experienced and trusted advisors at the helm. Millennials are five times more likely than Boomers or Xers to feel comfortable having their parents negotiate their salary and benefits (M-Factor survey). But for the other generations this can be problematic.

On one hand, there are specific issues to consider, such as how to cope with a co-worker who is too dependent on parental guidance or how to handle privacy issues when a parent inquires about a child's performance on the job. On the other, cultural clashes arise when the Millennials' tight-knit interface with their folks leaves the other generations scratching their heads or deeply annoyed.

One Traditionalist engineer was part of a multigenerational team that did facilities maintenance for a college. A recent Millennial hire had all the right credentials to succeed but seemed to be floundering. He was disorganized and not completing projects. Finally the Traditionalist took him aside to see what the problem was.

"I know I'm not doing great," explained the Millennial. "But I've taken home all the project notes and work orders and my dad is putting them into a spreadsheet so I can organize my time better."

The Traditionalist was taken aback. After coming up through the school of hard knocks he couldn't imagine asking his dad to do his work for him. "What a wimp," he thought, shaking his head. "This kid's never going to make it."

Every generation carries with it certain assumptions about how we interrelate with parents in childhood and how we redefine those relationships as adults. The Millennial in the story above probably felt he'd developed a good strategy for improving his performance. Obviously the Traditionalist felt otherwise. When these values collide, misunderstandings ensue, relationships are damaged, and the work product is affected. It pays to be able to take off your own generational lenses and see how parenting norms have changed as we prepare for a new reality at work.

PARENTING EVOLVES

Traditionalists, aka "the World War II generation" according to Tom Brokaw, author of *The Greatest Generation*, "...were mature

beyond their years in their twenties, and when they married and began families, it was not a matter of thinking 'Well, let's see how this
works out....'" They were the last generation "in which, broadly
speaking, marriage was a commitment and divorce was not an option." Parent-child relationships were often strained as parents—
toughened by a depression and world war—encountered the more
permissive society in which their children were coming of age, "a
time when excess not deprivation, was the rule, when their government lied about a new war, when the concepts of duty and honor
were mocked." They raised their Baby Boomer offspring to believe
they could be anything they wanted to be, but the parents weren't
about to do it for them. Kids were expected to sink or swim on their
own initiative, and it was OK if they learned the hard way by being
dropped into the deep end.

During the time when Baby Boomers became parents, changes
had occurred in society and new rules for raising children had
evolved. Family size became smaller and adults could focus more
attention on fewer kids. Modern psychologists like Dr. Spock began
to tell us we could influence a child's success by taking a more active
role in their development, from reading books to helping with homework to coaching Little League. Boomers rebelled against their own
more authoritarian parents, whose "my way or the highway" style
seemed rigid and unfair. Coming of age in an era where individual
rights were increasingly emphasized, Boomers felt they owed their
kids a fuller explanation than "You'll do it because I said so." As
social restrictions and taboos loosened, it was more acceptable to
talk to children about topics formerly considered "for adults only,"
and Boomers were determined to be more open communicators
than their parents had been. Authoritarianism was out; quality time,
communicating, and collaborating were in.

Gen Xers also were affected by social change as they had children
of their own. Many felt their parents had been unavailable to them
due to long hours at work or because of divorce. The Women's Movement allowed mothers to have more options but it also meant many

women were forced to make tough choices between getting home and getting ahead. Xers who felt lonely coming home after school to an empty house or shuttling between blended families vowed they would be more present in their children's lives. Forget *quality* time, they were longing for *quantity* time. As a result, a recent survey from the University of Texas at Austin found that even though it's Boomers who have been tagged "helicopter parents," Gen Xers are proving to be even more intensely involved (earning them the flattering new name "Black Hawks!"). And don't think it's just affluent or white-collar parents who are guilty of this heavy duty involvement; the same study found that "helicopter parenting appears to cross racial and ethnic lines, as well as socioeconomic status."

Changes in the way people live also triggered new ways of parenting for Boomers and Xers. The rise of the suburbs meant kids were farther from school and activities and needed more chauffeuring. No more grabbing a basketball and heading off to the local park. Today parents spend hours shuttling children from one activity to another. Fortunately, the advent of technology has helped parents struggling to do it all. With mobile phones and the Internet, Mom could actually leave the office in time to get home for dinner as long as she logged on after bedtime. Dad could connect with the kids from his job site via cell phone to help with homework and double check that Junior got to debate team practice on time.

But as much as technology has increased the ability of parents and children to be connected, living in a world that feels less safe has further fueled the rush to stay in touch. All it takes is one school shooting to play out on your television screen and those cell phones and PDAs are set to speed dial. In fact, after the tragedies of Columbine High School and 9/11, many schools dropped their bans on cell phones and pagers in classrooms because parents insisted they have a way to reach their kids in case of an emergency.

One Baby Boomer commented, "I remember being in college when my grandpa died. My parents had no way of getting hold of me other than calling the main phone at my dorm and asking someone to put a note under my door to call home. The day of the Virginia Tech shooting incident, I think I called my son about twelve times. I can't imagine how I would have felt if I couldn't reach him!"

Fears about violence and crime have increased parent-child interdependence. Fewer kids walk to school today or wander the neighborhood unsupervised. Instead parents accompany them to the bus stop and escort them to structured playtimes that not only seem less risky but more educational.

One other subtle factor crept into the parenting equation over the past few decades: the belief we can control the way our kids turn out. In other words, if we do everything right, from receiving the best prenatal care, to obtaining the proper immunizations, to enrolling in the "right" schools, to providing the ideal enrichment activities, we can create outstanding children. The pursuit of this goal has led parents to view their offspring less as kids and more as their greatest achievement yet. Suddenly it's not just a parent-child relationship, it's parent-protégé.

Our M-Factor survey found that of all the generations, Boomers are the most optimistic about the Millennials entering the workforce and the most eager to see what they will be like. That's a plus for the workplace because Boomer parents have a good rapport with Millennials and are likely to relate well to them at work. This is in part because parents have gone beyond being authority figures and role models to also being colleagues and buddies. When it comes to working through challenges, today's parents don't give orders, they consult and pitch in. Whether it's co-authoring a fifth grader's report on South Africa, yelling advice from the soccer field sidelines, or hiring a tutor to improve testing skills, Mom and Dad have been a crucial source of input for the Millennials.

Combine these changes in society with a goal of creating the best brood on the block, and we shouldn't be surprised that we now see a hands-on, heavily involved style of parenting—what Tom Brokaw describes in *Boom* as "the most over-managed generation of children in the history of the planet." It's hard to criticize any parent whose mission is to play an active role in their kid's life. But what do you do when the mission continues in full throttle beyond childhood?

THE FAMILY GOES TO COLLEGE

We saw this with the transition to higher education. Hands-on parenting didn't go out the window when Junior went out the door. Visit almost any university Web site today and you'll find page after page dedicated not to students, but to the *parents*. From college selection to settling in, parents are involved in the process. Now even freshman-orientation programs include a slot for mothers and fathers, complete with their own special handbooks.

For many, this is a new twist. When most Boomers headed off to school, they were lucky if Mom and Dad helped unload the car and

Borgman © 2004 & 2005 *The Cincinnati Enquirer.* Reprinted by permission of Universal Uclick. All rights reserved.

haul the lava lamp up to the dorm room before peeling out of the parking lot and not looking back. Today, parents are so involved in the college process that Winona State University in Minnesota recently rolled out a special course designed by the counseling center. It's aptly titled "How to Let Go," and focuses on teaching parents the skills they need to support their child without micromanaging.

When Boomers wanted to communicate with their own parents, making long distance calls from school was a big deal. They waited patiently until after 9:00 p.m. on weekdays to get the best rates. And dads constantly nudged everyone to "Make it quick; this is expensive." Now, with the explosion of affordable communication options, it's not uncommon for college students to speak with or text message parents multiple times a day.

A small, private liberal arts college recently dropped its century-old tradition of taking visiting parents on a campus tour while their offspring registered for classes. It seems the adults were spending the whole tour on cell phones with their children debating the merits of calculus over history of the Roman Empire.

"It just wasn't worth it," one college administrator explained. "Why try to separate them when it was so clear that the parents and kids wanted to tackle registration together?"

This is typical of the types of adjustments savvy college administrators are making to serve their newest, most demanding clientele.

Are we done yet? Nope. Often parental involvement keeps right on going after school orientation. You'd think after finding a college, applying, making a selection, moving in, registering, and getting settled, the folks might want a breather. You might picture the parents taking the phone off the hook, pouring a glass of wine or two, cooking exotic foods, reclaiming the TV remote, and basking in the fact that there was a little more peace and quiet, not to mention room, around the nest. Not so. Parents don't have time because their return to school doesn't end when they drop the kids off at the dorm. A recent online poll by Experience, Inc., found that 38 percent of students admitted their parents had either called into or physically attended meetings with academic advisors, and 31 percent of students reported their parents had called professors to complain about a grade. Just as Dad was willing to argue with the ump at a baseball game about a bad call, he's ready to go toe-to-toe with the prof about whether his kid really deserved a D.

MILLENNIALS ON RECORD

"For each generation, the goal is that your kids have it better than you had it and can do the things you wished you could have done. And more than ever there is a focus on higher education. Parents are *so* focused on the education. They say things like 'Don't get a job if it's going to take away from your studying in college.' But then those kids are missing out on important experiences that shape their view of the world. They are coming out of college too ideological because they haven't had as much time in the real world. Bottom line: it comes down to the parents."

— *Steve Mell, age 25, electrical engineer, Century Engineering Inc.*

More than just ensuring their protégés get perfect grades, parents are staying on the job to make sure their own work—spending years planning for how to pay for college—is getting an A+ as well. Who blames them, as costs have skyrocketed! Trade schools, technical schools, colleges, universities, and postgraduate institutions have become much more expensive in adjusted dollars, and loans and scholarships are harder to get. Education beyond high school is eating up a bigger portion of the family's income, and savvy parents are going to be sure they get their money's worth. As a result, a 2006 survey by College Parents of America found that over half of parents surveyed were "much more" involved with their children than their parents had been during their college years. Alecia Thiele, associate professor and academic coordinator of clinical education at Clarke College, commented, "We are seeing a change from the hovering helicopter parenting to *stealth bomber parents* who are much more demanding of the *why's* than they were before. Parents no longer 'hover,' they get in your face. They want accountability. They want to know where their tuition money is going and what marketable skills their kids are going to have when they come out of school. In many ways, money has become the focus of college education."

While it creates challenges for college and school administrators, increased parental involvement can have its upsides. A recent survey by UCLA's Higher Education Research Institute found that 80.5 percent of incoming freshmen said their parents were involved the "right amount" in activities related to choosing and enrolling in college. No big shocker there, as what kid wouldn't be in favor of someone helping them make such a crucial life decision? But the result appears to be students who are more engaged. A report by the National Survey of Student Engagement found that college students who reported high levels of contact with their parents or guardians were more satisfied with their education and had deeper learning experiences. Interestingly, responses differed among students of different ethnic and racial backgrounds, with 43 percent of Latino students saying they would like their parents to be *more* involved.

So, while increased parental engagement is ruffling feathers and causing more work for college administrators, it may also be creating a better educational experience for students. The question is, will the same be true as Millennials move from college to the next life stage—full-time employment? How far should a parent's role extend when it comes to careers? Will the workplace see parental involvement as an advantage or an irritant? And how will the generations react?

WELCOME TO THE WORK WORLD, MOM AND DAD

Xer Chuck finished the last of his e-mails and shut down the computer. If he headed home right now, he could beat the traffic and maybe get in a workout. On the way out he saw Millennial Chelsea headed his way. "Great," he muttered. "She's going to stop me to talk more about the research report. Apparently our eight other conversations today weren't enough." Because he was responsible for another section of the report, the boss had asked him to be a "resource" if Chelsea needed help. As much as Chuck wanted to step up to the role, he was hoping any more "resourcing" could wait until tomorrow. He tried to veer off into the copy room and make a beeline for the side door but she cut him off.

"Chuck, I have feedback for you on the report."

Chuck was caught off guard. The boss was out of town and they weren't delivering their drafts to him for another week. How could she already have feedback?

"My dad," beamed Chelsea, "is a marketing V.P. at Westlake Investments so I asked him to go over our drafts and he gave me a ton of ideas. It's so cool 'cuz he never says YOYO."

"Yoyo?" stammered Chuck.

She spoke very slowly and deliberately. "You're On Your Own."

Chuck was already too annoyed to even pretend he knew what she meant.

She cheerfully continued, "Anyways, don't be bummed, I mean, he really likes your writing, he just has a couple tweaks on your analysis."

Chuck was speechless and could only wish that he was OHO (on his own). Collaborating with Millennials had already pushed him out of his comfort zone. But collaborating with a Millennial's dad was in another stratosphere.

Ask a Boomer or Xer how they would have felt if their parents had followed them from college to work, and they'll tell you they would have died of embarrassment. Ask Millennials about it, and they say, "Why not?" In our M-Factor survey, over 10 percent of Millennials said they would "feel comfortable having my parent/s call the boss if there is a problem," compared to just 1 percent of Gen Xers and Boomers. While 10 percent isn't a large number, it's significant, and it's a huge increase over prior generations.

Studies show Millennials hold their parents in high regard and welcome their input. According to the Robert Half International report titled "What Millennial Workers Want," one in four Millennial workers consults his or her parents when making employment decisions. Should we really be that surprised? After all, they've been observing Mom's and Dad's professional journeys all their lives. They've watched the painful ups and downs of their parents' career paths and know that forces like globalization, fluctuations in the economy, mergers, and competition can put jobs at risk. They also understand how important it is to get off to a good start—that what they do today will set a tone for the rest of their careers.

MILLENNIALS ON RECORD

"Before I go to my parents, I always think about what they would say...and I'm always wrong! They always bring something up that I would have never thought of. They give me a good work-life balance. They will constantly remind me that yes...I have a lot of work to do but don't forget that you have a life, too. That helps me make better work decisions. They keep me grounded."

— *Syed Zaidi, age 26, ERS senior consultant, Deloitte and Touche, LLP*

Millennials are, understandably, worried about making mistakes and are going to use every tool at their disposal to make the transition to work less fraught with pain and risk. Enter Mom and Dad.

They've experienced a lot in their careers, not all of it pleasant, and are eager to use their knowledge of the work world to help their kids avoid some of the mistakes and miseries they experienced.

"When I got my first job in real estate," explained Dwight, a successful Baby Boomer developer, "my parents didn't have a clue how to help me. I was the first one in my family to graduate from college, I was in a field they didn't know anything about, and I suppose they thought I'd figure it out. Once I was married and had kids, I'm sure they assumed I was a grown man—I was twenty-four—and it was none of their business. I have a lot of skills now, and I'm sure as hell not going to let my kids flounder if I can use my experience to help them."

Just how much are Boomers helping their Millennial children with the transition to work? In a Michigan State University survey of employers, 26 percent said parents actively promoted their son or daughter for a position, 31 percent said parents submitted a résumé on behalf of their offspring, and 41 percent said parents obtained company materials for their kids. It looks like Millennials have figured out they have free access to some of the best and brightest consultants money can buy.

And, access to parents will only increase when, instead of using cell phones or text messages to reach their mother or father, Millennials can simply poke their heads into the living room. According to a survey by Collegegrad.com, the #1 Entry Level Job Site, "Among 2009 U.S. college graduates, 80% moved back home with their parents after graduation, up from 77% in 2008, 73% in 2007 and 67% in 2006." Why not? In addition to a ready supply of advice, it's a great way to save money for paying off college debts or buying a first house.

While Traditionalists, Boomers, and Xers can't imagine moving back home with their parents, they better start getting used to a work world where parents are moving in with them. But why assume this means time-outs and grounding? The arrival of Millennials' parents might present a potential boon for the workplace. Millennials who have strong relationships with their parents are more likely to feel comfortable connecting with their elders at work.

MILLENNIALS ON RECORD

"My parents are such great resources for me it would be foolish *not* to look to them. They have 'been there' and 'done that' and I want to use that knowledge. The networking component alone is immense. I can't even tell you how many leads or phone numbers I've gotten through my parents. To call them only parents is such an understatement. They are my mentors, tutors, and friends."

—Ian Winbrock, age 21, market research analyst, ZAP, Inc.

Millennials like Ian will be more eager to collaborate and enjoy interactions with the other generations, and they will be a more receptive generation of mentees. That being said, there is no denying this family-involvement tsunami will create a workplace awash in uncomfortable new situations. We are already hearing from Traditionalists like Ed, who is in charge of training programs at his company. Ed has been tasked with developing remedial classes for newly hired Millennials, because their parents encouraged them not to work during high school and college and they now lack basic skills such as workplace etiquette and customer service. Or from John, a Gen X graphic designer who now has to put together a quarterly newsletter for parents of Millennial new hires highlighting all the recent developments at the company—something he just doesn't have time for. Or from Boomers like Carol, who is in charge of recruiting and has to explain to the executive committee that she needs a bigger budget so she can redesign job fair materials to include frequently asked questions posed by parents.

This is only the beginning. Reports are in and co-workers are struggling with a lack of independence among Millennials who have been accustomed to getting loads of coaching from parents. Some are uncomfortable grabbing a project and running with it on their own for fear of making mistakes. When conducting our M-Factor survey we were surprised to find that nearly half of all Millennials expressed the concern that they don't get enough *formal* feedback on the job. This may be reflective of a desire to have a much better idea of where they stand. Having been praised lavishly at home, they can also be hypersensitive to criticism and easily discouraged by failure. In the M-Factor survey, while only a fourth of Millennial respondents (24 percent) said their own generation is poorly prepared to handle feedback on the job, almost twice as many (40 percent) of all respondents think this is true. Given the fact that parents have played a big role in helping them set goals, some are complaining that Millennials seem passive about inventing and fighting for their career paths, expecting their future to be laid out for them in detail instead.

Clearly, Mom and Dad's influence is being felt on multiple levels at work, and workplace harmony and productivity will depend upon the generations coping with this reality rather than fighting it. Whether in tight economic times when many companies are short-handed or as the economy recovers and work demands increase, every generation needs the Millennials to hit the ground running and shoulder some of the workload. Then maybe it's not such a bad idea to make a little extra room for Mom and Dad.

MAKING WORK WORK FOR YOU

This leads Baby Boomers to feel a bit like Jekyll *and* Hyde. While they would love to complain about their new hire's lack of independent thinking, they might be too busy text messaging advice to their own child, who's preparing for a noon meeting with a supervisor. For Xers raised to operate independently, it's hard to understand why Millennials want so much face time and input or why they are uncomfortable operating independently. Here are some guidelines for approaching the parent/workplace dilemma:

• **Save judgment for the courthouse.** When we ask audiences what they think of Millennials, the first words out of people's mouths are usually judgmental. We hear things like entitled, clingy, needy, or spoiled. It's easy to judge someone whose relationship with their parents appears to be poles apart from your own, but that doesn't mean the Millennials' relationships are wrong—they're just different.

One Boomer middle manager commented, "I remember feeling annoyed when my co-worker kept telling me how his parents did things, how they became successful. Then I realized what he was telling me was how much he admired them. That's pretty neat."

• **Be specific about boundaries.** Just like there are parental controls for television and the Internet, workplace policies limit how parents can or should be involved. Colleges and universities have led the charge in tackling this issue. For example, at Clarke College when students and parents are together for new student orientation, they make everyone aware of FERPA (the Federal Education Right to Privacy Act). Under FERPA, school officials can't give out any information to a parent unless the student first signs a waiver. Right then and there, during orientation, students are given the opportunity to waive their FERPA rights, thus giving their parents permission to talk to their professors, see their grades, and examine their bills online. When asked what percentage of students sign these waivers, the answer was "99.9% waive their rights to privacy." The reason? Mainly because their parents are paying for their education.

Workplaces need to be similarly prepared to deal with privacy policies. Most human resources professionals will tell you it is not appropriate to give out information about an adult employee to anyone, period. So, if you get a call from a relative asking about anything from a performance issue to how they can help their loved one be more successful, it's appropriate to say you're not allowed to violate privacy by discussing it. Cindy Pruitt, director of compensation in the Winston-Salem office of law firm Womble Carlyle Sandridge & Rice, related an instance in which a young summer associate received a harsh review for a piece of writing. As Cindy put it, the supervisor "bled all over her paper." The summer associate came to Cindy almost in tears because she had been so harshly graded. Cindy tried to comfort her by reaffirming that she was a good employee and was held in high regard by her peer group, and said, "You can't be perfect from the beginning. We're not beating you up; we just want you to do your best." The next week, sure enough, she received a call from the summer associate's mother wanting to know what happened and why she had received such harsh criticism. Cindy had to tell the parent that she could not discuss her daughter's performance for "legal and lots of other reasons." She also told the mother that her daughter is an adult and as an adult, she would handle the situation.

If you're uncomfortable and need the right wording, ask HR. And, while you're at it, ask about any other rules of the road that might help you navigate. For example, our M-Factor survey uncovered that Millennials are the most likely of any generation to feel comfortable telling their manager they are looking for a new job. This kind of honesty is great, but managers need to be coached on how to handle it. Rather than treat the employee like a traitor, supervisors might want to uncover why the employee is dissatisfied and what the company could have done differently to retain him or her.

Beyond employment issues there are the legal ones. More than one company has run into the problem of Millennials taking work home and sharing it with family members. Managers and co-workers need to know what the company policies are on confidentiality, intellectual property, and privacy. An employee might be allowed to take a laptop home to work remotely, but it might violate policy to transport the company database off the premises or to show this information to people outside the company. Familiarize yourself with the guidelines and be prepared to communicate them. Millennials have grown up in an era of open source information. In fact, they are the least likely generation to worry about giving out private information, such as credit card numbers, online. You can assume they won't know your company's privacy requirements unless you teach them.

• **Coaching doesn't stop with Little League.** The Millennial generation is showing up on the job with the least amount of work experience in decades. For some that's because job opportunities for teens and college students dried up during the recent recession. By August of 2009 the number of teens who wanted a job but couldn't find one reached 25.5 percent, the highest level since the government started keeping track in 1948. This means once they do graduate and find full-time employment they will have had fewer formative work experiences than prior generations. For others, the lack of work history is due to family choices. Often, parents who can afford it would rather see their kids take on other types of challenges that will look good on a college application or a résumé. The good news is, while Millennials might be working less they aren't just playing Wii games and drinking Red Bull. They have traveled, volunteered, and participated in a variety of sports and activities. All along the way, they've been coached. And not just by the professionals carrying clipboards and wearing whistles. They've been coached by good ol' Mom and Dad.

When Millennials show up in your department, they not only

will *accept* coaching from you, they'll *expect* it. When assessing these new hires, assume that while they have lots of skills that apply in the rest of the world, they may lack hard-core business know-how. They are going to need your input on basic drills like how to deal with the office bully or how to treat your biggest client. If you wait around for them to learn via the school of hard knocks, you risk having them head out the door as soon as the knocking starts. You also risk them making costly mistakes that could have been prevented if you'd just spent a little more time going over the playbook.

• **Maybe father does know best.** Even though it might be tempting to mention to a Millennial that Pops isn't on the payroll and Mom doesn't understand the business, why risk offending? Several Sutter Health hospitals and medical groups in California's Central Valley have Employee Activity Committees that plan events throughout the year. They recently became aware that a lot of employees were bringing their parents to organization- or employee-sponsored functions like holiday parties and local sightseeing tours, and were happily enjoying themselves right alongside Mom and/or Dad. Instead of seeing this as a problem, leaders view it as a sign that employees are proud of where they work and want to share the experience. For them, including parents fosters commitment and pride among employees.

If Millennials come to you touting parental opinions, ask questions about how the advice applies. And be willing to admit to yourself that once in a while even the folks have good ideas. One young sales rep who still lived with his parents approached his supervisor and admitted that his Mom had told him he needed to improve his work habits. He felt bad about the feedback and wanted to discuss this with his boss. The supervisor handled the conversation admirably, asking for specific examples and quizzing the employee on how he felt the mother's observations applied in the workplace. What she had observed was that he kept numerous programs open on his computer's desktop, even when doing work for the company, and was constantly interrupted by e-mails, or dings from people trying to instant message him. The supervisor agreed with the mom's assessment that this was an inefficient way to get work done and they brainstormed a daily schedule that would allow for both concentrated "thinking" time and unstructured "communication" time. By being open to parental input, the manager created a teachable moment for a young employee.

- **If you can't beat 'em, invite 'em in!** While the Millennial is the one signing on, you can assume Mom and Dad are weighing in, so why not reach out to them? Smart organizations are turning parents into allies in the war for talent. Fortune 500 company C.H. Robinson Worldwide, Inc., noticed that Millennial recruits were often accompanied by parents who drove them to interviews and/ or stayed in hotels with them. Sometimes they even got closer than the parking lot. Carmen Baas, a recruiter at C. H. Robinson, commented: "We recently had the father of a candidate call one of our sales reps to talk about his son's job offer so he could make a decision on whether or not his son should come work for us. I've also had parents attend career fairs in lieu of their children who had prior engagements." But rather than resist the wave, C. H. Robinson decided to ride it. To cater to the Millennials' needs for parental involvement, they created packets to be mailed to parents simultaneously with their child's offer letter. That parental information packet includes marketing material on C. H. Robinson so the parents can learn more about the organization, as well as information about the benefits package, so parents can review it for their child. They then give candidates about a month to accept or decline the offer, because they realize Millennials will need time to sit down and talk it over with their top advisors: the folks.

If you're trying to reel in the best and brightest you need every possible lure you can muster. Ernst & Young now distributes "parent packs" to students during information sessions at college recruitment fairs. Recruiters from General Mills send welcome baskets to parents of new hires filled with nostalgic products. Since it's far better to have Mom and Dad in your corner, General Electric has begun running recruiting ads aimed at parents in campus newspapers and on schools' parent Web pages. They sport catchy headlines like, "Let us take your son or daughter off your payroll and put them on ours."

- **Once they've signed on, keep inviting them back.** Why not hold a yearly open house or plant tour and encourage the whole family to attend? Merrill Lynch, for example, holds a parents' day for interns' families to tour the trading floor. How about an awards celebration targeting younger employees where parents can join in applauding Millennials' achievements? Why not include the family in mailings of company press releases? After all, if your organization has an achievement to brag about, why not give Mom and Dad something new to put on the fridge?

SO, WHAT'S A MILLENNIAL TO DO?

We've talked a lot about how each generation can understand and relate to Millennials in the workplace, but Millennials can play a huge role in creating intergenerational synergy. For one thing, they can realize that although they have close, collaborative relationships with their parents they will have to develop new ways of relating to Xers, Boomers, and Traditionalists at work where the family dynamics they are accustomed to at home are not necessarily going to be appropriate.

Toto, I Don't Think We're in Kansas Anymore.

Millennials have learned from their parents to be respectful of diverse cultures. We've ushered them on field trips to natural history museums, glued straw into cardboard box dioramas of the Serengeti, and outfitted them in costumes for international awareness day. Now it's time for the "kids" to put their cultural sensitivity to work...at work. One of the best methods Millennials can use to get off on the right foot in a new workplace is to approach it with the same curiosity and consideration they would give a foreign culture. A Millennial who signs on for a Save the Children gig in Botswana would undoubtedly study local customs, language, and taboos before showing up. Why should the workplace be any different? Take that same cultural awareness, apply it to learning the system at Acme Widget, and BANG...your chance of being successful just increased by 300 percent.

What should Millennials do when entering an exotic new civilization masking as their first job? Pick up on the prevailing customs. Find out who the chief is and how he or she leads the tribe. What do the tribal leaders wear? How do they behave in meetings and other types of powwows? When is it appropriate to listen or to speak? How do the most influential tribe members communicate? If the chief likes to have face time with his or her inner circle, then stop e-mailing and show up. Too many Millennials assume they can behave the same way at work as they did at home. If it's OK with the folks, it must be OK with the boss, right? When they miss key cultural signals they get branded as clueless or not management material.

What should Millennials understand to make their forays into the workplace jungle successful?

• **Recognize it's your manager, not your mom.** Millennials should avoid trying to relate to the other generations at work the same way they do to their parents at home.

Millennial Lakisha kept her eyes on Donna as the meeting progressed. A Baby Boomer, Donna had loads of experience, a real competitive drive, and plenty of intensity. She knew how to keep her arguments logical even in the face of rising conflict. Lakisha had spent a lifetime watching her mother take on challenges in much the same way. Her mom had that same gritty logic and self-discipline, and you couldn't rattle her even if you tried. Lakisha knew Donna was a good person to watch if you wanted to get ahead in their company.

Donna left the meeting exhausted. Her skirt felt too tight and she kept having hot flashes during the meeting. The boss had asked the same dumb question eight different times, which made her feel like she wasn't explaining herself. She had to keep taking deep breaths to avoid losing her temper. Partway through the meeting her laptop froze and Lakisha jumped in and fixed it in front of everyone. The whole experience hadn't been pretty, but she got the OK on her department's new budget, and that was the main goal.

Donna walked out with Lakisha, who looked young, annoyingly fresh, had no dark circles under her eyes, and had piped up with several good ideas when Donna felt she was floundering. When Lakisha turned to her and said, "You remind me so much of my mother," it was the last straw. To Donna, that meant old, sweaty, and technologically incompetent. She had no idea that Lakisha's mom was a super role model or that the comment had been the ultimate compliment. Lakisha couldn't fathom why Donna looked ticked off and walked away.

While Millennials might adore their folks and have superb rapport with them, workplace relationships are bound to be different. It's important to assess the prevailing conditions before assuming anything. Consider Donna and Lakisha. Lakisha jumped in and fixed the computer because that's what she had done countless times for her parents. They were always grateful. It never dawned on her that fixing Donna's computer in front of her boss and peers might have made Donna look inadequate or worse, antiquated. Telling Donna she reminded Lakisha of her mom was meant as a compliment, but Donna didn't want to be reminded of her age in a company that was becoming more and more youth-oriented. She also didn't like the annoying roles that come with being a "parent" to her new hire, like having to nag, lecture, or remind Lakisha. What she really wanted was a professional, respectful, results-focused relationship. For Lakisha, positioning herself as the "kid" probably wasn't a great strategy either. Soon she was going to want to take on bigger roles with more authority. If she looked too young or was perceived as someone's child, it was going to be a lot harder for her to seem credible and get ahead.

• **It pays to be patient.** While it might be acceptable to walk into the folks' house and declare that their old TV is eligible for the Smithsonian, in the workplace such a comment will be much less welcome—at least until trust has been established. While parents might be used to it, seemingly confident higher-ups can be deeply offended when criticized for their way of doing things. They might have been responsible for how things are, or they might have spent the last six years trying to change them. Instead of saying, "this customer service system is from the Stone Age!" Millennials will get a lot farther by asking, "What are our goals for customer service?" Instead of diving in to "fix" perceived shortcomings immediately, Millennials should ask how they can help. While it might be hugely frustrating to see that a new place of employment is not only behind the times but is in some ways archaic, patience is the best tactic.

• **If unsure of the rules, Millennials need to check the playbook.** Where parents never hesitated to comment on anything from who a Millennial is dating to what they should do with their hair, bosses are often uncomfortable talking about "soft" issues like personal hygiene, dress, grammar, or etiquette. Rather than wait for an uncomfortable situation to escalate, Millennials can alleviate pain on both sides by asking for input. For example, before attending a meeting the new employee could check with the boss to see if he or she is properly attired. This creates an opening for the supervisor to comment on a potentially touchy topic, and helps both parties be more at ease with the dialogue.

THERE'S NO PLACE LIKE HOME

Gen Xer Rob sighed as he completed yet another frustrating interview. Would it be unprofessional to pound his head on the table in front of a twenty-one-year-old? This college student had shown up late for the scheduled appointment time wearing a wrinkled shirt and was ill prepared.

First question: "How much do you know about our company?"

The response was a cocky, "Not a lot, really. Maybe you could fill me in." Rob felt like throwing his latte at the wall, but since the walls of the interview rooms at HQ were painted a trendy new shade of cappuccino, it wouldn't make much of an impact.

Later, Rob headed home to take his son Jasper, a burgeoning pitcher, to baseball practice. Jasper appeared in a wrinkled uniform that obviously had not been washed since Tuesday's practice. They were running late.

"Who are you playing tonight, son?" he asked.

"I dunno, Dad. You have the schedule."

"But how are you going to get that no-hitter if you haven't studied the other team?" he replied as he fumbled with his Black-Berry. "Here you go, Jasper, you're playing the Sidewinders and their coach is named (scroll, scroll, scroll) Chuck...No wait (scroll, scroll). It's Charlie."

"OK," responded Jasper as he put on the earphones and settled in to watch a backseat DVD. Rob, meanwhile, continued to drive while drumming up as much information as he could find on the Sidewinders.

In the parking lot of the Little League field, Rob briefed Jasper before sending him out to the mound. When the game started and Rob settled in to watch, his mind wandered back to the unfulfilling interview he'd conducted earlier that day. "I just don't get who's raising these irresponsible kids!"

One of the funniest moments we experience as keynote speakers and workshop leaders is that moment when an exasperated roomful of Boomers and Gen Xers tell us how frustrating Millennials can be and then ask us how they got that way. It's astonishing how people struggling to manage Millennials at work don't realize they are the same people who are raising them at home.

We like to ask the following question: "Boomers and Xers, how many of you as teenagers ever had a part-time job where you might have had to work on Christmas Eve?" Then we ask, "How many of your Traditionalist parents would have let you call in sick or lie so you could get off work?" Then, the coup de grace: We ask, "But how many of you have let your own child blow off a shift or even quit a job so he or she could go on the family vacation, get an extra night at home with the folks, or go to a party they really wanted to attend?"

Gotcha!

That's where it starts. What we sow when raising our future workforce is what we will eventually reap. But strangely, there's a big disconnect between our own parenting behaviors and what we hope to see happen at work.

The good news is that in many ways parents have actually raised the kind of future workforce any of us would be proud to hire. One of the best qualities an employee can have is the willingness to question the status quo and ask the tough questions. Millennials are happy to do that in spades, because we've made our kids part of the family "team," seeking their input, listening to their points of view, and empowering them to take action.

MILLENNIALS ON RECORD

"I wouldn't say I was my mother's friend but I was an 'equal voting member.' If I was polite and reasonable and logical, then my opinion would be heard and oftentimes it would influence the final result."

—Bobbie Godbey, age 27, program coordinator, West Virginia University

Millennials represent approximately $200 billion per year in buying power. They don't just spend on themselves (although they obviously do plenty of that). They also spend on family purchases such as groceries, electronics, home furnishings, vacations, and more. We help them do their research, we coach them on decision-making, and we allow them to make choices. All this builds confidence and capability.

What else have parents done for Millennials? We've given them options. This generation has seen more places and had more diverse experiences than any before. As one MOR commented: "Our parents make the alternatives available to us to give us a richer life experience. My mom really encouraged the outside opportunities saying things like 'you'll have your whole life to work!'"

We always get a laugh when we ask audiences, "How many of you know Millennials who have traveled to more places than you have?" We've enabled them to see the world, if not face-to-face then via film, television, books, and the World Wide Web. They bring plenty of personal experience and perspective with them to the workplace.

MILLENNIALS ON RECORD

"Traveling the world doesn't help you become a better accountant. But it helps you see the world a little bit differently and be more understanding when you run into those bureaucratic walls. It teaches you how to work with other people and to weather challenges a little bit better."
—Dale Till, age 20, Northeastern University student working full time at the Institute for International Urban Development

Another gift? We talk to Millennials about virtually everything. Money? Sex? Politics? Drugs? Terrorism? You name it, we've found a way to have a dialogue about it, and this creates a sense of open communication that's invaluable on the job.

Bravo mothers and fathers—take a bow. Your protégé really is worth bragging about. But before every button on your shirt pops, read on. There might be a thing or two you can add to that parent-

ing handbook that will create an even better future workforce to
fuel innovation and ingenuity:

- **Allow kids to fail.** People learn best and fastest from making
their own mistakes and fixing them. It's painful to watch a child
flounder, but in the long run children become more resilient and
resourceful if they have to deal with failure once in a while. One of
the biggest fears of today's business strategists is that we are producing a coddled workforce of straight "A" students who are afraid to
go out on a limb for fear they'll fall. American innovation was born
out of metaphorical scraped knees and bloody noses. A generation
that's been told they shouldn't even touch a doorknob without applying antibacterial hand sanitizer may not have the rough and tum-
ble qualities needed to compete in a global dog-eat-dog economy.

- **Hold them accountable.** In today's jam-packed family life,
it takes more time to hold a kid accountable than to do the job
yourself. We need to slow down and make sure that when we put a
child in charge of something, they get it done. Whether this means
showing up on time for dinner, preparing properly for that first
part-time job, or turning in assignments at school, we need to teach
our children that responsibility is a huge part of being an effective
team member and a critical factor in success. Over the past five years
countless employers have complained to us that they resent having
to "police" Millennials on what they consider to be basics—things
like showing up on time, meeting deadlines, or following through
on promises. While it's possible to teach these things in the workplace, the most successful employees learned about accountability
years ago from Mom and Dad, at home.

- **Teach them "work" is not a "four-letter" word.** In fact, it
can be a pretty fulfilling and meaningful activity. The United States
has come a long way since the days when just having a job was
enough. Today we expect our jobs to complete us as human beings,
fulfill us, and employ our gifts and talents. But our ways of talking
about work haven't evolved much from the days of the blacksmith

limping home from the forge and announcing he got kicked in the head. Instead of making sure our kids hear about the positive aspects of our work, we moan about long meetings, bad bosses, and stupid policies. That's fine, because it's part of the reality. But often we miss the opportunity to say, "I made a difference today, I built something beautiful," or, "I made a really cool presentation in the meeting and felt great about my speaking skills." We need to talk about the gratifying aspects of work, and we need to explain the hard steps we took to get there. Kids need both a vision of what's possible and a realistic perspective on the sacrifices that are part and parcel of being successful.

• **Cut the cord, or at least give it some slack.** The knock on helicopter parents is really quite simple. It's that they aren't allowing kids to grow up and become adults. We know that the period of adolescence is lengthening in U.S. culture, extending well into the twenties and even the thirties. As the age for marriage and children moves further out, as education takes longer to complete and debt rates are higher, many young people today stay dependent on their nuclear families for an extended period. Today many are moving home until they can find a job, pay off debts, or save enough money for a house that is becoming increasingly tough to afford. Or they move home because it's easy, it's comfortable, the laundry gets done, the big screen TV is really big, and oh yes, they like their folks and think they make stellar roommates. But as long as they have Mom and Dad on speed dial it's too easy to avoid taking on the risks and responsibilities of adulthood.

Psychologists tell us young people benefit when parents set expectations that they act more like grown-ups. Participating in household chores, taking on specific expenses (such as their own car insurance and repairs), making progress paying off school loans, or saving a set portion of weekly pay toward the goal of moving out are examples of this. Parents also do their offspring a favor when they cease "caretaking" behaviors that were appropriate when the kids were younger, such as waking them up in time to go to work or class, doing their laundry, or picking up their rooms. Moms and Dads tell us they see these small tasks—like changing the oil in a daughter's car—as ways of showing affection. Instead, why not wait until Saturday and show her how to change the oil herself? After all, investing in a child's autonomy now will have a direct impact on her ability to support you in the future!

- **Sometimes the reception can be too good.** We all know people who text message, call, or e-mail their kids constantly. When Lynne was on a recent boat trip up the British Columbian coast, the pilot announced to passengers that the ship would soon be in position for a few minutes of cell phone service. In perfect sync, every parent on the boat whipped out their mobile phones and dialed the "kids" who were on average at least age thirty. The sad thing was they had only been away from shore for two days! An online survey by the advocacy group College Parents of America found that a third of parents communicate with their college-age kids one or more times a day. Sure it's nice to stay close, but what message are

"YES, MOTHER, I TOLD YOU, I'M DOING FINE ON MY OWN AT COLLEGE.... HEY, COULD YOU LOG ON AND FIND MY SCHEDULE, ORDER MY BOOKS AND CALL ME WHEN IT'S TIME FOR CLASS?"

you really sending? While one child might hear "Mom loves me," another might be thinking, "I can't do this without them." It's why we called this chapter "Connected Via the Cordless Umbilical." No one can tell a parent or child how much is too much, but we can ask the question: Do we hurt or help the connection when we are willing to unhook?

Every new generation has brought with them its own perspective that ultimately made positive contributions to the workplace. Traditionalists' military background set the tone for loyalty to institutions and an unremitting work ethic. Baby Boomers' competitive drive challenged the status quo, shook things up, and took professionalism to a whole new level. Gen Xers, who were unwilling to pay the same price for success they saw their parents pay, pushed for work-life balance and the workplace flexibility many of us are enjoying today. Undoubtedly, there will be elements of the close Millennial-parent relationship we can all learn from. For example, because Millennials tend to see their folks as smart, interesting, and helpful, they are likely to view their bosses that way, too. This can only be a benefit to managers who must engage young employees.

Yes, it will require work to provide the input, feedback, and mentoring Millennials demand. It's even more work to include their parents. But ultimately these might just be the bonds that create the long-term loyalty every employer dreams of. Or, that keep an employee from hopping to your biggest competitor when the going gets tough.

Think of it this way: If you're having a hard time hammering home a message with your new hire, maybe having the parents on your side isn't such a bad thing. Instead of thinking of them as meddlers, just think of them as managers you don't have to pay.

three

ENTITLEMENT

JUSTIN. Millennial Justin was eager and excited for his job interview with the local Veteran's Administration Hospital in a department providing services for the homeless. Given that he had a degree in social work, a summer internship with a local nonprofit, and a volunteer position helping homeless people through his church, Justin felt he had a lot to offer. He had prepped hard for the interview. He searched the Web to learn everything he could about the V.A. He read articles on the challenges facing the homeless in his city and county. He talked with his college placement office about pay ranges for these types of jobs, the benefits he could expect, and opportunities for advancement. He'd even stopped by his parents' house for a strategy session on interviewing. Justin's mom helped him frame questions to ask and his dad, a corporate executive, did a mock interview with him.

A Generation on a Silver Platter?

"You're a fantastic candidate, son," Justin's dad proclaimed. "They're going to love you!"

After the interview, Justin phoned home. "How did it go?" his parents asked breathlessly.

"I'm not sure," responded a disappointed Justin. "I don't think we connected."

ERIC. Baby Boomer Eric had been with the V.A. for twenty-five years, nine of those as supervisor of the caseworkers, and he prided himself on being a good interviewer. He knew the history of the department, the challenges they faced, and the types of candidates who would work well in the V.A. system. Over the years, Eric had made a lot of sacrifices to serve homeless veterans. The caseload was heavy and the work could be exhausting. He was a vet himself, so the job meant more to him than just a paycheck. After the interview with Justin, Eric stomped back to his office.

"How did it go?" asked a co-worker. "That kid had a great résumé."

"I didn't click with him," responded Eric. "He barely let me talk about the department or the population we serve. Instead he asked a million questions about how fast he could advance, how much money he would make, how much vacation time he would have, and how he could get the types of cases that most appealed to him! Right, like we're going to sift through the homeless and find the more attractive cases for some spoiled punk! Oh, and he asked how much feedback and mentoring he could get from me. How about what he could *give*? I know entitlement when I see it, and I'm looking for someone with more of a service orientation."

A generation gap at its saddest. Two people who might have had very compatible interests and goals were sidelined by a concept that's become widely known as *entitlement*. The real loss is that neither of them was right or wrong; they were unable to look at the world through the other's generational lens.

You hear it all the time . . .

- "These doggone Millennials expect the moon!"
- "It's all about what we can give *them*. What about what they can give us?"
- "I would never have been that cocky when I was that age."
- "They want to be running the department in three months."

However people phrase it, everyone seems to agree that Millennials are the entitled generation. In our M-Factor survey, when respondents were asked which generation is the most entitled, Millennials won by a landslide! Traditionalists, Boomers, and Xers who had to pay their dues feel Millennials push too hard and ask for too much too soon. It's become a real source of resentment in the workplace.

WHAT IS ENTITLEMENT ANYWAY?

Based on the hundreds of interviews we've done, accusations of "entitlement" arise when . . .

Millennials have the guts or the gall to ask. "If you hire me for this sales job can I have a company car?" That doesn't seem like an unreasonable question, unless you're talking to someone who was with the company nine years before he or she got a car.

Millennials expect perks or praise before they've earned it. "Can I get Friday off? I know I've only been here two weeks but I have seven vacation days coming to me."

Millennials come off as spoiled. "Great, my Millennial intern just told me he would have to quit unless he could work on a project with one of our international clients. He said he's planning on living overseas for a while!"

Millennials appear too big for their own britches. "I could definitely ace that project if you want to hand it over to me—I'm really good at that." What Millennials see as confidence can come off as cockiness to the other generations.

Millennials ignore the hierarchy. "I hope you don't mind, boss, but I e-mailed our V.P. to suggest we change the software program we've been using—it's bogus and too slow." This comes off as rude at best and insubordinate or downright threatening at worst.

So, are the generations right when they accuse the Millennials of being too entitled? In some ways, yes. This is a generation that has been raised to expect a lot and to ask for what they want. Up until 2009 they found jobs relatively easy to get and have been willing to change jobs if they are unhappy. The U.S. unemployment rate in 2000, when the leading edge of Millennials turned eighteen, hovered around 4 percent. Even when that number more than doubled in June 2009, and new graduates struggled to find jobs, Millennials continued to express high expectations for how they wanted to be treated at work and what they expected to accomplish.

However, we believe the accusation of entitlement gets tossed around too readily and is often a cover for other issues. It's easier to blame the Millennials for being spoiled than to examine what's really going on. For example, sometimes Millennials are griping because a certain job is uninteresting, or a particular manager is not very good at handling feedback or doling out praise. At other times, what some see as *entitlement* might just be *engagement*. If an employee is constantly agitating to do more, that might be a really good thing.

The pivotal question is: To what extent is entitlement a problem or an opportunity, and what are the best ways to deal with it?

MILLENNIALS ON RECORD

"I hear a lot about the 'I-Generation'—kids being obsessed with themselves and a little too self-indulgent—and I have trouble with that. I think that inherently, adolescents are self-indulgent. It is more of an age thing than a generation thing. Once we get to the workplace it all evens out."

—Ava Jackson, age 22, artistic learning coordinator,
California Shakespeare Company

WHERE DOES ENTITLEMENT COME FROM?

When you ask Millennials about entitlement, their insights help a lot. Bobbie Godbey of West Virginia University, commented, "We are a more diverse group of people, but not just ethnically and culturally. Millennials have been able to experience a lot of things previous generations weren't able to experience until much later in life. And because of that we are more restless. . . . If something wasn't working out, we moved on because we had so many choices." To Bobbie it's not about disloyalty or being spoiled, it's about using the opportunities available to find the right fit.

It's not surprising Millennials see jobs this way. Because many Millennials came of age during relatively good economic times, and because they followed in the wake of the much smaller Gen X population, they've historically been in demand. More recently, however, the economic downturn that began in 2008 may have put a damper on the "entitlement" attitude. Results from a 2009 national student survey showed less than 20 percent of 2009 college grads who applied for jobs actually had one when they graduated. Compare this to two years earlier when 51 percent of 2007 grads left campus with a job in hand. According to a February 2009 report from the National Association for Colleges and Employers (NACE), companies surveyed were planning to hire 22 percent fewer grads from the class of 2009 than they hired from the class of 2008. Some 44 percent of companies in the survey said they planned to hire fewer new grads, and another 22 percent said they did not plan to hire at all for spring 2009.

Millennials already in the workforce saw their companies go through layoffs and downsizing during the period from 2008–09, and many told us that for the first time in their lives they felt lucky to have a job. For the Millennials, the bad economy has pushed the pause button on getting ahead but they still plan on hitting the play button, or even fast forward, as the economy bounces back. In fact, as the U.S. unemployment rate reached 9.5 percent in June 2009, a survey by Adecco found that 71 percent of full-time employees age eighteen to twenty-nine said they were likely to look for new jobs as soon as the downturn reversed. And even in the face of a recession, Millennials we interviewed who were employed continued to express a desire to do more in their current jobs and progress more quickly. Our M-Factor survey, conducted during the economic dip, revealed a continued confidence among Millennials, with 61 percent saying they felt optimistic or somewhat optimistic they could find a job if they needed to.

Millennials also appear to be a bit more relaxed about finding that first job than prior generations. *The Economist* reported that in response to the poor economy many industries were offering deferred start dates to new hires, "giving them six months to a year to travel or do public service" before coming on board. Credit Suisse offered around six months' salary to new employees who agreed to start a year later. That way they locked in the talent they needed while giving the organization time to recover from the downturn. A vice president of human resources with a Fortune 500 company reported that her organization had continued making offers to top graduates throughout the recession with the proviso that they receive a small stipend in exchange for agreeing to postpone their start dates. She was amazed to find most Millennials were quite content to wait, and commented, "We Boomers would have balked at such a deal, but the Millennials seem content to move home, travel, or volunteer until it's time to start." Why are Millennials so much more easygoing?

Millennials knew they had alternatives from day one. When they visited the mall looking for part-time work in the early to mid–2000s they were likely to see HELP WANTED signs in just about every storefront. And even if they accepted that job, it had to compete on the Millennial's calendar with a host of other formative activities like academics, sports, family time, and volunteering. Also, parental attitudes about work were more permissive. If you couldn't manage your work-school load, Mom was likely to suggest you drop your shifts at Abercrombie rather than miss the family vacation or skip hockey practice.

Think about what went on while Millennials were engaging in all those extracurricular activities. They were encouraged to take on leadership roles and help shape the organizations they joined. Parents, coaches, and teachers stopped ruling with an iron fist as they had in previous generations and encouraged Millennials to collaborate with them to achieve the right balance of activities. Millennials became used to having a voice and a choice. So should we be surprised if they feel "entitled" to the same level of engagement on the job?

MILLENNIALS ON RECORD

"What I struggled with most is that in college I was involved with a lot of organizations and held leadership positions in them. When I entered the corporate world, my struggle was less about the work and more about realizing my opinion didn't matter and my voice no longer held a lot of weight…I felt almost useless. Now, over the last four years, I do have more people coming to me for input, but it's been a long haul."

—Greta Hanson, age 27, promotions assistant manager,
Fortune 500 food company

Many Millennials have accomplished amazing things during their teen and college years. They've run their own nonprofits, managed budgets for their sports teams, participated in student government, and contributed to family decisions. Millennials have experienced responsibility and autonomy and at the same time they've learned to play vital roles as members of teams. They tell us that typically the teammates divided up the work according to what they were best at. One MBA grad explained it this way: "On our projects there were always people who were better at certain things, like you always needed someone who was good at finance. You just automatically deferred to that person for that part of the project. It didn't matter if they were younger than you or what major or work experience they had. If they were best at that, that's what they did." The same was true at home. If the kids were better at something, busy Boomer parents were more than happy to hand over the reins. "Honey, can you install this new antivirus software on Dad's computer?" Or, "Could you organize your brother's birthday party, you're so good at it!" were not uncommon refrains.

No wonder Millennials show up at work and are mystified by not being assigned to a project when they know they are better at it than everybody else. In our MOR interviews, many twenty-two- and twenty-three-year-olds honestly couldn't understand why they would be any less qualified for a job than a thirty-five- or forty-year-old if they had the right skills. They don't mean to offend; they are simply accustomed to a household, school, or work situation where job assignments are based on capability, not seniority. One MOR put it this way: "Even to this day, I get frustrated. I don't understand why I need five years of experience when I might be able to do the job really well after three. Those minimum qualifications are hard for me." At the same time, many of our MORs commented on how much they love working with the older generations because there's so much to learn from them. So it's not as if Millennials think they know it all. They just want to be acknowledged for what they do know. Rather than label them as entitled, perhaps we need to applaud their desire to make a contribution.

The tension around talent versus tenure has been complicated by the steady upending of the pyramid at work. For centuries it was assumed that employees who had been around a long time automatically knew more than the younger ones did. Today, that's not necessarily true. The tech boom meant that sometimes the person with the green hair had more know-how than the person with the gray hair. The age of specialization has intensified this divide. Because we see lightning-fast technological developments in many fields, it's common now for recent graduates in math, science, engineering, or nursing to know more in certain areas than those who've been in the workplace a while. A company that refuses to identify that knowledge and take advantage of it is not only frustrating young workers, it's wasting resources and squandering a valuable competitive advantage. Such a company is also bound to frustrate young workers who can clearly see they possess valuable knowledge.

To stir the pot even further, Millennials tell us that they don't always equate "experience" with being "qualified" for a job. Sometimes they see experience as *getting in the way* of having a fresh perspective. In that case, a younger person who is less locked into a certain way of doing things might be a better candidate.

You can see that the "entitlement" debate is deeper than we realize, with part of it stemming from Millennials' questioning the whole idea of seniority when it comes to who is best qualified for a job. One could argue a fiery generation with high expectations that is willing to challenge the status quo is a good thing for the workplace. Or, as Edward Roberts, founder and chair of the Entrepreneurship Center at MIT's Sloan School of Business put it, "This country has always needed a base population of cocky entrepreneurs . . . we've never needed these types as badly as we do at this very moment."

THE DARK SIDE OF ENTITLEMENT

There wouldn't be so much angst around entitlement if it didn't have a very real dark side. Traditionalists, Boomers, and Xers are justifiably worried about Millennials' work ethic and loyalty. They are concerned about being fair to more experienced employees who have paid their dues. And, they are apprehensive about overconfident new hires being given responsibilities they aren't prepared to handle. When our M-Factor survey asked the generations how well-prepared Millennials are to succeed in the workplace, *over half* the respondents said they felt Millennials were either unprepared or poorly prepared to be effective.

Raised by parents who built their lives around their offspring and showered them with constant streams of praise to build their self-esteem, this generation shows signs of being far too impressed with their own value and importance. The Aspen Education Group reports that 16,400 students took the Narcissistic Personality Inventory (NPI) between 1982 and 2006. In 1982, one-third of students scored above average on the test. In 2006, that number was over 65 percent. Clearly something has changed. While the accusation of entitlement has been exaggerated in many cases, it also has a root in reality. Here are the six drivers of entitlement we have identified:

1. **A cult of customization.** Baby Boomers had the big brands, from Levi's to Wheaties. Gen Xers had the anti-brands—the little companies that started out under the radar and morphed into a movement, like Apple Computer. While these companies are huge today, they've protected their antiestablishment image and continue to charm the marketplace with their "reinventing business" style. For Millennials, marketers turned away from big brands and anti-brands to "creating your own brand." Over time, just about anything could be customized to suit a young consumer's personality

and taste. From personalizing ringtones to customizing a new car with off-market add-ons, Millennials have been able to shape the world in their own image. Why not the workplace?

2. The self-esteem movement. Millennials have been praised to the skies by parents trying to help them feel good about themselves. The Aspen Education Group points to what they call the "runaway inflation of speech" as a culprit in the Millennial generation's healthy sense of itself. "No girl is pretty; she's drop-dead gorgeous. That guy is a genius (not merely bright)." This *praise inflation* is playing out in the workplace in ways that make the older generations cringe. Lands' End and Bank of America, for example, have hired consultants who serve as "praise teams" to teach managers how to compliment employees using e-mail, prize packages, and other displays of appreciation.

The jury is still out on whether or not the drive to establish a healthy self-esteem in kids has succeeded. Studies have shown that kids who are told everything they do is great develop a shakier sense of self than those who are given honest feedback. The young people who received a balance of positive and negative input were better able to judge their own performance and exhibited less stress over their choices than those who were told everything was good. This is certainly playing out in the workplace, where Millennials can't seem to receive negative feedback without being traumatized by it. Or, as Deborah Stipek, dean of education at Stanford University put it, "I have a box of Kleenex in my office because they haven't dealt with [criticism] before."

ZITS © ZITS PARTNERSHIP, KING FEATURES SYNDICATE

3. **"I want it yesterday."** In our sped-up, tech-driven world, when kids have wanted something they've been able to get it. Children longing for a certain toy don't have to wait days to get to the mall or months until their next birthday. They can walk to the computer, find it on the Internet, and use a gift card to pay for it instantaneously. This is playing out at work when Millennials expect growth, development, and promotions at a pace that takes the boss's breath away.

MILLENNIALS ON RECORD

"I walked in the door thinking that I could be the CEO. With every job I've wanted to learn as much as possible and then move on to the next thing. I want to live a complete and full life so taking in as much knowledge as possible is the most realistic way to do that. And I want to move up as quickly as possible. That might be unrealistic from the job's point of view, but I don't think of it as unrealistic."

— *Nikki Schmidt, age 29, manager of business programs, The Conflict Center*

4. **Changing attitudes toward work.** Ask Traditionalists about work and they are likely to say, "You're lucky to have a job." They'd lived through the Great Depression or its aftermath, and they knew the fear of doing without. Ask Boomers about work and you are likely to hear, "Get something with a future." This generation wanted to earn, achieve, and stand out from the crowd. Ask Xers and they'll tell you, "Create a career where you can land on your feet." Having lived through the dot-com boom and bust, and having watched their parents give their lives to their jobs only to end up downsized or divorced, Xers thought about surviving first and thriving second.

Ask a Millennial about work and they'll tell you they have choices. They have been raised by parents who told them, "If you're going to work as hard as we have, do something you care about." Richard

Sebastian of St. Cloud University's School of Business explained it this way: "They're told they are special. They're told they can accomplish whatever they want in life, that they should go for their dreams, and consequently they . . . have this inflated sense of importance . . ." Millennials are looking for jobs where they can express themselves and their unique gifts and are disappointed when the workplace doesn't support this.

5. The grading system has changed.

David put the car in park and looked in the rearview mirror. His seven-year-old son, Jonah, looked back with a smile and gave him two thumbs up. It was Jonah's first day of T-ball.

They jumped out of the car and within seconds were greeted by a Boomer coach named Rob.

"Welcome to the Sidewinders little buddy, you must be Jonah. Hey, are you ready to have some fun?"

Jonah nodded.

"Well remember. That's what this is all about. Don't worry when it's your turn to bat, you get to keep swinging until you hit the ball. We don't have three strikes."

Jonah glanced at David, confused. David shrugged his shoulders as coach Rob continued.

"Now listen. Everyone will get a turn at bat and then we take the field and the other team comes up to bat. We don't do three outs because it wouldn't be fair and not everyone would get a turn at the plate."

Now Jonah really looked puzzled. This approach was not covered in the "kick T-ball butt" speech his dad had given him on the way to the field.

Rob continued, "And finally little buddy, we don't keep score!"

Jonah and David were baffled. If we don't keep score, how do we know who wins?

Rob concluded, "Now get out there and have fun!"

As Jonah jogged out to meet his team on the field, David couldn't help but wonder whether this game would last until January. It didn't, and the T-ball experience turned out to be a great lesson for Jonah. At the end of this and every game of the season, there weren't any tears or silent treatments on the car ride home. There wasn't any bragging about a future in the Baseball Hall of Fame. There wasn't even a running tally with the team's wins or losses. (Although if you asked any of the parents they definitely could have told you the score!) There was just a seven-year-old boy who loved playing the game. All the kids got along great, cheered each other on, and were constantly happy.

But David's euphoria faded a bit as he flashed ahead fifteen years to when all of the Sidewinders would be old enough to join the workforce. He couldn't help but picture the first day on the job: "Surprise, surprise guys, around here you'll be lucky if you get two strikes. We don't let you keep swinging until you hit the ball. In fact, we expect you to be able to hit the ground running. And finally boys, around here we actually do keep score and we definitely want to beat the competition."

David wasn't sure who was in for a bigger shock, the Sidewinders or corporate America.

6. Trophies for everyone! There's one more societal shift that has fueled the entitlement furor. In our competitive capitalist environment, "A" has always been linked to achievement. You do the best work and you get the top grade, the highest pay, or the most recognition. However, as attitudes have changed so has our system of grading. Now you don't get an "A" for achieving, you get it for attempting. A recent study by researchers at the University of California, Irvine, found that a third of students surveyed said that they expected Bs just for attending lectures, and 40 percent said they deserved a B for completing the required reading. As Jason Greenwood, a senior kinesiology major at the University of Maryland put it, "I think putting in a lot of effort should merit a high grade. What else is there really than the effort that you put in? If you put in all the effort you have and get a C, what is the point? If someone goes to every class and reads every chapter in the book and does everything the teacher asks of them and more, then they should be getting an A like their effort deserves."

We've raised Millennials with phrases like, "The results don't matter, as long as you did your best," and "Even though you lost, I'm so proud of how hard you tried." While praise may build confidence, it doesn't necessarily set you up to bury the competition. Imagine a team of engineers assigned to design the next space shuttle being told, "Whatever happens, we'll be happy if you just try your best."

Lynne spoke at a conference for high-potential young engineers at a major oil company recently, and a senior executive was asked how new hires could make sure they're on track for plumb international assignments. He responded that as much as he wanted to retain all of them, and as much as he would like everyone to have these opportunities, the best assignments would go to the highest performers because that's what makes a company competitive. "You will have to excel and you will have to stand out from the crowd," he told them. Lynne wondered if he would have needed to explain that concept a decade or two ago.

In this chapter we've discussed six drivers that have contributed to the perception of entitlement among the Millennials. Now here are a series of solutions for dealing with entitlement organized around "Four Rs"—recruiting, retention, rewards, and respect—along with ideas you can use to manage your team or your own career.

RECRUITING

When we dig deep into the roots of entitlement we often find the wrong expectations were set right from the beginning. If you've looked at a large company's recruiting Web site lately you have to admit the presentation is pretty dazzling. They highlight so many enticing aspects of the organization you can't imagine why *everyone* wouldn't want to work there. Sometimes the razzle-dazzle continues into the interviewing process. It's natural that recruiters and hiring managers want to put their best foot forward, but prospects need to find out if the shoe really fits. Company representatives make the culture, the jobs, and the experience seem irresistible. But too often they fail to paint a realistic picture. Millennials wind up in jobs that aren't anything like what was described. When they complain, they are accused of being too demanding or too entitled. To avoid dissatisfaction down the road, recruiters need to be honest about what candidates can expect, and candidates must tune in to reality. Here are some tips:

• **Paint a realistic picture.** Millennials will demand from day one what the other generations have spent years trying to earn. For example, our M-Factor survey found they are just as optimistic about achieving work-life balance as both Xers and Boomers, even though they are just starting out. If you're recruiting, talk with candidates about the ups and downs of working in your environment. Discuss how successful candidates succeeded and where unsuccessful ones went wrong. Describe a typical day. You stand to lose some candidates by veering away from Fantasy Island, but better to lose them now than be marooned on that island with miserable Millennials six months into the job. One accounting manager put it this way: "We talk with candidates about exactly what sorts of hours will be required. In slow times, they will have an easier schedule. During tax time the hours increase exponentially. We have ways of easing the situation, like we supply dinner five nights a week during tax season and we have a workout room in our building. We also provide a concierge to run errands for people putting in long hours—picking up dry cleaning, etc. But the reality is you are likely to work twelve-hour-plus days during certain times of the year, and we don't want people to be misled about that."

- **Put tech 2 work.** A number of employers now use everything from Web sites to videos to help demonstrate "what it's like to work here." From illustrating what your campus looks like to demonstrating a "day in the life" of an employee, technology can take some of the burden off recruiters and help you create a realistic depiction of your workplace.

- **No blind dates in the workplace.** Encourage candidates to talk with current employees about how they like the company and what they do in their jobs. You run the risk of a good candidate being scared off by something they hear, but it's better to raise issues early while they can still be resolved. For Millennials new to the work world this can be a little intimidating but also extremely valuable. Interviews with current employees will provide a good sense of cultural fit and offer a chance to ask more honest questions than they might be comfortable asking the *recruiter.*

- **Beef up your internships.** In our MOR interviews, the Millennials who most frequently had expectations that were well-aligned with their actual jobs had done internships with the company or a similar organization before being hired full time. Children's Memorial Hospital in Chicago, for example, was struggling with turnover among young nurses. Instead of moaning about what a spoiled crop of Millennials they'd hired, they looked a little deeper and found that their on-boarding process was failing to set nurses up to succeed. They instituted a beefed-up internship program with mentoring and extensive training that has curbed turnover by more than 50 percent and increased job satisfaction.

Liberty Diversified International, a privately held diverse portfolio management company, hires a new batch of interns every semester. As the shift from Gen X to Millennial applicants took place, they noticed Millennials weren't as excited by the program. The biggest surprise was that this had nothing to do with the work, but rather with the title *intern.* Millennial applicants wrinkled their noses as they explained *intern* implied stapling, grunt work, temporary duties, and a less than 100 percent contribution. So, rather than look at reinventing the whole internship program, Liberty simply re-branded it. Millennials can now apply to be a "professional development associate" or PDA, which sends the message they are there to learn valuable skills for future careers.

Too often accusations of entitlement arise because employees don't feel the job they have been given is what they were led to expect. When it comes to entitlement on the recruiting front, realistic communication can alleviate misunderstandings for workers, managers, and companies.

RETENTION

The struggle around entitlement is probably most painful when it comes to retention. Boomers and Xers tell us they feel their backs are up against the wall when they've invested in grooming and growing a Millennial only to find out the new employee expected something different and is threatening to leave. While the recent poor economy made younger workers more hesitant about job hopping, don't think for a minute they won't leap the minute conditions improve. That willingness to walk if they aren't satisfied can feel like a slap in the face to older workers who put up with plenty of grunt work when they started their own careers. A Boomer managing director of a large regional theater company explained it this way: "When I started out in theater, I would have done anything to be part of that world. I swept the stage, cleaned the makeup rooms, acted as prop boy—anything just to be around the theater. Today's theater management grads see it as a business management job, and they look down on a lot of the small tasks I had to do and learned to love."

Once the Millennial expresses unhappiness, there are two choices: resent it or identify the issue and deal with it. Unfortunately, resentment is often the most popular choice. Bosses get mad, and eventually they get even. But they don't get the problem solved.

Sometimes it is truly a bad match and both sides would be better off cutting their losses and moving on. If you have honestly evaluated a Millennial's complaints, have tried to respond fairly to them, and are still experiencing a problem, you might simply have to let that person go. Other times, however, the perception of entitlement can be overcome and the relationship can be worked out quite satisfactorily. Here are some solutions:

• **RecogniZZZe boredom.** Parents who thought they could escape the cries of "Mom, I'm bored" by heading off to work will be surprised to find they're hearing it at the office. One of the most common complaints we hear from Millennials is they don't have enough to do, or enough to do that is interesting. In one survey, of the 75 percent of Millennials who said they were unhappy at work, 61 percent said they were bored.

You can imagine the reaction from the older generations when told by a Millennial the job is boring: "These kids think they're too good for the job! When I was their age I held that position for years and I didn't complain!" Today, expectations around work have changed and skilled Millennials feel justified in letting bosses know they could do more. Meghan Bromert, one of our MORs, commented, "What they don't understand is why we are changing jobs. It is mostly out of boredom or not being challenged. When we were growing up, we were balancing three sports, honors classes, and volunteer work. We were good at multitasking." So it's not necessarily that Millennials feel "entitled" to take on more or new tasks, it's really about staying stimulated.

Another MOR commented, "Entry level work feels like a huge step down from what we were doing prior to being hired. Why would they want to waste our capacity like that?"

Too often the real reason people label Millennials as pushy, spoiled, or entitled is because we don't know what to do with them. Many managers are unclear on what next steps they *can* offer to an employee who is bored. We gave the keynote speech at an event sponsored by a major U.S. insurance company a couple of years back. During the break Lynne was approached by three Millennial women who spoke in whispers: "We don't know what to do. We work in customer service and we're bored out of our minds. We finish all our work by 3:00 and then we sit there. But if we surf the Internet to fill the time we get reprimanded. If we ask for more to do our boss is mad. He says this is how the job descriptions are written." We wanted to go back and interview those Millennials for our book, but oddly enough they were no longer with the company.

The problem was an insecure supervisor who was afraid to address what these employees could really do. He didn't want to challenge the status quo by pushing to rewrite job descriptions. He clearly didn't want the powers that be to find out that staffing allocations might need to be reconfigured or his department's productivity could be even higher. And the Millennials were seen as "entitled" if they said, "This work is too easy, we're getting done too fast, and our jobs don't make sense."

Too many job descriptions haven't been updated in decades. Technology has made many positions repetitive and dull. Ask yourself, is this really entitlement or is it something else? If employees are pushing for more, find out what you can do to reconfigure jobs, add responsibilities to employees who are highly capable, or give additional rewards where they are merited. Learn what career paths are available for your peak performers. But don't be paralyzed by fears that you don't know what to do with demanding, capable Millennials who are truly engaged.

• **Mix it up.** Bosses, if your Millennials are hungry for more to do don't accuse them of being entitled. Take something off your plate and serve it up on theirs. Boomers are the worst generation at delegating. They hate to let go of the things that have earned them a seat at the table. And of course they're convinced no one could possibly do things as well as they have. Boomers, the more you can let go the more it frees you up for something else. If your desk wasn't piled to the ceiling with unfinished projects perhaps you'd have available space to take on a new assignment you'd actually love.

For independent Xers, delegating to Millennials can seem like a huge time sink. The more you hand over, the more you have to teach and mentor them. But remember, your biggest time commitment is during the ramp-up phase. Once employees get comfortable with new tasks your reward will be increased productivity and possibly the opportunity to take on new challenges yourself.

MILLENNIALS ON RECORD

"After my first intern position here I really thought about leaving because I didn't feel I was being used well. In my new role, I've been given the chance to manage projects. That makes me want to stay because I want to see those projects through."

—Luke Norman, age 24, program manager, Center for Community Leadership, United Way

• **Address career jitters.** Millennials who express concerns about whether they are doing enough or if they are getting ahead fast enough are often labeled as "entitled." But maybe those are exactly the right concerns for an employee to have. When we interview employees who are happiest in their jobs, they tell us they are learning a lot, they are challenged, they are being coached and mentored, and they see they have a future with the company.

If Millennials are anxious, perhaps one of these ingredients is missing. Try to get to the bottom of it. Do they feel they are being mentored? Do they know what their next career step or learning opportunity might look like? The good news is this doesn't mean they always need to know exactly which box they are headed for on the org chart. Millennials are less worried about their actual title or whether they will have a dotted-line reporting relationship to a certain person or department and more worried about whether they are contributing. Reassuring employees about how their contribution is making a difference can be key. And sometimes it helps to have more than one place to turn to when concerns arise. The Womble Carlyle law firm has created two lines of mentoring. The first-line mentor is the associate's supervisor and is aptly called a "supervising mentor"; the second-line mentor is a "resource mentor," who can be from a different practice group. The reason for this two-tiered approach is that the first-line mentor is the associate's boss, and it's not always possible to discuss matters candidly, especially personnel issues. A second mentor gives the associate another person to turn to who might have a different perspective or be less personally involved in the issue.

MILLENNIALS ON RECORD

"The biggest thing is communication style. We are used to instant communication and feedback. When we work with generations who aren't that way, it's so difficult to stay motivated."

— *Julie Rinaldo, age 30, NPI engineering supervisor, Arrow Electronics, Inc.*

For Millennials who are anxious about their progress, point out specifically how the things they are doing in their job are serving the company, as well as how they are building long-term career skills.

• **Share the dream.** When asked about ambition, one MOR told us this: "We are freaking rock stars! Our brains are constantly going. We are thinking about everything from world hunger to war all the time. Not that the other generations aren't thinking about these things, but it's like our generation has an instinct to care about the world and figure out how to change it." Another MOR countered, "Our generation thinks we are the only ones who ever wanted to change anything. That's why we come off as seeming entitled." They both have it right.

Millennials are tremendously passionate about making the world a better place. But they appear entitled when they act like they're the only ones with a dream. Talking to them about how their work fits with the company's vision can help them feel more connected.

We've been talking about how to get around the entitlement roadblocks when it comes to recruiting and retaining Millennials. But the entitlement issue also rears its ugly head around . . .

REWARDS

Jenna was clearly disappointed with the pat on the back she received after working for a month on a research report for her department. Her boss, Gen Xer Trey, had thanked her personally, but he could tell she felt let down.

"What does she want," he muttered to himself, "a medal? A standing ovation? Should I take out a full-page ad somewhere?" He was bummed because he'd gone out on a limb with their Boomer boss to convince him Jenna could handle the project. Trey had even stepped up and requested that Jenna's name be on the report cover with the other Boomer department heads. That was a stretch! The Boomers had been appalled. Then they decided it made them look more hip to show that both an Xer (Trey) and a Millennial had participated on the project.

Trey had a lot of Millennials to supervise and they were so needy all the time. It wasn't enough to say thanks or to put a note in their personnel file. What did they want from him? He thought about the big chart with gold stars on it he'd seen at his son's preschool. "Maybe I should get one of those," he muttered.

Trey headed down the hall to his best work buddy's office. Gino had worked as a recruiter and was more tuned in to the Millennial mind-set.

"Dude, you have to think Millennial," Gino advised. "Rewards don't have to be so complicated. Like, Jenna's into collaborating.

Didn't she get a ton of people to help her on that project? And she likes to get the big picture. As I recall she interviewed several senior leaders, right?"

"So?" asked Trey.

"So you should invite her to the final presentation. She doesn't have to say anything, but she could at least see how it's received by the committee.

"Plus, she puts in a lot of hours. I saw her here the last two weekends. Why don't you give her a personal day off as a reward? Or, if you can't swing that, how about letting her use the office football tickets? I know she's a huge football nut. She ran the Fantasy Football pool for the office this season."

"Got it," responded Trey. "I can do this."

As four generations prepare to manage and team up with Millennials, it's going to become clear that every generation sees rewards in its own way. Whichever generation you're from, you can assume Millennials won't necessarily be motivated by the same things that turn you on. When they show disappointment or ask for something different it's going to be way too easy to think they are acting entitled. One Millennial offended the CEO of a small company by saying he didn't want to receive a holiday turkey since he was a vegetarian and would rather have a donation made to the local food bank instead. The CEO saw him as unappreciative while the Millennial was simply trying to avoid wasting the company's money.

It's great if you can figure out what kinds of rewards *do* mean something to Millennials, but it can be tough if you're not from that generation. For independent Xer Trey, being invited to attend one more meeting wouldn't have sounded like a reward; it would have sounded like a big boring drag. It didn't dawn on him that it might be a thrill for Jenna. How do we peer inside Millennials' minds and figure out what's meaningful for them? Here are some tips:

• **Rewards don't have to be BIG to be meaningful.** Toys, tickets, or time off can all be ways to show you noticed a Millennial's performance. Gift cards and gadgets are great, too. How about decorating a Millennial's chair, or letting them plan the next party? At conventions, instead of handing out tote bags and coffee mugs, meeting planners have started giving attendees a thumb drive or an environmentally sensitive water bottle with no PCBs. Millennials are thrilled. When you can get inside the mind of another generation small things can go a long way.

- **Collaboration can be its own reward.** Ask Jenna, and we bet she'd tell you that being chosen to handle the office Fantasy Football pool was a reward. Ask a Boomer and they'd say it was one more "duty," but Jenna had a ball with it. A reward can mean something as simple as collaborating on a special project.

- **One reward does not fit all.** Remember this generation is all about customization. Whether it's a tangible reward or a new responsibility, make sure the Millennial knows why and how it was chosen just for them. One card shop franchise manager chose an employee of the month and rewarded her with a CD mix of her favorite music downloaded from iTunes. She also used the store's card-making software to design a set of note cards with the employee's name on them in a style she would love. The cash outlay wasn't large and the buzz among employees was priceless.

- **Reward while it's still rewarding.** If you thought Gen Xers were impatient, stand back. When a Millennial turns in an assignment you're likely to get an e-mail ten minutes later asking if you received it and a text message five minutes after that asking if you got the e-mail. We will need to pick up the pace of feedback and rewards if we want to maximize their value. A gift certificate to Amazon.com isn't half as meaningful a month later as it would have been on the day of the accomplishment.

- **Recognize the team.** One MOR told us that when interviewing for promotions within her firm a mentor coached her to say "I did such and such" instead of "we" because she needed to impress decision makers with her accomplishments. The Millennial commented on how hard it was to say "I" after so many years of working in teams. A number of Millennials told us they didn't feel it was always important to be rewarded individually, as long as their team won the prize. This team orientation is a real ace in the hole for business and it makes sense to reward it. But competitive Boomers and independent Xers don't always think along those lines. If you're racing toward the finish on a project, why not set up a team competition with prizes for the winners? Then stand back and see what your Millennials can really do.

If the old rewards aren't working, don't assume you have to spend a fortune to update them. It might just be you need to look at incentives from a generational point of view. A lot of what gets called "entitlement" can be chalked up to two simple things: attitude and gratitude. Millennials go wrong when they portray an attitude that makes the other generations feel inept, threatened, or unappreciated. They go doubly wrong when they are ignorant or insensitive. The trouble is one generation doesn't always know what is insensitive or rude in the eyes of another. We've talked about entitlement when it comes to recruiting, retention, and rewards. Now for the last, and potentially most loaded one of all... respect.

RESPECT

Veronica was a Gen Xer who set aside thoughts of making it big in corporate America after college and joined the public sector. She worked in HR for a progressive city in northern California, and was proud of how much change she'd been able to bring about in a short time. She had created the city's first bi-lingual recruiting Web site, gotten senior leadership thinking about hiring young talent, and instituted a program to slow the rate of Boomer retirements until they could build more bench strength. As the only Xer in a Boomer-dominated world, Veronica had fought to earn her place at the decision-making table. Now it was time to tap into the Millennial generation. Her first interview was for an entry-level HR position and the candidate looked promising. Enter Chandra, a graduate of a good local university. Sharp and well-prepared, she made a great first impression—until this exchange . . .

VERONICA: Tell me a little about why you want to work in city government.

CHANDRA: I like the mission of local government and the potential to make a difference in people's lives. I think I would like the variety, too. One day you're working on parks and the next day it might be parking. I guess I just worry that change comes so slowly it might be frustrating. Are you able to see the results of what you do?

VERONICA: Actually, we're one of the most progressive cities around. We have incredible benefits, flexible schedules, a super work environment, and really compelling vision, so I'm surprised you'd see us as slow.

CHANDRA: No doubt you have done some great things, but what about the bureaucracy that tends to go with government? How do you deal with that? I've been following that toxic waste dump issue in the paper and it seems like nothing ever gets decided.

VERONICA (to herself): Well, something just got decided because you sure as heck aren't going to be working for me. Talk about toxic waste!

If you think about the dialogue above, Millennial Chandra actually had reasonable concerns, both about the pace of change being potentially frustrating and the challenges of working in a bureaucracy. She wasn't wrong to have some apprehension about the city being slow moving, but it was her tone that sent the conversation off track. She appeared unimpressed by the many positive benefits Gen Xer Veronica listed, not seeming to realize that Veronica might have been the very person responsible for putting those in place.

Her worst offense was probably the most subtle. By implying the city was doing a poor job of dealing with the toxic waste issue, she made Veronica the bad guy. It's quite possible that the waste site had been created by a disreputable company and now the city employees were tasked with finding the will, the means, and the money to fix it. These acts of dedication that public servants commit every day often go unnoticed, but they shouldn't be invisible to someone applying for a job there. Think how differently the conversation might have gone if Chandra had done her homework with a different focus . . .

VERONICA: Tell me a little about why you want to work in city government.

CHANDRA: I am fascinated by the breadth and variety of what cities actually accomplish on behalf of citizens. I like the idea of being able to make a difference. But I know it can be a slow process sometimes. I am curious, how do you handle the frustration when you can't make change happen fast enough?

VERONICA: I try to focus on the things we *can* accomplish. For example, from an HR perspective we're one of the most progressive cities around. We have incredible benefits, flexible schedules, a super work environment, and really compelling vision. I'm proud of that.

CHANDRA: I can see why you would be. I have compared a number of public sector employers and this city has so much to offer. I would like to know more about your career opportunities, but I also want to know about your mission. Like, I've been following the toxic waste dump issue and it seems like the city employees are not going to give up until they can get it resolved. I have a lot of respect for that.

VERONICA (to herself): And I have a lot of respect for you.

Look how the dialogue changed. Chandra didn't give up trying to get the answers she needed. Instead she took a different tack and used tact. She worked from a place of respect and acknowledged her Gen X interviewer as a change agent. She didn't insult the bureaucracy but politely asked how Veronica dealt with it. She presented herself as a person sensitive enough to navigate the politics that will inevitably pop up on the job. She showed curiosity about the challenges the city faced and found a courteous way to address a tough issue. You can see that after only a few sentences these two established an atmosphere of politeness and respect. Entitlement didn't rear its ugly head. From here it would be much easier to talk about the sticky parts of the job. So how does this play out for those of us in the real world? Here's how . . .

- **The Golden Rule is still in effect.** The most important thing Millennials can do in any interaction with the other generations is show respect for where they've been. This means doing some homework and acknowledging the accomplishments of the organization, the department, or the individual before challenging the way things are being done. Instead of saying to a Traditionalist, "I'm bored and I want to talk about how I am going to get promoted faster," Millennials should try saying, "You've had such a long and rewarding career here, I would like your input as to how I can be successful in our company."

If you're talking to Boomers, acknowledge the struggles they've had and the progress they've made: "You've survived through three major recessions. Can you give me some pointers on how to deal with the current downturn?" Or, "What was it like to be the first woman vice president in our company's history? I bet I could learn a lot from you."

One of the greatest laments we hear from Traditionalists today is that the Millennials aren't interested in the company's past. Boomers regret that Millennials don't seem to appreciate the battles they've won, for example in the areas of civil rights or women's rights. Gen Xers tell us Millennials don't appreciate the hardships they have endured, whether fighting to move the company to a new software platform or crusading for visibility in the shadow of the Baby Boom. Most people in the work world have overcome obstacles to get to where they are today. The best way to gain respect and not come off as entitled is to honor them.

- **Respect goes both ways.** If you're recruiting Millennials, don't make assumptions about what they do or don't know. They may look like the kid who mows your lawn, but they might also be capable of mowing down the competition if you give them a chance. Ask about the experiences they've had in school, in work, and in life. Talk with them about how these might translate to your workplace. If you're managing Millennials, ask which parts of the job seem easy and doable to them. That's how you uncover hidden talents. Ask them also where they think they need support or coaching—oftentimes they want input from you but weren't sure how to ask. Be aware that respect also comes through in your language. Millennials don't want to be called "kids" or spoken to in generalities: "Your generation has no respect for the old ways!"

Don't make assumptions about what Millennials think. You're far better off asking than guessing. For example, many managers we interviewed expressed concern that Millennials would think their career paths were advancing too slowly. But in the M-Factor survey, when we asked respondents whether career paths where they work advanced "too slowly, just right, or too fast," Millennials were more likely than Boomers or Xers to say that in their workplace career paths advanced "just right."

• **Switch from "they" to "we."** Politicians have gotten into lots of trouble for rudely referring to groups as "those people," yet we do it all the time with the generations...."Those kids never look up from their PDAs—you can't make eye contact!" Or, "These new hires are so cocky, it's like they know everything!" All we can say is, *those people* who talk this way are creating generational divides, not bridging them. A trick we suggest in our BridgeBuilder® training classes is changing the "they" to a "we." It's such a powerful way to speak. Think about a conversation between supervisor Carl and long-time employee Rose:

ROSE: Those Millennials are driving me nuts. Always asking questions, bugging me for feedback, wanting to be rewarded for every little thing. They need to get a grip.

CARL: Our Millennials are some of the best new hires we've made in a long time. We're lucky to have them on our team. If Millennials want our feedback, Rose, it's because we have something to teach them."

The dialogue above brings up another point. We also need to:

- **Stick up for each other.** You all know the person on your team or in your department who has something negative to say about everyone. What we have never understood is why that person has so much power. Why does a single negative soul have more influence on morale and attitudes than ten positive people? And what can we do to combat it? Quite simply, we have to stick up for each other. That's what happened in the dialogue above. Rose tries to go negative and Carl refuses to go with her. There's power in that. Here's another example between two Millennials:

JASMINE: Yeah, like our boss is the most slow-moving creature on the planet. I looked up "sloths" on Wikipedia and I think I have found Carl's ancestor!
J.P.: Whatever, Jasmine. Carl is going slowly on this proposal because he has to get it approved by like ten committees and he has to find the money to finance it. He's working his tail off so we can do the project, so get over it!

There's incredible strength in sticking up for each other across generations. Here's another one . . .

HARRIET: Well Edna, you sure have your hands full babysitting for your team! Do those new hires know anything? What are they, Gen Y? Gen Z? I mean, I saw how they were dressed for work and almost had a bird. I thought they were from janitorial!
EDNA: I know. I saw a Millennial in the elevator the other day and I wanted to ask him if he was dressed to go to band practice!

But the truth is this group of new hires is so sharp you can't believe it. They're the reason our department is number one in productivity, and since they came on board I can honestly say I never had more fun!

Try it out for yourself the next time you get caught in the entitlement cross-fire. Among the Four Rs—recruiting, retention, rewards, and respect—the most powerful is respect, and standing up for one another is the simplest and perhaps the most profound tool we can deploy.

• **Don't confuse entitlement with engagement.** Millennials who are coming to you for feedback, coaching, advice, mentoring, or input are not necessarily doing it to be annoying or because they are spoiled. It might be because they are actually *engaged*. We mentioned this earlier but we feel it merits repeating as we talk about respect. Millennial Jenny Dotson, senior meeting manager with the National Association of College and University Business Officers, explained it like this: "We were raised to work *with* our parents, not for them. We admire them and want to please. We take that with us to work. When I check in with my boss, it is not because I am insecure, but because I want to make sure I am pleasing her with what I am doing."

Employees who request more responsibility might not be pushy and greedy, they might be *eager*. Workers who keep asking about that next career move aren't necessarily making waves; they might actually be turned on and wanting to progress. Ann Miller, who serves as corporate culture specialist at Liberty Diversified International, made this point: "I often hear from more senior employees how taken aback they are by how comfortable Millennials are speaking directly to executives. There is a trust level with them that they can feel comfortable saying what they think. Rather than see this as disrespectful, I challenge our culture to see it as a gift that we have been given. In an age where we don't have time to waste, it is refreshing to get it all on the table and not have to guess or beat around the bush."

MILLENNIALS ON RECORD

"The other generations probably don't know that we are hungry to learn. Not all of us are lazy and just getting by. I love when people will teach me something. My supervisor is really good at that. She won't just give me an answer, she'll teach me something. We are curious. We ask a lot of questions. But that isn't us being disrespectful or us trying to challenge someone. It's just us being curious."

—*Samantha Fogliano, age 25, senior account executive, Surge Worldwide Healthcare Communications*

Whether it's around recruiting, retention, rewards, or respect, the entitlement question will continue to plague the Millennial generation for the foreseeable future. Those who cope with it the best will be managers, co-workers, and Millennials who recognize the issue and address it head on. Sometimes Millennials will need to change their attitudes or at least find ways to communicate so they don't come off as spoiled and demanding. Other times managers will need to question their own responses to being challenged and admit that sometimes Millennials have a point. We can make jobs more interesting and career paths more compelling. We can become better at communication and feedback. Most importantly, we can focus less on our personal responses to the other generations and more on the best ways to get work done. Ultimately that's best for everybody.

Back at the V.A., Traditionalist Eric sat in the interview room with his arms crossed over his chest. He wasn't happy about giving Justin a second chance, but the kid had called him directly and made a compelling case.

"I know I didn't listen well in the interview," Justin explained, "and I apologize. I was just so excited to finally have this chance that I came on too strong. I have worked hard to build my résumé, I really believe in your mission, and if you give me a shot I think I can prove to you that my heart and my work ethic are in the right place."

Eric shook his head and grinned. How could you say no to that?

four

MEANING

It was another Monday morning. Ariel stared longingly at the framed college graduation picture on her desk and remembered how on that day she truly believed she would make a difference in the world. She sighed as she pondered how it was possible that only a year later she had left the world of endless optimism and entered the world of endless paperwork.

Ariel worked at an insurance company where mantras like "ethics over all" and "the customer comes first" were drilled into her head on a daily basis. No wonder her company had continued to be profitable in a bad economy. The organization wanted policy holders to know that even when the rest of the world felt shaky, the insurance side of their lives was secure.

She understood how the company was helping clients, but she didn't feel like her job contributed to the mission statement tacked on her cubicle wall.

Who Am I, and Why Am I Here?

At the same time, Ariel knew she was lucky to have a job. Half her friends had been laid off from other companies while her position was secure. The people she worked with were nice and wanted her to succeed. So why the nagging sense of dissatisfaction?

Ariel went to talk to her Gen X boss, Eddie. "Do you ever feel like there's something missing?" she asked.

"What do you mean?" Eddie countered as he shuffled through stacks of claim reports. As a victim of the dot-com bust he felt relieved to work for such a stable company.

"I meet all my goals; I process the right number of claims per week; and I receive good evaluations," she explained.

"That doesn't sound like a problem," said Eddie, not looking up from the forms.

"I just feel flat about what I'm doing. What does it all mean?"

Eddie sighed. "The meaning is you have a place to work with a steady job and a good future. We have flexible schedules, paid time off, family leave. Look at all you've learned already. Come on, Ariel, this isn't philosophy class. Stay busy, meet expectations, and you'll get promoted in no time." Eddie dove into his pile of papers again with gusto.

"But what if that's not enough?" Ariel thought to herself.

Later that day she ran into Reg, a Millennial team leader in the same claims department.

"Reg, help. I do a good job, but something's missing."

"I know what you mean," he responded. "I felt that way for a while, and then I went on some client visits. You know—when you are processing a claim, but you have to check out the situation in person? Once I started meeting face-to-face with policyholders and could see how we really help them, everything changed. It wasn't just pushing paper anymore; it was changing lives. Plus, a lot of claims reps don't want to do the fieldwork so I'm helping the team out, too."

"Wow," breathed Ariel. "We don't do that in our division. We have field reps who handle the site visits."

"Go anyway," advised Reg. "I'll even take you. It's worth it."

Ariel was encountering a trend experienced by the hundreds of Millennials we've interviewed over the years. They want a good job in a stimulating work environment. They want good pay and good bosses, too. But beyond that they want to find meaning in what they do.

Few books written about Millennials have touched on this vital trend. To skeptical Xers the Millennial search for meaning can sound like just one more way to avoid the realities of grunt work. To Boomers who aren't sure they've resolved their own questions about purpose, the Millennials' quest can seem like something more appropriately tackled in church or on a shrink's sofa. Traditionalists who spent years climbing the ladder might wish Millennials would just buckle down, pay their dues, and *earn* the promotion to more meaningful work.

But countless comments by Millennials about searching for meaning on the job told us we'd better take a closer look.

Some of you might be thinking, "Great, I work for a manufacturing company; it's not exactly the Peace Corps. Why do I need to know about meaning?" Or maybe you're thinking, "In shaky economic times, people ought to be grateful just to be working." We understand the skepticism. When your assembly team is frantically trying to get an order crated and shipped, and a Millennial informs you he or she doesn't feel fulfilled, it's tempting to drop them in a box and ship them out with the next order. When you've seen co-workers laid off and hear a young employee complain that the job is boring it's hard not to want to launch into a lecture about gratitude.

But the truth is for many Americans, work is much more than what we do; it's who we are. Millennials have been raised by parents who told them, "If you are going to work hard for a lifetime, find something to do that has meaning for you." They've encouraged them to give back and volunteer, and they've talked with Millennials a lot about what kind of work might make sense to them. It's not enough to find work; you might as well find a job that means something.

THE MEAT BEHIND MEANING

Many of the Millennials we interviewed who love their jobs talked incessantly about meaning—the feeling they were making a difference. A lot of those who expressed dissatisfaction cited the same value. That is, they felt their work lacked meaning and passion, which in turn made them want to leave. This often comes as a surprise to the other generations who argue that Millennials will find meaning in their work once they pay their dues and learn the ropes. Meaning, in other words, is higher up on Maslow's hierarchy of needs and you can earn access to it over time. Not so, the Millennials would argue. Why enter a job if you can't play a meaningful role? Why work if you aren't making a difference for somebody?

Millennials place a premium on the psychic income they derive from work, according to Molly Epstein, associate professor in the Practice of Management Communication at Emory University's Goizueta School of Business. She goes on to say, "Millennials will choose workplaces and employers that provide an environment where they feel valued, have freedom to work on projects that are important to them, and are recognized as individuals. . . ."

An upside of the search for meaning is that while it may require some thought, it doesn't cost a lot. Companies that can't pay as much in salaries and benefits can still engender loyalty and engagement by scoring high on the meaning index. Millennials talk, text, and tweet incessantly about what they do in their jobs. Organizations that find ways for Millennials to express their passions and do meaningful work will benefit hugely from positive buzz. They will also increase loyalty and reduce turnover.

Sometimes it can feel like providing meaning for Millennials is an insurmountable task. How is a person supposed to recruit, retain, manage, do their own job, *and* provide meaning to these pesky new hires? It's not like there are big "meaning" budgets carved out for managers to spend. But the costs of not paying attention to meaning are also considerable. Millennials are more than willing to leave a job if they don't feel fulfilled.

> ## MILLENNIALS ON RECORD
>
> "My dad has been at the same company for almost thirty years. The way older generations were raised is you find something and stick with it. With our generation it is about finding your passion. If you aren't happy, quit and find something else! We are much more open to switching majors, changing careers, and starting fresh."
>
> — *Julie Strand, age 23, sales representative, C. H. Robinson Worldwide*

The search for meaning isn't just a feel-good approach to management, it's a necessity when it comes to finding, engaging, and keeping this passionate generation. According to the Kelly Global Workforce Index, 51 percent of young workers surveyed were prepared to accept a lower wage or lesser role if their work contributed to something "more important or meaningful." Among Millennials, the willingness to sacrifice pay or title in exchange for more meaningful work was evident across all countries, and most pronounced in the Asia-Pacific sector. According to Christine Hassler of the *Huffington Post*, "The majority of the thousands of twenty-somethings I've interviewed have all said they'd choose a job where they felt like they are really contributing to something over a higher-paying job with more menial responsibilities."

Our biggest "aha" about meaning is that it might just be the lowest hanging fruit you can pluck to get the most out of this new workforce. We know it's important to Millennials, and most of your competitors aren't doing it. Getting your arms around meaning can be a huge competitive advantage. The goal isn't to create a training camp for future Gandhis; it's to discover how Millennials' search for meaning can inspire truly great employees and become a savvy strategy for recruitment and retention.

WHAT EACH GENERATION MEANS BY "MEANING"

Whether you're the boss or the employee, meaning can be hard to understand and hard to achieve. Yet, nine out of ten of our MOR interviewees said meaning wasn't just important, it was *the most important factor* in their work lives. When asked about money, our MORs said they assumed they'd be earning a good living. But when asked what was most important in a job, it was knowing you were "making a difference." While it sounds soft and fluffy, the search for meaning is actually part of the Millennial employee's DNA.

MILLENNIALS ON RECORD

"I think it's crucial to have meaning. I'm torn on what major to choose because I want to choose the one that can help me make a difference and help people. If I don't make a difference in a job, then I don't want to stay."
—*Samantha Fryer, age 21, artistic learning administrations manager, California Shakespeare Theater*

Wait a minute, you might ask, is the Millennial generation's drive for meaning really so unique? Don't Traditionalists, Boomers, and Xers want to make a difference, too? From what we can uncover, not exactly. For one thing, prior generations viewed careers differently.

Traditionalists. This generation was raised in an uncertain environment with fewer social safety nets. Many of their parents were immigrants desperate just to have a job and support a family. Untold millions toiled as laborers so their kids might have a better future. Ask them about meaning, and they were likely to say, "I work to ensure a better future for the people I love." Traditionalists also found meaning in "a job well done."

Baby Boomers. Hardworking Traditionalists enabled the Boomers to become the most educated generation ever. By toiling relentlessly and saving rigorously, the Traditionalists were able to give their Baby Boomer kids the opportunity to do better than they had done. Boomers focused on achieving and getting ahead. They understood they would have to work their way up through the hierarchy. If you paid your dues and played your cards right, you could eventually ascend into the really *meaningful* roles. People on the bottom did the grunt work; you could make a difference once you got to the top. That might take years, but it didn't matter as long as you got there.

The exception to this for Boomers was public service. Inspired by President Johnson's Great Society initiatives and impressed by the impact of the broad social movements (driven by Traditionalists) of the 1960s—such as voters' rights, women's rights, and civil rights—many Boomers believed a great career could be shaped around serving the public good. Baby Boomers oversaw the vast expansion of organizations that "made a difference," from government agencies to nonprofits to large, global NGOs. National goals were organized around the greater good, such as when President Kennedy challenged the nation to work together to put a man on the moon, or when President Johnson created the War on Poverty. Doing that type of work gave Boomers a built-in sense of meaning that suited their idealism and the belief they could change the world. At the same time, these rapidly expanding organizations gave competitive young employees plenty of room to rise to positions of influence, where they could jockey for power with the best of them.

Generation X. When Gen X came along, survival became the predominant strategy. Those who graduated into the tough economy of the early nineties had a hard time finding jobs and were told they would be the first generation that would fail to do better than their parents. While the accelerating economy of the mid- to late-nineties and the tech boom created lots of job opportunities, Xers were also influenced by trends that encouraged them to hang onto their

skepticism. They saw major "service" institutions called into question, such as the military, organized religion, hallowed nonprofits,
and even the presidency. Corporate layoffs and downsizing, the dot-
com bust, the recession of the early 2000s—which was exacerbated
by 9/11—all shaped the attitudes of Gen Xers toward their careers.
Since work could go away at any time, better not put your whole
identity into it. Gen Xers found meaning beyond jobs, engaging
in extreme sports and hobbies, major travel, and increased personal
time with friends and families.

Would Xers like to do something meaningful? Of course. But
that seemed a hard goal to achieve and survival was more important.
Each time we have surveyed Gen Xers about their workplace preoc-
cupations, their focus has been a defensive one. They want to keep
learning and growing so they can continue to get ahead, they want
to make themselves as valuable as possible, and they want to culti-
vate the ability to land on their feet should things go bad. When
Xers talk about meaning, they most often focus on the struggle to
achieve work-life balance. They are the first to tell you that meaning comes more from logging off than from logging on. Why?

During the birth years of Generation X, the number of working mothers crossed the 50 percent threshold. At the same time, the
push to move outward to the suburbs that began with the Boomers
continued. During the birth years of the Baby Boomers the percentage of families living in suburbs grew from 15 percent to 30 percent.
By 1980, when the last of the Xers were being born, that number
had grown to 45 percent. The result was more isolated families and
more parents absent from home. Throw in the high divorce rate
and Gen X offspring were not only the most likely to come from
a broken home, they spent a lot of time alone. According to the
authors of *Millennial Makeover*, the amount of time Generation X
children spent with significant adult role models dropped to about
fifteen minutes per day. It's no wonder when they got to the workplace
they targeted work-family balance as their #1 career issue, and one
can infer, their greatest source of meaning.

Millennials. As Millennials came of age, cultural observers noticed another shift. After the divorce rate reached a peak in 1981, it declined steadily until 2000. (At its peak the rate was 5.3 divorces per 1,000 people. It dropped to 4.2 in 2000.) Experts disagree on the reasons why. Some say it's because more couples chose to live together without marrying; others say couples were more determined to make marriages work. Whatever the reasons, the steadily declining divorce rate had an impact on Millennials. As families stabilized, they shifted focus and began concentrating more on kids. The amount of time children spent with significant adult role models rose from minutes to several hours each day. Parents expanded their roles beyond that of authority figures and ramped up their roles as teachers, coaches, mentors, and friends to their offspring. They quit telling their children what to do and be, and started asking them about their interests, desires, and talents. Frustrated with trying to be good at everything, Baby Boomer parents began encouraging their Millennials to specialize and find the areas where they could truly excel. Sports and hobbies became more serious, with practices held multiple times per week and sports "seasons" expanded to encompass half the year. On the education side, teachers increasingly used the "discovery" method of teaching where students were asked to do a project that appealed to them, rather than be assigned something from a pre-set list of topics. The self-actualization movement of the sixties, seventies, and eighties took root in parenting. Boomers and Xers didn't just want their kids to be successful; they wanted them to be fulfilled!

Many managers roll their eyes when they hear they are now at least partly responsible for helping Millennials find meaning in their work. Other managers see it differently. "That has always been the role of a good leader or manager," explained one experienced Boomer. "Aren't we all charged with helping employees see the vision and values that go hand in hand with the work we do? Isn't that how we build pride and commitment?" Perhaps those who resent the Millennial search for meaning are simply unaccustomed to seeing it in employees so new to the work world.

Some managers might respond: "Finding meaning for everyone else is not my job; it's *their* job." Yes, that's true, too. Employees need to take responsibility for seeking meaning in their work, whether this means mentally reframing what they do, lobbying for assignments that will inspire them, or working hard so they can step up to greater responsibility.

Leadership gurus Jim Kouzes and Barry Posner have come to define this balancing act as the art of *inspiring a shared vision* between leaders and those they lead: "At some point during all this talk over the years about the importance of being future-oriented, leaders got the sense that they were the ones that had to be the visionaries...What people really want to hear is not the leader's vision. They want to hear about *their own* aspirations. They want to hear how their dreams will come true and their hopes will be fulfilled. They want to see themselves in the picture of the future that the leader is painting. The very best leaders understand that their key task is inspiring a *shared* vision, not selling their own idiosyncratic view of the world."

Millennials raised to be collaborators with their parents, teachers, and peers are now looking for leaders willing to collaborate with them on creating meaning in what they do. And they don't just consider meaningful work *nice to have*; they see it as a *must have*. Time and again they told us, "If I didn't feel a sense of meaning in my work, I would have to leave." The good news is Millennials define meaning very broadly. Once employers understand what makes this new workforce tick, they will be able to find many ways to help Millennials experience meaning in their work, and thus encourage loyalty and engagement. We've identified six *meaning motivators* to help you understand exactly what Millennials "mean."

MEANING MOTIVATOR #1: MILLENNIALS WANT TO MAKE A DIFFERENCE IN THE WORLD

Millennials have been raised with a global awareness of everything from political issues to poverty and the environment. They have been expected to volunteer and give back, both by parents who had a history of social engagement and college admissions officials who began to factor such activities into the super competitive college admissions process. In many ways, Millennials see it as their job to clean up messes made by previous generations. When it comes to work, if they are going to be spending hours of their day on a job, they want to feel they are making a dent.

MILLENNIALS ON RECORD

"I love that I'm part of an organization that is trying to improve health care and provide care for patients...Of course I can have a job that just pays my bills, but meaning for me is contributing to something bigger and improving things for other people."

— Stephanie Bononi, age 25, associate, ZoomCare

Many organizations do themselves a disservice by failing to let Millennials know about the great work they do in making the world a better place and how employees can play a role. In our M-Factor survey, over 90 percent of Millennials said that having "opportunities to give back via my company" was somewhat important to very important when considering joining an organization. Sadly, only 26 percent agreed that their company did a good job addressing it. We suggest you:

• **Gloat about giving.** When recruiting Millennials, make sure your Web sites, print materials, and even the recruiters themselves emphasize your contributions to society. Cindy Pruitt, who has worked with the summer associate program at the Womble Carlyle law firm, reported noticing new concerns expressed by those being interviewed. Rather than being solely focused on their potential future employment, recruits have been lobbing questions like: "What's your commitment to pro bono work?" and "What's your approach to giving back?" Before focusing on how they can make themselves valuable to the firm, these young people want to be sure they are joining a firm that is making a difference in the world.

A Millennial interviewee who works for a major U.S. insurance company put it this way: "For me it is very important that the company I work for has a strong philanthropic plan. It's not enough to just be *in* the community, the company needs to be a *part* of the community."

Companies should tout the programs they've developed for taking a role in global and community well-being. But many are shy about publicizing the good they do. One aviation association, for example, refused to publicize that they often use donated private corporate jets to fly critically ill children to distant medical centers for treatment. "We don't want to highlight that these companies are spending money on private planes in a tough economy, even though they are donating their jets when idle to needy causes," explained an association leader. Other organizations are simply uncomfortable tooting their own horn. "As a company, we're the strong, silent type," explained a long-time client of ours. "We do amazing things, but we don't brag about it—that's just our personality." These reasons to avoid the limelight are perfectly valid and should be respected. But in many cases, it's not only OK to brag, it can be hugely rewarding. The companies that do it best tie their good works to their missions as well as to the interests of the audiences they hope to reach. Here are a few stellar examples:

- Best Buy's "@15" program offers its young Millennial consumers more than just the knowledge that the company is giving back; it goes further by giving them the power to control where the money goes. The Web site reads: "Best

Buy is donating $1 million, and you decide where it goes. Not your parents. Not your teachers. Not Best Buy execs. Not a group of government officials. You. It's simple. Powerful. And you make the decisions. Just think of all the good you can do." And if that wasn't enough to engage Millennials, all the featured charities help teens in need ranging from a college prep program for African American teens to the Pacer Center's Teens Against Bullying.

- Microsoft's Web site, in addition to a slew of programs ranging from disaster response to low-income support, features a unique technology that allows visitors to click on an interactive world map to see the impact of the company's efforts in each individual country around the globe. Unique stories at a local level allow visitors to connect with efforts more deeply than through a generic company mission statement.

- At North Face, they don't just support causes, they have chosen the umbrella cause of sustainability and work to support it in everything they do. They boast of how the company runs on 100 percent renewable energy and how its products are earth-friendly. In addition, they feature sustainability grants and volunteer efforts aimed at employees and customers alike.

- Starbucks features the Shared Planet program, an innovative way to engage the Millennials' desire for complete transparency when it comes to a company's business and charitable practices. Starbucks publishes its "Global Responsibility Report" online as well as information about ethical sourcing, environmental stewardship, and an entire section dedicated to community involvement. It also shows how each consumer can have an impact by pledging to use reusable coffee mugs and save ten cents on every cup of java.

What if you're not one of the big guys like those we just listed? We would wager you are no slouch at giving back, but you might just need to do a better job publicizing it. Perhaps your Web site could feature pictures of employees who took days off to volunteer, or who donated their vacation or sick days to a fellow employee in need.

Even as you showcase philanthropic interests through Web sites and outreach programs, make sure your recruiters know how to talk about them. Whether your company wins awards, donates employee hours to a cause, gives money, or sponsors special events, the bottom line is these are things Millennials want to hear about, and they can create valuable social capital with prospective employees as well as with the communities in which you do business.

MILLENNIALS ON RECORD

"I see the world as an opportunity for a lot of improvement. I don't think I would feel good if I wasn't working to help improve it,"

— *Kristin Richards, age 27, program supervisor, CivicWorks*

• **Demonstrate how deeds can be donated.** Most Millennials have been able to find time in their high school and college years to lend a helping hand. In his excellent book, *Grown Up Digital,* Don Tapscott cites a study by the Higher Education Research Institute stating that in 2005 some 83.2 percent of incoming freshmen had volunteered the previous year—and 70.6 percent did it on a weekly basis. However, now that they are signing up for full-time employment, they are worried about when they will find the time. Therefore be ready and able to address specific options you make available for employees to have the opportunity and the time to give back. Last summer KPMG organized an "Interns for Literacy" program, and every one of their 1,500 U.S. interns participated in literacy programs in their local markets. Along with full-time employees, they handed out books, took on roles as readers, and raised both money and awareness about the importance of literacy. Manny

Fernandez, KPMG's national managing partner–university relations and recruiting, said this was in part because the firm had conducted brainstorming sessions with college students they hoped to hire and found that over 70 percent were involved in volunteering at their schools.

Do you offer days off for volunteering—paid or unpaid? Do you sponsor a special project that is unique to your company? Do you have a policy that allows employees to set aside part of their salary for charitable causes? Or a Web site that allows them to search for volunteer opportunities in the community? Whatever it is, make sure Millennials know about it and have a chance to get involved.

Greater Twin Cities United Way in Minneapolis/St. Paul has been successful for years with its corporate giving campaigns that enable employees to donate a portion of their paychecks to the United Way. As the Millennials have come along, the United Way has evolved to enable younger donors to have more options for getting personally involved with giving, from participating in decisions as to how contributions will be allocated to donating their time to programs in the community. One example of how Greater Twin Cities United Way is working with Millennials is its Emerging Leaders program, which allows young people to get involved in volunteering, advocating, and giving. According to Randi Yoder, senior vice president of donor relations, "This year we are proposing a number of engagement opportunities for the Emerging Leaders. For example, small groups of employees can raise $5,000 to move a family from emergency housing into permanent housing and then provide a caseworker who will help direct them to job training, new schools, financial planning, emergency food, etc."

According to Randi, the emerging leaders "like to get personally involved, and they love having a specific, tangible goal where they know they are making a direct difference in people's lives."

Whatever your involvement with philanthropy, make sure you're prepared to let job candidates know about how they can participate in helping your company give back.

MEANING MOTIVATOR #2: MILLENNIALS WANT TO FEEL THEY ARE CONTRIBUTING

MILLENNIALS ON RECORD

"If I was moved into a role where I was doing tasks a 'monkey' could do, it would definitely make me want to leave."

— *Kate Jakubas, age 24, materials engineer, Elkay Manufacturing*

The *monkey* comparison was used frequently by our MORs to describe lack of meaning. Here's what Julie Strand of C. H. Robinson Worldwide said: "I know I'm not curing diseases or anything, but I do contribute to my workplace. I didn't want mindless work that a monkey could do. I want to be able to apply my skills." A big part of this is helping other people. Many of our MORs who were happy at their jobs attributed it to their understanding of how they made a difference for the boss, the customer, or others on their team. Unfortunately this isn't always clear to younger workers. In our M-Factor survey, when asked whether they know how their work contributes to the organization's vision/mission and strategy, Boomers were the most knowledgeable. Millennials showed the least certainty about how their work contributes. This is a communication opportunity for organizations hiring Millennials. Here are some tips:

• **Make jobs come alive.** Up until recently it was tough enough just to post jobs on Web sites, but technology has come a long way. Savvy companies are realizing their Web sites are the first place Millennials go to learn about them. While it's important to put forth your organization's best attributes, the trick with Millennials is to make jobs come alive. Millennials want to be able to imagine themselves actually working there. Some companies post pictures of current Millennial employees, where you can click on an individual to read about (or see a video on) what they do in their job and what has meaning for them. Other companies post written, video, or photo diaries of an employee's first year that paint a graphic picture of the employee's connection to the organization and the work. Lockheed Martin's Web site invites visitors to watch video testimonials by employees who transitioned to the company from college or the military or who have joined Lockheed as experienced professionals. These options help give job seekers an idea of where they might fit in and what their initial experiences might be like.

Claiming "People flourish at KPMG," the company's interactive Web site lets visitors select a value proposition such as Global Opportunities, Life Balance, Mentoring, or Supportive Culture and learn through videos what attracted a certain employee to KPMG. They can also interact with a Flash presentation to follow a career path.

The U.S. Army offers a "virtual guide" on its site to assist in navigating its numerous job categories. Visitors can answer simple questions on the "Match Your Interest" page, they can go to "Option Seeker" to prioritize their preferences, or choose to use the "Army Career Explorer" to find jobs for which they might be qualified. All this helps the job search feel more like a personal exploration that allows Millennials visualize themselves in the future workplace.

• **Train recruiters to "show me the meaning."** Just as Web sites and recruiting materials are being retooled to reflect the Millennials' desire for meaningful work, recruiters are adjusting their pitches. When the goal was simply to focus on the required skills and competencies of the job, recruiters were not expected to chat about potential new hires' passions. It was natural to blow right by the "meaningful work" portion of the conversation and focus on the future: "You'll learn the ropes, observe the experts, and then one day you will step up to be an account executive yourself!" "Fine," today's Millennial is thinking, "but what if I want to make an impact right now?" Recruiters from every generation need to be tuned into Millennials' hot buttons so they can comfortably talk about where meaning can be found in the job at hand. This isn't rocket science, but it does require recruiters to understand the multitude of ways Millennials search for meaning.

• **Put "meaning" on your menu.** Marc Kielburger, author of the *New York Times* bestseller *Me to We* and CEO of the internationally acclaimed nonprofit Free the Children, said it best: "Businesses need to think like nonprofits because that's what today's youth do. One of the best questions a business can ask itself is: 'What's your cause?'" What Marc is advising is really quite simple. Whatever you pride yourself on doing well, especially as it benefits the community, the public, the customer, the environment, or the world, is *your* cause, and you need to make it known to job candidates. You may not be running Doctors without Borders, but you are doing something that benefits somebody somewhere or you wouldn't be in business. Millennials want to know about it and feel a part of it.

"Our message has always been that you should come to work at the Federal Aviation Administration (FAA), become an air traffic controller or an aviation safety inspector, and you will earn great benefits," explained Ventris Gibson, assistant administrator for HR Management. "To be honest, for my generation of Boomers, that message worked just fine. We recently started to publicize the new and exciting things the FAA is doing but weren't talking about them in the recruiting process. Now we really hammer home the idea that if you come to work at the FAA, you can be part of changing the agency that will change aviation. We talk to Millennials about how they can lead the aerospace industry and make their mark in the world, and it has really worked. It used to take us a lot longer to recruit the best and the brightest and now that we have changed our value proposition, they land on our doorstep."

What if you're not reinventing the aerospace industry? A paper company that owns a large recycling plant ran the numbers and found they keep millions of pounds of paper out of landfills every single year. Suddenly a rather mundane operation took on an environmentally friendly role.

How about a food company whose mantra is "we bring families together." Their entire culture and marketing strategy is about making it easier to prepare and consume food so family members have more time to spend together. That's a lot more appealing to Millennials than if they just talked about getting their products on dinner tables at a certain price point. Of course you have to think hard about whether or not you mean it. Millennials will have their radar up for value propositions that don't ring true. But today many businesses are engaged in making the world run better, safer, faster, or more economically, and we can and should tell the Millennials that story.

• **Link Millennials to the cause.** Once they're in the door, we need to periodically connect Millennials back to the meaning of what they do. In other words, remind them of the "cause" they signed up for. This can be as easy as talking about how they make a difference for the company, the customer, the team, the community, the world, and their own career. More than one of our MORs expressed the benefits of doing so like this: "Having meaning in my work makes the little, meaningless tasks easier to swallow." Another refrain we hear over and over again from Millennials is that meaning doesn't have to be saving lives or curing cancer. As long as they are making a difference for somebody else, that's often enough. Consider these Millennials working in three very different environments:

> • Ashley Strub (ALK-Abello): "I want to help my customers solve problems. For me that has meaning because I'm helping someone else."
> • Ava Jackson (California Shakespeare Theater): "What makes me stay? I feel like I'm helping kids and offering something really amazing that they wouldn't have had the opportunity to do if not for our company."

- Bobbie Godbey (West Virginia University): "Because of my job, it's easy to personify meaning. I can see the students I have helped face-to-face. While it's not saving the planet, it's a pretty clear sense of accomplishment. It makes the mundane days much more tolerable."

Most of us don't work in positions that will enable us to save the world. But we can still show Millennials how seemingly small interactions can make a real difference.

- **Help Millennials find the meaning behind the mission.** Another mistake leaders make is to assume the company's mission statement does the job all by itself. We hate to say it, but a plaque above the receptionist's head with words like "service" or "people" isn't enough all by itself. In all of our interviews with MORs around meaning, the company mission statement was never mentioned. Either it's not deemed important, or organizations aren't doing a good enough job making it relevant to Millennials.

Companies that excel at engaging Millennials go out of their way to tie the new hire's work back to the mission of the organization. Jeni Nichols, founder and CEO of Sonoma Leadership Systems, put it like this: "This generation is asking to participate, at a very young age, in shaping the direction of their work and even their organizations as a precursor to buying in. They want to have a voice, but not just for the sake of being heard. They want to have a voice so they can feel committed and so they can truly participate in making a difference."

Rick King, the global head of technology and operations for Thomson Reuters, observed, "We learned right away that Millennials were not going to wait ten years to make a contribution. They want to know from day one how they are contributing." Thomson Reuters instituted the "Line of Sight" program that got every leader in the organization communicating the goals of the company to their employees as part of their reviews. In addition, managers worked with employees to establish their individual goals and objectives then drew maps for each employee that connected their individual goals with the organization's. "We wanted to make sure Millennials could visualize how their personal goals aligned with the overall mission of the company," explained King. The result? Since starting Line of Sight, retention and engagement have improved.

MEANING MOTIVATOR #3: MILLENNIALS WANT TO BE INNOVATORS

In our M-Factor survey, when asked how well-prepared Millennials are to succeed in the workplace, 92 percent of Traditionalists, Boomers, and Xers gave them high marks for their ability to create and innovate. Millennials have mastered an ever-evolving array of gadgets and have acted as "consultants" to family and friends on everything from how to program cell phones to buying flat screen TVs. It's natural they will want to continue using these competencies when they show up at work.

Of course there are times when new ideas and improvements meet with resistance, and this can be discouraging to a confident and competent Millennial. Not only is the meaning gone, but so is the wind from their sails. One of our MORs who chose to remain nameless said, "I am constantly looking for a new way to do something. I always want to innovate and revamp to make things better. The older generations are more of the mind-set that it's worked for the past twenty years so we are going to stick with that."

We said Millennials received high marks for their ability to break new ground; we didn't say the other generations got high marks for being able to deal with it. But this is something every generation needs to pay attention to, for two reasons. First, innovation, when done right, benefits everyone. If you're too overworked or exhausted to worry about a new way of managing the inventory and a Millennial wants to take on the project, hallelujah! Second, the ability to find smart, creative solutions to problems at work gives Millennials a sense of meaning that connects them to the organization. Here are ways you can nurture the inner innovator:

• **Find opportunities for them to innovate.** In our national survey we asked respondents to give us one positive word and one negative word to describe Millennials. The top positive ones were tech savvy, creative, energetic, and innovative. This generation has come of age with a constantly evolving stream of technologies and tools, and has developed a high level of adaptability. Constant change doesn't faze them; in fact, it excites them. Brace yourself, because this generation is going to walk in the door and from day one tell you all the ways they could help you do things smarter, faster, and better. Some of you will find this annoying. People who are successful naturally have a sense that the way they do things now is pretty good. When someone who looks about experienced enough to valet park your car tells you they can revolutionize the way you do business, it doesn't feel helpful; it feels offensive. And if they spend all their time bugging you about the next big idea it's natural to wonder if they are getting their *real* work done. But consider the flip side. Here we have a generation of Millennials eager and excited to come up with ideas to help us work smarter. Why wouldn't we take them up on it? Especially if it keeps them happy and provides an opportunity to find meaning in their work.

Lisa Perez, SPHR, vice president of Human Resources for Tecton Hospitality and Desires Hotels told us, "Rather than leave everything to senior management, we try to involve a cross-section of associates from different departments in problem-solving. It is important to us to include the younger generations and ask their opinions, as they get to identify, analyze, and deliver solutions to problems. We love when Millennials bring ideas to the table that aren't even from hospitality. It turns into a winning situation for everyone. As a result, all of our associates feel empowered in making our properties the best they can be for our guests." In a recent associate survey response to "I feel that my job, what I do and what I contribute, is important," Tecton/Desires scored 95 percent.

• **Show them the ballpark, then give them the ball.** While Millennials tend to have great ideas, they won't know the parameters and potential pitfalls that can make or break a successful project. The search for meaning can become a search for the Holy Grail if you don't provide Millennials with a map. However, that doesn't mean you have to micromanage the heck out of them. Whenever we ask Millennials about working with Baby Boomers, the first thing we hear is how much Boomers love process diagrams and flow charts. They asked us to remind Boomers you don't need to organize an innovation summit just to reinvent the filing system. In all seriousness, ground rules are great but if you tell people exactly how to do something it doesn't really count as inventing. *Do*, however, talk about your expectations. Get them thinking in advance about key considerations such as:

> • How much time do you expect them to spend on the project?
> • Whose help will they need? (And do you need to alert these people?)
> • When and how will you check in?
> • What is the budget?
> • What are the "untouchables"—the aspects of the project that no way, no how will they be allowed to change?
> • What do they need to do to prove the project is viable (i.e., cost analysis, time study, interviews with other stakeholders, etc.).

When supervisors aren't this organized, Millennials should take the bull by the horns and make sure they get the answers to these questions themselves. Nothing creates a plunge in the "meaning meter" like pouring your heart into a project only to find out there was no real commitment to supporting it.

• **Hold Millennials accountable.** Assigning a pioneering project, no matter how small, can be a fantastic learning experience for
Millennials, and add meaning in the process. But it is only going to
work if someone is willing to coach along the way. It's tempting to
get caught up in the Millennials' excitement and tell them, "Yes!
Go for it!" and be thinking, "Now just go away!" No matter how
much you wish that a Millennial could just go off and solve the in-
tractable issue that has been bugging you for months, don't give in
to the temptation to hand it over and disappear. You don't want to
find out a few weeks later they've waded into a quagmire of politics
and problems you now have to resolve.

Managers often make the mistake of thinking Millennials who
constantly check in looking for feedback are insecure. Not so.
This is a generation that's been coached, counseled, and structured
throughout their busy lives. Millennials check in often so they know
they are on the right track. They don't want to waste time making
mistakes or heading off on tangents. One Millennial assigned to
create a shared calendar system for a small consulting company said
this: "If I could, I would run a USB cable from my boss's brain right
to mine so I could download everything that's already been done
on this project. Then I wouldn't have to waste time going over territory that's already been covered."

There are two pieces to holding Millennials accountable. One
is checking in so both of you can make sure they are on the right
track. The second part is teaching them the discipline of completing
a project according to the specs, on time, and on budget. You don't
need to micromanage, but regular check-in meetings are a perfect
way to learn what your Millennials' skills are. And what could feel
more meaningful than having a boss who is willing to coach and
correct or, ideally, deal out praise?

• **Remind them every team still has a coach.** At some point
a Millennial will come to you with a great idea that makes perfect
sense, and you are going to have to say "no." Warning: This can be
tough for Millennials to take. While they've had a lot of structure in

their lives around *what* they are going to do, they've had quite a bit of leeway to decide *how* they want to do things. Millennials find a lot of meaning in expressing their own personal style through inventive projects. When you say "no" to something they've proposed it's going to seem like a slap in the face. Try to avoid having this be a surprise. Remind Millennials periodically that you are going to have to judge each new idea on its merit and that sometimes even good ideas aren't going to fly. Then go the next step and talk to Millennials about "why." They often have no idea how many other projects are stacked up on your department's plate, how tight the budget is, or how a challenging political climate might make the project nearly impossible to complete. The fact that you took the time to hear a Millennial's proposal and give thoughtful reasons why it can't be done will go a long way toward building trust.

• **Add "Innovator" to their job description.** Millennials are natural consultants. They've been doing this at home for years, and they'll look forward to being a resource for you too. We suggest putting this skill set to work. Let's say you're installing new payroll software in your HR department. This is an activity that many clients tell us pushes them to the verge of a nervous breakdown because it means a huge learning curve for users and it usually results in lots of complaining and the need for plenty of technical support. That is a perfect and meaningful opportunity to assign a Millennial team to coach the other generations, answer questions, and talk people down from the ledges when things go bad. Our experience has been that Millennials are patient and eager to help. We seldom see the aggravated eye roll that would have been a young Xer's or Boomer's response to a really dumb question. Millennials are used to showing Dad how to program the TiVo—for the twelfth time—so it's only natural they are willing to explain patiently to a co-worker how to enter data into the new system.

Before you deploy them, consider providing generational coaching to your Millennial SWAT team. Teach them how the other generations will need to be addressed. Explain how a Traditionalist might be threatened by a new way of doing things, why a Boomer is so pressed for time, or why an Xer might be embarrassed at not having their arms around the new technology. Give them the skills they need to help the other generations over the hump and you've created a real powerhouse.

MEANING MOTIVATOR #4: MILLENNIALS WANT TO BE HEARD

Time and again Millennials have told us it isn't about whether all their ideas are accepted; it's more about feeling someone is willing to hear what they have to say.

MILLENNIALS ON RECORD

"At staff meetings I am asked for my opinion, which is great. I can speak up without fear of being shot down. I see my opinions listened to, considered, and *some* turned into actions. That keeps me here."
—Dale Till, age 20, Northeastern University student working full time at the Institute for International Urban Development

You might be thinking, "Doesn't every generation want to be listened to and have their ideas considered?" Of course, but Millennials seem to want it sooner. A Boomer starting out might have been aggravated if no one was listening, but would be much more willing to say, "Well, when I've been here as long as my boss, I bet they'll listen to me, too." Not so for the Millennials. They want to be heard *now*.

• **Can you hear me now?** If you're managing Millennials, assume they are going to want a regular opportunity to give ideas and input. This doesn't have to require hours of one-on-one time. It could be a roundtable where the team gets together for the express purpose of discussing new ideas.

One contractor held monthly meetings with his construction team leaders to talk about how each home renovation project was progressing. To help develop young leaders, he asked his top people to bring one high-potential Millennial along each time they met and assign them to deliver updates. As part of the assignment, each team had to present something interesting they had learned from a project to share with the others. The Millennials were thrilled to have their presentations heard and dove into uncovering something new or innovative to share. A side benefit was that the owner of the company and his team leaders got to see all the up-and-comers in action, which helped them with succession planning. After a project was completed, it was interesting to hear from the Millennials' teams about how meaningful it was to see the blueprints come to life. But the most meaningful aspect was not cutting the ribbon; it was cutting their teeth at the update meetings, where they got to feel they were truly contributing.

Over the past decade, U.S. Bank has developed a number of innovative programs that offer a more diverse work experience for employees and connect them back to the meaning of what they do. "We recognize that our employees are our most valuable asset, and that remaining responsive to our employees' changing needs and points of view is one of the key ways we retain our position of strength in providing top products and services to our customers," explained Mary Blegen, director of Employee Engagement and Leadership Development.

As U.S. Bank launches new initiatives, a key objective is to ensure that new programs are effective from all employee or customer perspectives. It had become apparent to the senior leadership of the organization, however, that the Millennial point of view was not always well represented during the design process. As a result, in January 2009, U.S. Bank introduced its newest employee engagement project, the Dynamic Dozen. Initiated by president, chairman, and CEO, Richard Davis, the Dynamic Dozen is a group of twenty-something U.S. Bank employees that serves as a sounding board for new initiatives. Each member of the Dynamic Dozen was selected by a vice chair from each of the company's core business lines. Selection was based on the Millennial's outstanding level of performance, commitment to innovation, and exhibited willingness to share their creative concepts with their managers and teams.

"Being selected for the group is a top honor," says Dynamic Dozen leader Mac McCullough, U.S. Bank's chief strategy officer and head of the Enterprise Revenue Office. "We'll use this group's fresh ideas and intellect to keep U.S. Bank competitive and ahead of the curve."

At their first meeting in February 2009, leaders realized the value of the Dynamic Dozen would extend well beyond their function as a focus group for new products and programs. "As we listened to their initial feedback around the work before them and the tools they would need to best perform this work," explained Mac, "we began to see how the Dynamic Dozen represents a perfect opportunity to watch a Millennial work group in action. We are learning about this age group's expectations as employees *and* consumers by seeing how they react to the questions we've posed and how they interact with each other to develop and present their work product."

At the request of their Employee Engagement and Leadership Development (EELD) group, one upcoming project for the Dynamic Dozen will be to review U.S. Bank's current benefit calculator and how they can potentially improve the tool to make it more useful for younger employees. EELD director Mary Blegen expressed the value of the Dynamic Dozen's input on this project: "While the impetus behind the Dynamic Dozen was to create a focus group that would give us perspective on our twenty-something customers, we're seeing the benefit of their perspective as employees as well. It's like having the cake *and* the icing." Imagine the benefit for a generation in search of meaning to have their ideas heard by top leaders *and* to be able to make an impact on programs that serve customers and employees.

- **Show them how their ideas fit.** We mentioned Millennial SWAT teams earlier. But you should also think about creating a Millennial "SWOT" team. Many of you have probably run into the concept of SWOT analysis somewhere along the way. It's a model for analyzing a company or product's strengths, weaknesses, opportunities, and threats (SWOT) in the marketplace.

Whether you use this or another model, it's a great technique to teach to Millennials who want to advocate for an idea or innovation. Author Bruce Tulgan describes this as providing "context" for Millennials. His point is that Millennials feel more engaged when they can tie their work back to the bigger picture. Assigning processes that help them put their work into context provides meaning. (See the diagram on page 112 for some tips to help create context.)

If you want to make it even more meaningful for you as a manager, see what methodologies Millennials might be able to teach you. Millennials learned processes in school to help them to work through issues as a group. One of those might be valuable in your workplace. When you assign a project, ask them how they would typically analyze the opportunity. See if they have an approach that's worth trying. You'll learn a new method and they get to showcase what they know—a true win-win. And what could be more meaningful than that?

- **Teach them how to show and tell.** When it's time to roll out a new idea or program, it's not the time to lay off on the coaching. Millennials will be eager, excited, and armed to sell their pet project. This is still high-risk territory. Millennials have done loads of presentations in high school and college, often at the varsity level. But that doesn't mean they are ready to step up to the big leagues. Find low-risk ways they can practice presentation skills until you scout out their abilities (and their flaws). Give them small assignments to present in staff meetings or to a client. If you've created a PowerPoint deck, let them tell you which three or four slides they feel most comfortable presenting. Debrief afterward to help them analyze why they were persuasive and how they fell short. Millen-

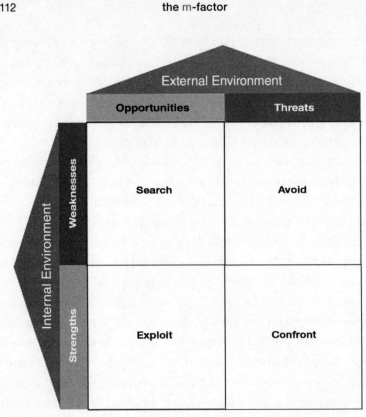

nials derive meaning from playing a valued role. Be clear on what you expect. Are you angling to get them more visibility? Or do you need to protect the project's credibility by presenting it yourself? It's perfectly appropriate to have them attend the team leader meeting and sit politely in the back saying nothing. Just don't forget to coach them on *what their role is* (sitting and not talking) and *why* (so they learn how the meetings run and who the personalities are in the room).

Even if their role is to listen and say nothing, you still need to debrief. Ask them who were the influencers in the room, or which presentations were most persuasive. Quiz them on why one idea got shot down and another one flew. Only via this process will they develop the skill level—and you develop the comfort level—to let them fly solo. When you do give them the chance to soar, make sure not to shoot them down. Unlike Xers, who were just happy to find someone who was paying attention, Millennials find meaning when they know they are contributing. New presenters are going to make mistakes, misunderstand a question, or flub an answer. We all learn that way. Just take a few notes, give constructive feedback, and let them try again.

Millennials should not assume they can run before they can walk when it comes to presentation skills. They might have been the MVP in graduate school or flown solo on a regular basis when they worked for AmeriCorps, but that doesn't mean the skills will cut it at Acme Corp. Millennials should study the best presenters in the organization and ask for advice on what works. Above all, they need to be open to hearing constructive feedback. It's a waste of time thinking that because you graduated cum laude in speech communications from Oberlin, your boss can't possibly be right about your ineffective communication style. Assume he or she has a point and see how you can improve.

So we know Millennials want to make a difference, to feel they are contributing, to be innovators, and to be heard, but that's not all there is to meaning.

MEANING MOTIVATOR #5: MILLENNIALS WANT TO KNOW THEY ARE SUCCEEDING

This generation loves being part of a team and is happy to work toward the group goal. At the same time they will find more meaning in their day-to-day job if they know the effort they are putting in also is yielding individual success. This is a generation raised with standardized testing. They are accustomed to working toward a score and being rewarded for their progress.

Here are ways to think about motivating the individuals who work for you:

- **It's amazing what people will do for a gold star.** Remember the chore charts parents posted on the refrigerator with gold stars for everything from dish washing to bed making? Well, it looks like the chore chart has found its way from the fridge to the department's white board. Basically, what worked at home is not a bad technique in the office. To all those Xers rolling their eyes at this point, here's the good news: This might be the cheapest reward system you ever roll out. In fact, some of the smallest and most personalized rewards carry the most meaning. Rewards like movie tickets, or an employee's favorite artist's new CD, a subscription to a magazine, or even just a personalized e-mail work in spades with Millennials.

- **Praise them, with specifics.** For praise to be meaningful to Millennials, the main point isn't to tell them *that* they did well (trust us, they get plenty of that!); it's to tell them *what* they did well. As we mentioned earlier, this is a generation that strives to find context in what they do. They don't want to hear they did a good job working with a retail client in a store; they want to know precisely what they did and how that made a difference. This may take a bit more time, but it's also the best, most effective coaching tool you have. Millennials will work hard for praise and if you catch them doing the right things and reinforce *why* they're right, you're developing a smarter, more capable employee.

- **Take time out to give them a time-out.** Classic management theory is to catch employees doing something right and praise them. That's still fantastic advice. But we suggest you flip it around as well. With Millennials, it's a good idea to catch them making small mistakes so you ward off the big ones. A big failure is going to be much more troublesome for you as a boss or team member.

Plus, big failures are bad for morale. A Millennial employee who blows it on a large scale is likely to feel resentful you didn't intervene sooner to prevent the problem. MOR Rachel Rosen, working in retail for The Limited, expressed it like this: "At my old job, I really only got feedback at our formal feedback sessions. I had to think back over the last few months to remember what they were talking about. At The Limited, I get feedback right away. As soon as I deal with a customer, my manager will take the time to say, 'That would have been a good opportunity to offer the customer a rewards card.' That's great because within twenty minutes I can fix and improve what I'm doing. At the end of the shift when my manager says great job, I can leave feeling really good about what I did that day."

"We find our younger employees respond better to 'try to beat your high score,' than 'we need to increase profits.'"

Millennials aren't always the best at handling negative or cor-
rective feedback. In fact, in our M-Factor survey we asked about
Millennials' ability to handle feedback effectively, and *only 3 percent*
of respondents said Millennials did this well. This is a generation
that hasn't been allowed to fail a whole lot, so failure is going to feel
pretty bad when it happens. Far better to experience small failures
and have the meaningful experience of improving than to be devas-
tated by big ones. One tip we've seen work well is rather than blast
Millennials with tough feedback, try to ease into it by finding out
how far apart you are. The way to do this is to have them do a self-
evaluation first and bring that with them to the meeting. Whether
you're very close or miles apart, at least you know where to start.

In team meetings, Baby Boomer manager Duke noticed the Millennials shied away from discussing things that had gone wrong.
They were uncomfortable admitting they had let him down, and
they tended to downplay the effect their own failure had on others.
A former fighter pilot, he was accustomed to making a fearless and
honest assessment of operational mistakes after each mission. He
tried pointing out failures in matter-of-fact terms and found he was
terrifying the team. They held their breath and looked panicky the
whole time he talked. Then they spent twenty minutes trying to
justify their actions. Twice he ended up with a Millennial in tears.
Having been raised to expect all As, Duke's team was earning an
F in failure.

"What would I do if this was any other skill my team lacked?"
he asked himself. "We'd practice." So he built a failure discussion
into his regular team meetings in which he asked, "What happened
this week that didn't work that we can learn from?" Team members
had to write down an example, evaluate what happened, and bring
it with them to the meeting. At first the team chose things that
were pretty safe. "Our vendor didn't deliver on time and that held
up our delivery to the client."

"OK, great!" enthused Duke. "That's right to identify it. What could we do differently?" There was no blame, just a discussion of how it happened and what they could learn. Over time the team got good at it. In fact, one week his highest achieving Millennial walked past Duke's office and gave him a big "thumbs up" and a huge smile. "I've got a great failure for you, Duke, you're gonna love it!"

This is a generation that wants an A+ for everything. Your job as a manager, supervisor, or team leader will be to specifically point out what was *not* wonderful so people can learn from it.

Millennials can also take responsibility for learning to handle mistakes more effectively. They can practice owning the errors, apologizing, and seeking feedback on how to do better next time. We are frequently told by clients that Millennials don't want to hear negative feedback and can't handle constructive criticism. Be the one to prove them wrong.

MEANING MOTIVATOR #6: MILLENNIALS WANT TO EXPRESS WHO THEY ARE THROUGH WORK

This one is a little more complicated. Millennials have found meaning in their lives by spending years developing their own personal "brand"—one that is reflected in all the ways they communicate who they are. From individual taste expressed via clothes, to personalized Web sites or music mixes on their iPods, to inventing their own charitable causes rather than giving back through established channels, Millennials have found meaning in self-definition and self-expression. This generation is going to want to express their unique gifts and talents through their work. It doesn't help that they have been told countless times by their parents how valuable their perspective is, because now they are going to want the boss to see them through those same rose-colored glasses.

When Boomers entered the workplace vying with millions of

peers for the same job or promotion, they were happy to learn how to express themselves in whatever way the system or the boss dictated. They dressed for success and learned how to write a proper business letter. They studied internal politics and respected the hierarchy. That's how they got ahead. Not all Boomers realized their dreams, however, and they have encouraged their Millennial kids to do better. One MOR who now works in the nonprofit sector expressed the origins of her search for meaning like this: "I associated my mom's unhappiness with her work and my family's problems with her unhappiness. She had dreams of doing something in politics but she didn't do that, and it was always 'three years later and three years later and three years later...' She stayed with it but was never happy. I knew it was extremely important to me to have a job that made me happy. I didn't want to just 'get a job.' I'm sure if I lost my job it would be different. But I'm always asking, 'What do I *want* to do?'"

Millennials want to put their own imprint on the workplace from Day One. Another MOR described it this way: "We've always been told to find our *passion*. And it's like the search is ongoing. It's almost this pressure to discover why you were put on this earth and then find the perfect career to match that purpose." Conflicts arise because we have a workplace where norms exist for good reasons. New hires who don't respect the status quo won't be successful. Likewise, bosses who fail to find ways Millennials can express their own unique styles through their work will end up with a generation in constant search of meaning, only somewhere else. Here are ideas to keep in mind:

• **Personal branding is a good thing.** Bosses who have been scarred by battles over personal expressions such as facial piercings and tattoos are understandably nervous when we tell them Millennials want to find ways to personalize their work environment. They fear anarchy and wonder if they'll be able to put the genie back in the bottle once it's been set loose. But Millennials tell us they love the little things. They don't have to reinvent the office, but can they decorate their cubicles or design their own special look for a report? A manager at C. H. Robinson Worldwide, Inc. told us he allows employees to choose their own titles for their business cards from a list the company provides. Deciding on whether to be called a "logistics specialist" or a "carrier account executive" may not be a huge decision, but it gives them the freedom, in a sense, to create their own destiny. He said no one abuses it, and the choices of title have been very revealing.

Our Millennial Debra announced passionately to us during her first month of work that Century Gothic was *her* font and she did *everything* in it. We were taken aback. Lynne couldn't figure out if Debra was suggesting the rest of us should have our own fonts and show some personality, or if it meant no one else should even think of using Century Gothic. David couldn't help but think she needed to find a hobby! But this was an a-ha moment for us. Debra got excited about little things that were clever and fun and expressed her creativity. In an odd way, Century Gothic made every e-mail or document that she typed feel more personal and even more meaningful.

"OK," bosses say, "but what if they run amok?" We say, you're the boss and you get to set the tone. But it doesn't hurt to vary the pitch. At one convention where we spoke, the all-Millennial conference team was forced by headquarters to make sure every single presenter used the same (boring) company template for the slides. But to put their own spin on things they decided to play with our generational theme and created photo collages for every generation they projected on jumbo screens during the breaks. This was accompanied by a montage of generational music. The look and feel of the ballroom was transformed by their creativity and the audience got fired up naming the images in the montages and reminiscing about the tunes. Through their own search to make the project more meaningful for themselves, they made it more meaningful for attendees.

It's interesting to watch Boomers grapple with the Millennials' desire to find meaning by personalizing their work experience. After all, they were the generation that lived and died by the credo "express yourself." Then they entered corporate America and realized they could move up a lot more quickly if they cut their hair and donned a navy blue suit. We are firm believers that certain aspects of business need to be standardized. We are simply suggesting you allow creativity when you can. One Boomer boss in a marketing/advertising department of a nonprofit ran out of room to house all the Millennial interns, so he took a deep breath and told them they could configure the office any way they wanted as long as they could all fit and get their work done, and he didn't get in trouble with the fire marshal. He came back the next day to find all the desks pushed together into a giant island in the center, with the Millennials seated companionably around it. Just when he thought he was going to have to apologize for the lack of privacy, one Millennial intern said, "Thanks for letting us do it our way." Finding ways to express individual creativity, taste, and freedom can be the easiest, and sometimes the cheapest way to help Millennials find meaning on the job.

• **All those for bungee jumping, over here.** In our MOR interviews, the word "passion" came up time and again. If you can unearth an area of interest or a passion in one of your Millennials, it might pay to find a way to put that passion to work. This can benefit the organization as well as ignite a high-potential employee you don't want to lose. The General Mills Foundation is extending its work and funding into Africa with projects that help Africans become more economically sustainable. This work with Africa is new for the foundation. Lisa Novotny, V.P. of Human Resources, Technology, explained the challenge: "How do we not just give money but really be sure it makes a difference in alleviating hunger? They asked me to help structure how we evaluate programs. What strikes me is one of the people who is leading this for the foundation is a Millennial at a junior level in the organization. It is his passion to do this even though he's doing it in his spare time, and he has no idea if he'll get credit for it or if his boss will even acknowledge it. He did a couple of years in the Peace Corps before coming to our company, and he feels such a strong need to keep that going. I asked 'How do you still find the energy to manage that with your current job?' He has a prestigious MBA, and he said, 'It's kind of a struggle because it's so important to feel I am giving back to something bigger than myself, and after we're done with this project how am I going to figure out what I am going to do next?'"

Although General Mills is engaging Millennials in big projects, a project doesn't have to be huge to have meaning. Debra's most pressing passion around this book was that the voice of her generation be heard, so we put her in charge of organizing and conducting many of the MOR interviews. You've seldom seen anyone so charged up, and the project enabled her to become an advocate for our interviewees and their points of view. This was good for us and it's been great development for her.

Millennials will see more meaning in their jobs if they can become specialists in one or two areas unique to them.

MILLENNIALS ON RECORD

"I have become a go-to person for a number of projects, and it is really meaningful to have someone come to me because I can answer their questions. It keeps me engaged when people rely on me to perform a certain task that only can be done by me because I'm the expert."
— *Kate Jakubas, age 24, materials engineer, Elkay Manufacturing*

• **Exercise their expertise.** You have probably seen this a dozen times. A Millennial comes on board with a special talent, and soon he or she is taking on that skill for the whole department. It comes naturally because it's what they've been doing at home and in school. It starts with getting your nephew to help you choose a new cell phone. Then your daughter sets up your Facebook page. Next, your grandchild is designing your holiday card using your photos that she uploaded to a Web site. If it works at home we can flex our management styles to do the same in the workplace.

One company hosted a yearly charitable-giving campaign that had been conducted the same old way year after year. Contributions were dropping and the Boomers in charge were burned out. The thought of doing it one more year was about as appetizing as the rubber chicken served at the fund-raising dinner. They took a gamble and put Millennials from the marketing department on the job. They ended up with not just a revitalized campaign, but engaged employees who felt they were changing the world. These assignments, based on special interests or skills, don't have to take away from productivity. If we do it right, they enhance it by tapping into people's greatest strengths.

One day at a prominent paper company, a Millennial receptionist named Marci seemed anything but engaged in her job. Her Gen X manager, Doug, asked her if something was the matter.

"All I do is answer the phones, what's the big deal?" she said, sounding discouraged.

As tempted as her busy boss was to say, "Listen up Missy, change the attitude or you're out of here," he was concerned. Marci was the best receptionist the company had found after more than a few tries. He attempted to give her a pep talk but he could tell it wasn't sinking in.

Doug knew he had to do something.

The next day, Marci got a visit from the CEO! While she was surprised the CEO even remembered her name, she was more intrigued as he pulled up a chair next to her. He grabbed paper and pen and sketched out a detailed org chart with dotted lines from her spot as receptionist to every other box on the chart, right on up to his at the top.

He explained that with the price of pulp being so volatile competing on price was hard to do. The only way he has been able to differentiate himself from the competition was to offer the best customer service possible. His mission was for customers to feel the service they would get from his paper mill was too good to go anywhere else, regardless of changes to price.

Marci was now sitting up straight. The CEO continued to explain that her job was to be the face of the company. He then pulled out a copy of an e-mail he had gotten from one of his biggest clients. It stated how much it meant to the client to be able to do business with such a friendly and efficient company. The CEO explained to the Millennial that this customer alone had contributed seven figures to the company's bottom line.

He went on to state that every time this customer called and heard a friendly voice on the other end of the line, heard his name used, and was routed to the right person as quickly as possible, it made a difference. In the eyes of the CEO, Marci's job was invaluable to the company. He concluded with a sincere thank-you for the important work she did every day.

To say that Marci felt better about her job was the understatement of the year. She was more than engaged; she was proud. Had her responsibilities changed? Not at all. The only difference was that the entry-level job had meaning and a purpose. There was one more minor change to come, however. The next day the CEO stopped by again and put a new nameplate on Marci's desk that read "DIRECTOR OF FIRST IMPRESSIONS."

part three

managing day-to-day

five

GREAT EXPECTATIONS

It was six o'clock and Tom, a Boomer manager, was ready to wrap up. He had gone over his notes enough and wanted to be sure he got a good night's sleep before presenting his draft presentation in front of colleagues. The annual three-day board meeting was a month away and the pressure was on to stand out.

Tom was about to leave when he noticed that his new Millennial hire, Josi, was still at her desk. He felt badly he hadn't been more attentive her first few days, but she really seemed to be jumping in and getting things done. He called her over.

"Hey, Josi. Sorry I haven't been more available. I have been so caught up in the presentation."

"It's no big deal," she answered. "I totally understand. But it's only a practice. I'm sure you'll get some great feedback to make it really strong."

Is What You See What You Will Get?

Tom smirked. He didn't care if it was a practice. He wanted to nail it.

"Is there anything I can do to help?" she asked. As Tom thought about it for a second, she continued, "If it's OK to make a suggestion, I caught a glimpse of your slides and they're...uh...well, a little boring."

Tom was taken aback, but deep down couldn't disagree with her. He knew she had a strong marketing background, and she had made it known she loved creative projects. That was one reason her résumé had stood out from the stack.

"Here's the CD with my presentation on it. If you want to make some tweaks, that's fine. I'll check them out in the morning," Tom felt a stab of relief that he had given her something creative to do. He clicked off his light, and headed home.

The next morning, Tom was still a bit rattled. He had tossed and turned all night going over his points. The meeting wasn't for another four hours. Josi had left a CD on his desk, and when he launched the PowerPoint, he gasped as the company logo bounced onto the screen to the theme song from *Survivor*. His jaw dropped when he noticed that instead of the classic round bullet next to each point, flames on torches now flickered. No longer were executives quoted with their names showcased in Arial bold. Instead, a cut-out of each executive's head from his or her I.D. photo graced the screen with thought bubbles.

After Tom looked cautiously around the office and realized that he wasn't on *Candid Camera*, he yelled for Josi.

"What have you done?" Tom accused.

Josi was grinning and ready to say, "You're welcome," when she realized his shocked look was anger.

"You don't like it," she said slowly. Tom paused and then shook his head as though someone had just thrown a glass of water at him.

"Well, considering you just broke every design standard this company ever put in place," he answered, "not to mention making my sustainability plan look like a joke, you could say I have issues with this. This is the Board of Directors, not *Beavis and Butthead!*"

"But you said it needed livening up," she said with a shaky voice. "I just wanted to help."

Tom didn't know how to respond. The room was quiet as Josi backed out of the office. Soon after, Tom pulled up an earlier saved version of the PowerPoint, and continued to practice. Meanwhile, Josi sat in her cubicle thinking about pulling up some job search Web sites. Clearly she didn't belong.

What just happened? In the story, both sides had expectations about what the other side *knew*. When Tom said it was OK to spice up the PowerPoint presentation, he assumed Josi understood the serious nature of the content and would acquaint herself with the company's design standards. Josi, on the other hand, thought since Tom had hired her for her creativity he might like her to use it.

Expectations met? We don't think so! To a lot of Traditionalists, Boomers, and Xers, it feels like what used to be basic assumptions about work are all out of whack. Millennials are showing up on the job and confounding bosses and co-workers with misplaced notions about everything from what to wear to where they are going in their careers, leaving both sides frustrated.

MILLENNIALS ON RECORD

"Academia is so theory-based and kind of makes students feel like they are the second coming. And then they get out in the real world, and they feel like gurus that know more than older people. But the problem with theory is just that…it's just theory."

—*Steve Mell, age 25, electrical engineer, Century Engineering Inc.*

Why the mismatch? Basic expectations about how work is conducted get shaken up whenever a new generation arrives on the scene. When Generation X showed up on the job they threw the work world into a tizzy over issues like flexible schedules, work ethic, and job changing. A lot of companies are still trying to get their arms around these topics and are going to be shell-shocked when a whole new set of conflicts arises. And they are bound to arise. Early reports are in and established employees are finding Millennials to be a whole new ball game. When asked in our M-Factor survey about Millennials' preparedness to enter the workforce, only 7 percent of respondents from the other generations said Millennials are "ready, willing, and able to succeed."

This expectation gap is compounded by the fact that Millennials are impatient. They enter the work world with a ticking time clock in their heads that says, "I want to hit the ground running and start making a difference, now!" The time frame for getting comfortable in a job is shorter than ever. In one study of Millennial turnover at a large hospital, newly hired nurses said they made the decision to stay or leave within just a few weeks of being hired. When we asked nursing supervisors how soon they checked in with new hires to make sure they were happily settling into the new culture, they told us they check in religiously *after the first six months!* That's a classic mismatch of expectations. Boomers expected to spend three to four years on the job before making a move. For Xers that time frame shortened to a year or two, so it makes sense the nurse managers would base their assumptions on prior experience. They hadn't shifted their expectations to coincide with a new influx of Millennials.

When expectations are set incorrectly during the recruiting and on-boarding process or they go unmet once the Millennial is on the job, it's a recipe for misery for all involved. That's why it's so important to manage expectations on both sides of the generation gap throughout the journey from job search to job satisfaction.

MINDING THE EXPECTATION GAP

Terrence took time out during a busy shift supervising Millennials filling holiday orders for a famous online retailer. He had spotted two of the newest hires and wanted to make sure they were doing fine.

"Danny, Emma, how's it going?" he inquired enthusiastically. The two glanced at each other before Emma responded cautiously.

"OK, I guess." They both looked away as if wishing they were elsewhere.

"You don't sound excited," urged Terrence. "Are you not feeling the holiday spirit?"

"Actually, no," said Danny. "This, um, isn't what we thought it would be at all. Your recruiters stressed how high tech everything is, but this assembly process is so inefficient. And they made it sound like it would be a more fun, more social environment. I mean, I know these are part-time student jobs but I was expecting the culture here to be more like the culture you portray on the Web."

Terrence was deeply dismayed. He had quotas to meet by holiday time and couldn't afford a lot of turnover right now. Honestly, he didn't know what the employees expected. The assembly area was clean and comfortable with an emphasis on safety. He wondered what the recruiters were telling people, and if other new hires had expectations that weren't being met.

Encounters like this are all too common. Recruiters are charged with getting qualified employees in the door and candidates are all too eager to hear what they want to hear about the upsides of the future job. The trouble starts with first impressions that don't match up with reality and often ends with the final impression of slamming the door on the way out. The alarming part isn't just the dollars and time being wasted on recruitment efforts that don't pan out. It's that too often the blame is on the Millennials. Leaders get frustrated with turnover and accusations start to fly: "We just seem to be getting the wrong Millennials; we need to hire different ones!" Or, "We aren't recruiting hard enough if we can't get better people!" Imagine if instead we heard, "Our Millennials aren't finding a fit here and we need to figure out what we can do to change that." Companies need to ask what they are doing to make sure Millennials are a match from the get-go and can kick off their new careers with a sense of commitment and confidence. If they're the wrong fit, companies need to take a look at their hiring and screening practices. If the Millennials are qualified but are failing to thrive, that's another set of issues. Too often the job experience isn't what was advertised. They are given less interesting work to do than they had hoped; they have less access to mentors; they are putting in more hours than expected; or they aren't getting ahead fast enough. Some of this can be attributed to a normal "shakedown" period. But the problem is also built into the way we recruit, onboard, and manage. There's a real difference between companies that are seen as best places to work by Millennials and those that have high turnover and bad reputations, and a lot of this boils down to managing expectations.

Organizations can diagnose the issues they are facing by asking these questions:

- Are we failing to recruit Millennials with the skill sets we need?
- Are Millennials willing to come on board but refusing to stay?
- Do they stick around but underperform?
- Are generational conflicts on the rise because Millennials are failing to fit in?

Once you have your arms around where mismatches lie, you can get more specific. Interview recruiters about the hiring process. Then talk with managers, supervisors, and co-workers about how well-equipped new hires are to do the job. Don't make it personal; focus on the specific tasks and outcomes: "In which areas do you wish our new hires were better prepared?" Don't let the discussion focus only on the negative. Ask for the upsides, too: "Where are the new hires excelling? What are the best skills they typically bring to the table?"

Just like judging in the Olympics, you probably have to throw out the highest and the lowest scores, but look for recurring themes. Are there certain areas where supervisors or co-workers need to compensate for Millennials time and again? Which gaps in expectations are proving to be the most costly? Which are impairing morale? Remember, some deficits are annoying, while others can be devastating to your business. For example, one construction firm expected that new hires would know what to wear to the job site during the bidding process, but this wasn't the case, and it wasn't a big deal to fix. But other new hires were making mistakes on bids because the procedures weren't taught to them.

You can also ask new hires themselves. After a decade of generational consulting, we continue to be amazed at how a group of Traditionalist, Boomer, and Gen X bosses will call us into a meeting and ask, "How can we understand Millennials' expectations better? Why are we having so many problems with the Millennials?" It hasn't dawned on them to ask the Millennials themselves.

MILLENNIALS ON RECORD

"When I graduated, I thought I was going to get this first-class job and be a successful marketing person. But those opportunities come with experience. I just thought I'd be automatically handed this great opportunity, but it wasn't the case."

—*Michelle Minter, age 24, fire claim representative, State Farm*

Invite a few Millennials who are flourishing in their jobs to talk about the experiences they had coming on board and how their expectations were or were not met. Ask them:

- What experiences helped them the most in acclimating to the new job?
- What could the company have done to help them be better prepared or get up to speed more quickly?

Some of these instances are going to be based on generational blind spots you couldn't have seen for yourself because you're not a Millennial. Even if your turnover numbers are low and the Millennials tell you you're doing fine, keep asking. When the economy takes a dip or the job market is tight, employees are more likely to hunker down and find satisfaction with what they have. That doesn't mean they'll stick around when opportunities open up again, unless you create the right environment right now.

One financial company collected feedback about their onboarding process from each year's class of new hires recruited from top business schools. One year they learned the Millennials wanted more group activities as part of orientation. Another year they found out the Millennials wanted opportunities to socialize with executives. The third year they were told that there was a huge mismatch between all the socializing that happened during onboarding and the way they were left to themselves once the job started. Over time this process resulted in an expanded mentoring program whereby new hires were assigned a peer "buddy" as well as an executive mentor to see them through the first year of employment. Employee satisfaction went up and attrition dropped substantially.

That's how organizations become employers of choice and uncover the cheapest recruitment and PR strategy on the planet. Plain and simple, do a great job meeting expectations as you bring Millennials into the fold and they won't hesitate to broadcast their happiness. And we don't just mean to a few friends sitting across the sushi bar. Suddenly they're bragging to thousands of Facebook friends about how much they love their job and you're receiving résumés from eager candidates. Plus, you didn't even have to show up at a job fair!

Exit interviews provide another means of gathering critical information about expectations. Companies don't often bother to do these with the youngest hires as they typically cost the least to replace. But all turnover is expensive. And why not get your arms around this new generation of employees as quickly as possible? Be respectful. Assure them (if appropriate) that you will still write a recommendation letter, but that they could help you and future new hires by explaining just what went wrong. One investment firm found that a series of Millennials left a particular department because they were the only Millennials, and the three high-level Boomers who ran the department were inaccessible. The firm made the decision to combine that department with another, moved the two areas into the same space, and created additional reporting relationships for the Millennials. The problem was solved and the high turnover disappeared.

LET THEM KNOW WHO YOU ARE

"If there are seventy-six million Millennials," asked one frustrated CEO, "why can't I find one?" Millennials won't come to work for you unless they can get to know you. That means managing expectations right from the first impression to the first day on the job. According to our M-Factor survey, one out of every three Millennials felt their company did not do a good job attracting their generation. We live in an age of guerrilla marketing. By the time Millennials get to you they've probably watched literally millions of commercials. They've seen countless campaigns that have entertained, engaged, and informed them. And even those flashy campaigns aren't holding their attention anymore. Since the advent of TiVo, Millennials can just hit fast forward! So is it any surprise that the black-and-white want ads that pulled in Traditionalists and Boomers aren't connecting with the tech generation, or the glossy four-color brochures with headlines about "work-life balance" or "continuous learning" that lured Xers aren't enough? Millennials expect to be dazzled.

When the networks roll out their new fall lineup, they don't wait for fall. Months before a premiere, audiences see trailers, read reviews, learn about the stars' hobbies and habits, and might even enter a contest to win a visit to the taping of a show. Come fall, viewers are already turned on and tuned in. The way to get a leg up on the competition is to be the first to tell Millennials that your "show" is the one to watch. Here's how:

• **Take advantage of "touch points."** Like previous generations, Millennials want to know you offer competitive salaries, benefits, and advancement opportunities. But what other attributes do you offer that are important to Millennials? We're not implying you should be dishonest or sell them on promises you can't deliver. Instead, we encourage employers to think about the attributes they can offer that might appeal to Millennials and perhaps haven't been communicated in ways that reach them. We're suggesting you think outside the generational box about the story you want to tell to Millennials, and then consider where to tell it. Savvy firms are using new "touch points" as strategies for getting their messages across to this next generation of recruits, such as:

• **Web sites: YOUrl.** It seems elementary, if not insulting, for us to tell companies and leaders that Millennials rely on the Web when it comes to learning about job opportunities. But many organizations have focused so much time and attention on the customer side of their Web presence they've treated the "careers" portion of the site like an ugly stepsister. Time and again we've clicked onto a client's career site only to find a single sentence stating, "No jobs are available at this time." Nice. Think about the interest and curiosity that drove a candidate to learn more about your company, and then think about the opportunity wasted. Even if you aren't hiring right this minute, you will be one day. Why miss the chance to talk to job seekers about what makes your place of business a great place to work? And even if that job seeker doesn't come to work for you, he or she might be your customer one day. Why blow the chance to tout what a great organization you have?

Too often a team will spend a lot of time and money on a new recruiting site targeting Millennials only to have their expectations fall flat. The reason is usually simple. If the site was designed by a group of Boomers, odds are the look, feel, and even the messaging will resonate best with, well…Boomers. Have you stopped and thought about whether your site appeals to a new generation? Does it convey value propositions that would appeal to a Millennial? What about how you convey these messages? While a 360-degree tour of your facility might seem silly to some, for a generation raised on multimedia, it could be the first click they make.

Then consider the tools you want to include. If you are still lauding the fact that you now accept résumés online, in the eyes of a Millennial this is like still celebrating that you survived Y2K. It used to be a competitive advantage to offer this high-tech option, but Millennials are beyond accepting it, they *expect* it and they wouldn't know any other way to apply. It's time to take your tech up a notch.

On the flip side, Millennials will be the first to call you out if it's all bells and whistles with nothing to back it up. You may have hired the most cutting-edge Web design agency but make sure you aren't abandoning content in exchange for creativity. Focus on the value propositions that make your organization a great place to work for Millennials. Most important of all, make your site useable. If Millennials have to spend more than a few seconds figuring out where to click, the next button they hit will be the "exit" button.

As you think about content, contemplate ways to make your jobs come alive for Millennials. They might log on to the site for the local hospital because they're interested in health care and discover

job openings in all sorts of areas they hadn't expected, from administration to IT, finance, and maintenance. Make it easy for them
to learn more. In certain Asian countries, PricewaterhouseCoopers
features the PwC Graduate Blog, where you can click on faces of
recent hires and read entries about their first year on the job. The
Saskatoon, Canada, Health Region gives visitors to their career site
the option to "take our site home" by downloading it onto your
e-reader.

Many clients have asked us over the years how to make a site
appealing to one generation without turning off the others. Our advice is let the generations self-select. Allow them to click to an area
for "ambitious graduates" or "experienced veterans," where they
can find what they need. Provide a range of tools that allow job
seekers to learn about you in the way they feel most comfortable. A
Traditionalist might want to read the CEO's blog, but a new graduate might want to start a live chat with a recruiter.

Finally, companies that aim for a competitive edge are making
the whole application process more transparent. You don't have to
respond to applications within fifteen minutes, but you do need to
let applicants know how your process works and what they can expect. Just like when you hit the "Order Now" button on Amazon.
com and within seconds receive an e-mail thanking you for the
order and telling you when to expect it, companies need to be specific and timely in their response strategies. That's the best way to
manage expectations right from the first contact.

• **New Media: Out with the boob tube—in with YouTube.**
Once you've identified the right messages and created an online
presence that reflects well on your company, it's time to think about
other uses for the Web. With new media evolving by the minute,
more and more touch points with Millennials are springing up.
What about inviting Millennials to sign up to receive a text message
when a new job opportunity in their field becomes available and
sending it right to their cell phones? If it's cost prohibitive to buy
air time for a commercial on network or cable television, what
about creating a commercial for YouTube? Hospital Corporation

of America (HCA) hosts their own "channel" on YouTube called "A Career at HCA," where candidates can chat, post, and read bulletins, and watch videos about careers with the company. Sites like these aren't expensive to maintain, and they provide "up close and personal" access to candidates never possible via traditional job posting methods.

KPMG got rid of flyers "because they all wound up in the trash at career fairs," explained Manny Fernandez, national managing partner–University Relations and Recruiting. So they developed a new approach for connecting with Millennial job candidates. "We are trying to give them an inside look at what it's like to be a first-year associate or to be an intern. When our interns go on overseas assignments, say to Australia, we arm them with a handheld video camera so they can capture the experience. Then we upload it to our KPMG-sponsored YouTube site. We hear time and again they want to know what the experience is like day-to-day, and we constantly try to capture the realities of that transition from backpack to briefcase." This is a great example of using a Web-based "touch point" to create a connection with Millennials. It's also a great way of managing expectations by presenting a fairly realistic portrayal of the jobs, since the videos are shot by Millennial employees themselves.

How about getting some of your superstar employees to start blogging about why they love their jobs and what they are learning every day? Rather than expect Millennials to read testimonials on your Web site, think about how you could repurpose them into a podcast that could be downloaded to an iPod or the newest Black-Berry. You don't have to reinvent the wheel, just roll it to some new places.

• **Tap into members of the tribe.** Touch points don't have to be high tech. Your best recruiters may be right under your nose—your own employees. It's hard to set false expectations when job candidates are being recruited by people who actually work there! Many of your Boomer and Gen X employees have Millennial children of their own or know friends of their children who would make great employees. Or, if you've just hired Millennials who love their jobs, wouldn't it make sense to empower them to share the love? Like it or not, Millennials may be more open to being recruited by a friend at a bar than the vice president of marketing at a career fair.

It's not new to offer employees some type of monetary reward if they refer a new hire to the business, but it's still effective. Some of these incentive programs have gotten even savvier by increasing the reward if the new employee stays for a certain amount of time. But rather than just dangle a monetary prize for employees who refer a new hire, why not arm these employees with the tools needed to hit the recruiting pavement? Give them sizzling paragraphs they can incorporate into a personal e-mail or text message to their family and friends. Update your team on entry-level positions you're trying to fill and describe your ideal candidate. Host a social gathering where employees can invite a Millennial they believe is worthy of meeting the gang.

• **Educating the educators.** The typical approach to those graduating from college is to host a table at the campus job fair or schedule interviews on campus visiting days. While this tried-and-true touch point has proven to be successful, companies are getting savvier with the materials they hand out and have made the connection more personal by inviting alums who work for them to stop by and "tell it like it is." If they can talk about a range of topics, from on-the-job stress to the in-office culture, it will go a long way toward helping job applicants match their expectations with reality.

And then there's the "off season" approach. Instead of relying on a handful of days to pull in candidates, create touch points that allow you to stay in front of students throughout the year. Approach your target school by department—from marketing to economics to business—and provide updates on what is going on at your company. Are there current and exciting case studies you could share with professors that would help beef up their curriculum—not to mention your exposure? Are you able to provide "experts" from your organization who would be willing to volunteer as guest speakers in class? Have you made sure the job placement counselors at each school are up to speed on your current hiring needs and where the opportunities are? Ask yourself if you are really top of mind for students and schools alike or just another folding chair at the job fair? What can you do to develop deeper relationships with those who are *already* coaching your potential new superstars at school and can help you both spot talent and set expectations?

MILLENNIALS ON RECORD

"I was really good at school. I was an excellent student. But I didn't know exactly what to expect from the workplace. In school, you read the syllabus, you do the assignments, and you are fine. But at work, it becomes a lot mushier. So it's harder to feel confident about what you will need to do to be successful."

— *Kate Jakubas, age 24, materials engineer, Elkay Manufacturing*

An international pharmaceutical company found they were having to do more and more recruiting at colleges just to fulfill their yearly targets. They found the competition kept getting tougher and it was becoming harder to stand out from the crowd at university recruiting events. "Eventually," explained a Millennial in charge of campus recruiting for the company, "we just decided to stop chasing so many schools and focus in on a handful. By being more targeted, our recruiters were able to spend a lot more time at fewer campuses. They were able to develop deeper relationships with the placement officers and with professors in the business and science departments. Even when the downturn hit and we weren't hiring as many people we were still able to get better candidates and create a tighter 'fit' between our needs and those we did hire." With that many touch points working on your behalf you have a much greater chance of marrying job applicants' expectations to your own, and you decrease the chances of an ugly divorce down the road.

THE COURTSHIP

So you find a few high-potential candidates, and on paper (or on screen) they seem perfect. Now it's time to meet them face-to-face and have a real dialogue. The problem with Millennials is sometimes these conversations don't end up being very *real* at all. The result? Expectations gone really wrong and opportunities wasted.

• **The Interview: Out of the board room, into the chat room.** How often do employers hire a Millennial only to scratch their heads a few days into the job and wonder if it's the same person they interviewed a few weeks back? The problem is we don't create interview situations that encourage Millennials to "get real." First, consider the candidate. We often hear recruiters say things like, "I'm not sure we even *want* a candidate who doesn't know how to interview properly." But that may be throwing the baby out with the bathwater. A new college grad might not know much about interviewing, but he or she could still be a great fit for your company. If you aren't finding the right fit with new hires, maybe it's time to set pride aside and give Millennials a leg up before they even walk through the door. Many companies today are using their Web sites and pre-interview materials to tell candidates the kinds of questions they will ask, the kind of information they seek, and even what is appropriate to wear. Some even suggest homework graduates can do to prepare for the interview and point them to Web sites or articles about the firm. It might not feel like your job, but it could keep recruiters from scratching their heads after a disastrous interview wondering why things didn't go as expected.

• **The offer or THE OFFER!** We all remember getting our first job and how excited we were. Or do we? When you make the offer, do your candidates feel like they just won the lottery or were just read their rights? Do you communicate only the terms, or do you sell the excitement? A little fanfare will go a long way toward exceeding expectations for a generation that has been coached to find work they care about and can be proud of. Give them something to brag about. Some organizations provide hip and cool "welcome packs." Others organize "get acquainted" events to celebrate new hires and introduce them to the firm. PricewaterhouseCoopers provides newly hired interns with a link to a private Web site hosted on Facebook where they can get acquainted before they start work and stay connected throughout their employment. This helps them form immediate friendships with peers, so they feel more bonded to the firm before they even start.

Some of you are thinking, "Sure, but our industry is in the toilet, it's not really the time to set off a fireworks display or give someone a prize just for signing on." We say you're wrong. If times are tough you can still build relationships and enthusiasm even as you set realistic expectations. Let people know you are facing challenges and yet you're still pumped up about adding them as a valuable new asset to the team. Millennials want to hear an honest assessment of the situation, and they really want to know they are still wanted and needed by the company. Don't let the wind out of the new hire's sails just because the company is facing the doldrums. If you have a job to fill and they can make a difference, let them know it. They are likely to add much-needed energy and passion that raises everyone's spirits.

LOOKING FOR LOVE IN ALL THE RIGHT PLACES

Companies frequently tell us they are recruiting where they always recruited, and suddenly the people they expected to shine are a bit dull or aren't working out at all. Unfortunately, rather than questioning whether they are recruiting in the right places, companies tend to stick with the status quo and recruit even harder, still expecting stellar results. Or they blame the candidates. "What's wrong with kids these days?' they ask us, "We keep hiring Millennials and they aren't working out."

Sometimes the Millennials you're recruiting truly aren't the right ones. One international consulting firm told us they had recruited from a handful of very elite colleges for decades. Recently they were finding their new hires lacked the work ethic and drive required for the job. To make matters worse, their new Millennial hires were picky about the type of work they wanted to do and disdained menial tasks. This was frustrating for partners who had to manage them, and it was costly for the firm to replace them when they didn't stick around. One partner commented, "The trouble is, at these schools many of the top students have never worked. They come to us expecting the moon and are offended by the idea of paying some dues."

Our suggestions? Consider the notion that you may be looking for recruits in all the wrong places. If your expectations are no longer being met, perhaps it's time to consider schools with students whose values or skills will provide a tighter fit.

If you know who you want to attract, but you're worried about competing against more exciting suitors, get to know what they have to offer. For example, if you're talking about the demanding hours your accounting firm requires during tax season, you might want to point out that your biggest competitor is known for being rigid about schedules while you allow employees flexibility to set their own schedules as long as they get the work done. Just as you want to set realistic expectations about your own organization, you can do so regarding the competition.

You might also consider new types of job candidates. During Millennials' formative years, the gap between the haves and have-nots in America has widened. This is a generation divided by differences in education, access to technology, and opportunity. Although the Millennials are poised to top the Baby Boom in size, there will be fewer workforce-ready candidates than in prior generations because jobs have become more skilled while fewer young people are getting the basic education they need to be employable. The U.S. high school dropout rate currently hovers around 30 percent, and it's as high as 50 percent in some regions of the country. As the economy improves and worker shortages intensify, a question for policy makers and employers will be how to enable more Millennials to get the skills they need to fill hiring gaps and become valued employees.

Employers experiencing severe worker shortages may need to explore this untapped population and consider how to get them up to speed. Abbott Northwestern Hospital in Minneapolis faced a huge challenge in staffing a health-care center in the Phillips neighborhood in the inner city. The neighborhood scared off skilled workers from other locations, yet it wasn't producing local grads with the right qualifications to work for one of the best employers in the area. They responded by creating their own workforce. Abbott Northwestern started their own training center right in the neighborhood, where willing students can get the education they need to fill jobs such as certified nursing assistant. Commutes are short and employees are putting their earnings back into the community where they live.

Another option is to partner with schools to create and educate the workforce you need. Thomson Reuters started a new program called "Hire4Ed" to introduce at-risk students to potential careers. The company paid the equivalent of one full-time salary and four students worked for the company one day a week and alternated on Fridays. The money earned went to the school to help subsidize the students' education. Bob Azman, senior vice president of Customer Services at Thomson Reuters explained, "This program benefits the four students who get to explore our organization and all the possibilities available here. Most of them are at-risk and wouldn't normally have this exposure. The school feels this program actually rescues them from a path leading to gangs or violence. However, make no bones about it, we benefit just as much, if not more. By getting to know them we are able to get a sense for who is coming down the pipeline and the issues we need to pay attention to so that we cater to the workforce of the future. For example, the students felt strongly that our organization should be more 'green.' Best of all, they are wonderful recruits. Thanks to Hire4Ed, we get on their radar *now*, so when they graduate from college or trade school they will think of Thomson Reuters as a place to start their career."

If you think you're looking in all the right places but aren't feeling the love, perhaps it means something has changed and you're not recognizing it. One Boomer with a Midwestern manufacturing firm said he'd always preferred to hire candidates from his alma mater. But he hadn't stayed in touch with how the school was changing. A land grant college, it had always attracted hard-working farm kids from surrounding rural communities. Over the past two decades the area had become much more urbanized and the student body had changed. They were less interested in the blue collar jobs the company had to offer. "We're rethinking where we can find the best match for our organization," he commented. "I needed to let go of my views on what school that should be and think about the people we need."

While many employers are quick to explore what is different or has changed with this new generation of recruits, organizations should also be asking how *they* have changed. Have your expectations shifted? Has work ethic become more important than technical skills? Are you really looking for math wizards, or do you need someone with more critical-thinking or problem-solving skills? As we confront the new wave of Millennials, we have to continually ask ourselves: "Do we truly know who we need and are we looking for them in the right places?"

In summary, recruiting is a lot like dating. Part of it involves managing expectations. You don't want to paint such an unrealistic picture of yourself that candidates are turned off when they discover what you're really like. At the same time, you want to tap into the touch points that connect with Millennials. Finally, you want to be clear about who your ideal candidate really is and make sure the places you're looking are going to result in the match you dreamed of.

WHY "ORIENTATION" IS A DIRTY WORD

So you hire the right Millennial and it feels like the perfect match. They're psyched, you're psyched, and everyone expects to kick it off with a bang. The problem is that by day two it's more like a bust and no longer seems like a match at all.

When we wrote our last book we had a chapter on orientation called, "Here's Your Boss and Benefits; There's the Bathroom." Our goal was to point out that most orientation programs hadn't progressed much past the old-fashioned, bare bones "tour-and-time-clock" approach. New hires may watch a video, sign forms, be shown around the building, and boom—they're expected to be ready to go with the motivation to power them through the next few decades of work. As we write this second book seven years later, not much has changed. Sure, some companies have revolutionized their orientation schemes, but others are still in a rut. Yet Millennials are telling us that the process of entering a new job and a new culture is important to them and that first impressions make a big difference. Unfortunately, many also are reporting that it wasn't what they expected. How can you meet or exceed expectations when you bring new employees on board?

Liberty Diversified International has a superb reputation, but some of the industries they are in, such as paper and packaging, aren't exactly the sexiest, so they have to keep employees engaged with a great culture and good management. Liberty recently beefed up its orientation program to ignite the younger generations. Calling it "Path to Growth," the theme centered around the idea that an employee's career would be a journey and with each step he or she would continue to grow as a professional. New hires even received a lantern and backpack to help them on their way. The concept was great and the backpacks were a hit, but as Millennials went through the program something wasn't connecting and expectations weren't met. The week was jam-packed with activities so that on some days new hires could meet as many as two hundred people. The problem was it only lasted a week. "At the end of the orientation," explained Ann Miller, Liberty's corporate culture specialist, "Millennials missed the sense of community they had so enjoyed during the program." The answer for LDI wasn't extending orientation, but rather extending the feeling of connectedness. They now conclude the week by assigning each Millennial a "Path Finder" who regularly checks in and is available to help the new hire navigate. "We are clear not to call these Path Finders 'mentors,'" explained Ann, "because that suggested a Path Finder always had to teach the new hire something. Instead, we positioned it as a buddy program where new hires could always feel someone was there for them, and it's worked."

Think about it...many Millennials have been courted like top draft picks during the recruiting season, so it should be no surprise they are expecting the first days on the job to feel like the Super Bowl. After earning the right to play on the team, why should a new hire have to go through a whole season before they start feeling good about their choice? Sometimes all it takes is a little more oomph up front.

BASIC TRAINING: NOT JUST FOR THE MILITARY

You can see that expectations are met or missed at a number of points along the way, ranging from how we reach out to candidates to how we make the offer and bring them on board. But you can't stop there. One of the biggest expectation gaps is still lurking, waiting to trip up well-meaning employers. It's the gap around job competencies. A candidate can be a perfectly good hire and still lack some of the skills needed to succeed.

There's a reason the military provides basic training. They want recruits to end up with the right skill-set for the job. It's all about expectations. When you go into battle you can count on your troops performing because you know precisely how they were trained. The military excels in this type of training, where expected competencies are clearly laid out at each step along the way. Unfortunately, in today's workplace the rate of change is so rapid that what prior generations called the "basics" don't seem to exist anymore. Something as simple as counting back the change from a sales transaction seems to have gone the way of the abacus. While Millennials bring many skills with them to the workplace, they are not always the skills their bosses and co-workers had expected. In fact, nearly 70 percent of Traditionalists, Boomers, and Xers in our M-Factor survey agreed that Millennials are "lacking in some basic skills." These mismatched expectations are causing some of the most painful workplace gaps.

Many of our clients are shocked by what they have to teach Millennials. As one Xer put it, "The things they struggle with just seem so obvious. I can't tell you how often I want to look a Millennial in the face and say, 'What were you thinking?'" One of our first Millennial hires showed up to observe one of our keynote presentations wearing torn jeans and cowboy boots. Imagine our embarrassment when our client commented to David, "Casual day at Bridgeworks?" Keep in mind, Millennials may have robust *life* experiences, but their lack of *work* experience means they won't automatically possess all the skills expected in the workplace.

While working at law firms, Dana Bartocci (now employer relations coordinator at the University of Minnesota Law School Career Center) and Stacey Tidball (now the assistant director of the University of Minnesota Career Center) both encountered interns who were competent in some aspects of legal research, but had never been taught to use legal indexes to narrow their searches before beginning an assignment. Instead, they went straight to the Internet, where much of the information is incorrect, or to paid professional research firms, which can get expensive. To remedy the situation, one law firm developed a basic training program called "Research by Book," in which they told student interns, "This is a book. This

is where you begin your research projects." Millennials were taught
the more effective strategy of beginning with a legal index—not
Wikipedia—and then talking to an experienced attorney to get additional guidance and instruction *before going to the Web*. Narrowing
the topic in a legitimate legal source before going to the Internet
was a basic skill that resulted in more targeted, accurate searches.

While the law firm example might seem extreme, we have to be
willing to recognize skill and understanding gaps in our own businesses. Educational styles and standards have changed since Boomers and even Gen Xers were in school. If you hired someone from
another country, it would seem natural to assess their skill-set and
find ways to augment it without shaking your head and wondering
how they ever got hired in the first place. With Millennials we get
agitated because our expectations for what a young person *should*
know don't always match up with reality.

When working with Millennials, take the time to communicate baseline expectations about working in your culture, such as
etiquette, forms of address, how to treat clients, what written communication should look like, how mistakes are handled, and the
other "basics" that form the company's operating standards. You are
bound to uncover interesting gaps in understanding. For example,
our M-Factor survey revealed that while work hours and attendance
were named among the top three most important etiquette issues
by Xers, Boomers, and Traditionalists, Millennials ranked them at
the *bottom* in importance. Clearly, generational expectations don't
always match up and we need to communicate about this. It doesn't
have to be in a formal class; you can do it as a natural component of
managing or mentoring.

Part of managing the expectation gap means sometimes unwritten rules need to be communicated. The HR team of a Fortune
500 food company ran into an issue with privacy. A Millennial employee was reviewing confidential payroll files as part of her job, but
she also looked up what several of her peers were earning and used
that information to approach her boss about getting a raise. The

Boomer and Gen X managers in the department were horrified that an employee in HR would use the information so inappropriately. However, one Boomer decided to do a reality check with a Millennial colleague. She went to the Millennial and asked, "If you had access to this information, would you know you shouldn't look up co-workers' salary data and use it as a basis for comparison?" The Millennial responded, "I would have no idea. And I am so glad you told me, because I assume if I have access to something it's OK to use it." The Boomer went on to say, "This was the first time it became clear that we had completely different expectations about confidentiality. We learned we have to be more concrete. We have to say, 'You can do this with the information; you can't do that.' Our company has always had very strong views on this, but we assumed everyone had the *same* views and we were wrong. Now we train new employees on these policies."

Unfortunately, rather than coach Millennials, we often blame them. We need to give each other a break, and where we see Millennials failing to meet expectations we need to coach and teach.

One nurse manager noticed Millennial new hires often showed up for a shift five, ten, or fifteen minutes late. That meant patient coverage was interrupted, and employees trying to end their shifts couldn't do proper hand-offs. The hospital had to pay overtime when workers failed to leave on schedule. Morale suffered as veteran employees made rude remarks about the tardy Millennials.

The supervisor took matters into her own hands and organized a short class for new hires on "what's expected when you show up." In it she explained the consequences of late arrivals, citing instances of patient care that went awry, communication that broke down, and paperwork that was completed improperly. She gave anecdotal examples of how employees' personal lives were impacted when they couldn't leave on time—like being late to pick up kids at day care. She talked about the bad reputation Millennials were getting around the hospital. Then she outlined what was expected, i.e., that ideally nurses arrived twenty minutes early to put things in their lockers, change into scrubs, grab a coffee, and coordinate with the shift before theirs. She talked about the benefits, to sanity, to morale, to the patient, to the doctors, and to the hospital itself. Then she talked about consequences that would be put in place if people were late.

She commented to us: "If you told me when I started out twenty years ago that I'd have to give a workshop on showing up on time, I would have said you were nuts. But this is a generation that's had a lot of flexibility in how they schedule their lives. They haven't worked a lot of other places, so they weren't thinking about the consequences. And from a business point of view I don't think they realized the toll the tardiness was taking. After we started doing the training, I'd say lateness dropped off by about eighty percent."

MANAGING EXPECTATIONS: GRAB YOUR WHISTLE AND GET READY TO COACH!

So…we've found the right candidate, gotten them excited about their choice, gave an orientation to kick off the experience, and covered the basics to help them be as successful as possible. Guess what? There's still potential for missed expectations once employees are on the job.

As Millennials integrate into companies, they are going to expect ongoing coaching and mentoring. Here is a summary of our best tips for managing both your own and your Millennials' expectations:

• **Recognize generational disconnects.** Some problems really are generation gaps. You might actually have to explain to your Millennial bank tellers that they need to call Traditionalist customers "Mr." or "Mrs. So-and-So," rather than by first names. Don't waste a lot of time lamenting the olden days when people had *respect*. Get over it and get on with it. Describe the behavior you expect and explain why. Millennials are adaptable. They'll get it.

• **Coach on explicit *and* implicit know-how.** Explicit means specific procedures, such as how to complete a tax filing or install an air-conditioning unit. Implicit means the intangible stuff, like how to sell an idea or make the boss look good. Both are important, but we tend to be more prepared to teach new employees about the explicit things and assume they'll pick up on the other stuff through osmosis. Don't make that assumption. Several clients have mentioned to us that Millennials had a hard time figuring out how to leave an appropriate outgoing voice-mail message. The bosses were annoyed by this until we pointed out that fewer and fewer Millennials are using voice mail, preferring instead to post, chat, or text. If you find yourself having the same conversation over and over with your new recruits you might need to put together crib notes on the way you'd like things done. It will allow the Millennials to be more effective and lower your blood pressure in the process.

• **Be a coach, not a nag.** Millennials have been coached all their lives, so this won't be new to them. But they expect to be treated like a darling, not a doofus. Their parents, teachers, and coaches have addressed them like valued team members. They'll anticipate the same treatment from you. It's easy to get huffy and start talking down to the new person when it's an issue you find completely obvious. But think about how often the situation has been

Used with the permission of Brian Crane and the *Washington Post* Writers Group in conjunction with the Cartoonist Group. All rights reserved.

reversed. How many times has a Traditionalist or Boomer asked a Millennial for help programming a new cell phone or ordering something online? Most Millennials are pretty darn gracious about these things. They drop into the chair next to us and start showing us what to do, even though it's beyond basic to them. We need to show the same graciousness in return. Just because they may not understand a basic rule of your game, doesn't mean they won't be crack players the minute they figure it out.

• **Don't fall into the parent trap.** David Grossman, the CEO of a graphic design firm, shared a story about how he had hired a new Millennial designer. A few weeks into the job, he noticed the Millennial almost never managed to show up on time at 9:00 a.m. He called the Millennial's cell phone to find out what the problem was and was dismayed when he discovered he had gotten the employee out of bed. The employee even thanked him for the wake-up call! David didn't question whether or not the Millennial loved his job, or even if he was a great designer. He just couldn't believe the employee wasn't remotely embarrassed to be awakened by his boss to get his you-know-what out of bed and into the office.

Boomers tell us it's easy to start parenting Millennials because these new employees are the same age as their kids. It's a familiar role but it quickly becomes a burden for both parties. Xers tell us they don't want to be made to feel "old" around Millennials, and they don't want to be responsible for them. "This isn't a dorm," commented one Xer supervisor in a large travel agency, "and I'm not about to act like the resident advisor." Part of managing expectations is looking at what we expect of ourselves. Suffice it to say we need to watch the boundaries when it comes to taking on the role of Mom or Dad at work.

• **If you're stuck, call HR.** In the battle to manage mismatched expectations you can't always be expected to know what to do. One Baby Boomer manager of a financial office blushed while admitting he felt paralyzed trying to talk about their dress code with Millennial females. "They, uh, their outfits are kind of, well you see, they're very . . ." He made some hand gestures then petered out and blushed some more. Lynne visited the office later that week and immediately perceived the problem. It was cleavage—too much cleavage for a financial institution serving the public. The firm was located in a warm climate and had gone to casual dress five days a week, but the young ladies in the office were greeting customers with much more than a friendly smile. As a Boomer male, the branch manager was in way over his head trying to address the issue, but he hadn't called HR for help. Perhaps he didn't want to sound like a pervert or be perceived as a wimp, but clearly this type of conversation was light years outside his comfort zone, and we shouldn't expect he would know what to say. In this case, help took the form of a female Millennial HR rep who called all the employees in for a short meeting to review dress code and firmly clarified that no part of the uncovered female bosom should be visible because it made customers uncomfortable. (Actually, we're pretty sure it made some customers happy, but we won't go there.) The point is, if you're out of your league on anything from tattoos to time cards to travel, ask for help. In the battle for understanding between generations you shouldn't have to go it alone.

• **Résumés aren't always all business.** So often companies don't uncover the full potential of a Millennial because we get so focused on what "business" skills they bring to the table. It's another form of missed expectations when we don't bother learning what else they can offer. Millennials may have had other educational, avocational, or volunteer experiences they can bring to bear in the workplace. Don't just ask new employees about their *work* experience; ask about their *life* experience.

• **Get over it and get on with it.** It's human nature for Traditionalists, Boomers, and Xers to expect that the way *they* did things was the best way. Sadly, times change. The old ways get replaced, and we have to move on. Millennials are never going to know a world with mimeograph machines and carbon paper. They've never culled through a card catalogue or had to crawl off the couch to change a channel. Likewise they may never learn how to figure out a tip in their heads or even read a map.

Keep your eyes open for what's next. An employer just told us that a Millennial in their office couldn't read a handwritten thank-you note because it was in cursive! Some elementary teachers tell us they are phasing out teaching cursive writing. Apparently the push to ensure children are technologically literate is replacing classic penmanship instruction in some schools. The only thing we can do is adapt. Let go of trying to train on the outmoded stuff and force yourself to figure out what is important now.

It was a month after Josi's PowerPoint debacle with her boss. She and Tom had smoothed things over and even laughed about it. They would always remember Josi's first week on the job. In the end, they both learned something about working together and were relieved it was only a practice presentation.

The office was buzzing as the board of directors was arriving the next day for the annual meeting. The PowerPoint looked amazing; Tom and Josi had worked their tails off and were ready to blow the board away. Tom was so impressed with Josi's work he not only invited her to the meeting, but also asked her to present the slide on future trends.

Managers were finalizing reports, staffers were moving briskly up and down the halls, and everyone was straightening their desks. Barbara, the CEO's assistant, rushed breathlessly past Josi looking panicked. Josi called out, "Barb, is everything OK?"

"No, we just got an e-mail from our accounting firm that the financial projections are different from the numbers we gave you for your presentation!"

"How can I help?" Josi asked.

Barbara stopped in her tracks, thought for a second, and then said, "How quickly can you change the PowerPoint slides?"

"Just give me a minute," Josi snapped back.

She raced to the laptop and opened the file. Then she paused.

While Josi knew she could change the PowerPoint at lightning speed, she didn't want to be struck by lightning twice. She took a deep breath and went to find Tom. The biggest thing Josi had learned about working with him was that they did best when their expectations matched.

six

THE NEED FOR SPEED

Andrew was pumped. He had been hired by a small marketing firm to help increase their sales, and he'd just gotten his first big lead. The client was a local bank that requested a proposal for a marketing campaign to help them promote their fiftieth anniversary.

"The president wants the proposal like, right now!" Andrew explained to Helen, a Boomer and the owner of the company.

Helen grimaced. It was Friday. She'd been putting in long hours and was looking forward to her weekend. "When do we have to get it to him?"

Andrew was a bit breathless, "I was planning on e-mailing it out to him Sunday so it would be in his inbox first thing Monday morning."

"Great!" replied Helen, trying to sound enthusiastic. She knew the bank's current marketing firm was pretty old school and she wanted to show them her company was more innovative. Plus she

Managing Worklife in the Fast Lane

really wanted to keep Andrew motivated. "Let's get going on this! How about if I order in pizza?" she responded, trying to put some pep into her delivery when the last thing she wanted was to miss another meal at home.

The two of them pulled a team together and spent Friday afternoon and evening brainstorming ideas. Everyone came back in on Saturday to create mock-ups of sample marketing campaigns. Sunday, Andrew and Helen e-mailed back and forth all day until the proposal was perfect. Andrew created a Word document with articles the bank could place when their anniversary rolled around, as well as a colorful and creative array of sample ads. He finalized a super pitch letter, ran everything by Helen that evening for one last check, and got the whole thing e-mailed out to the bank president by Sunday midnight. Mission accomplished! The weekend was shot but at least they had delivered a proposal in record time, sure to dazzle the stodgy bank.

The next morning everyone rolled in, tired but feeling good about the accomplishment. Andrew quickly opened Outlook to check his e-mail. Sure enough, there was one waiting from the bank president. He took a deep breath and read:

"Thank you for your e-mail. I will be out of the office this week on vacation with limited access to e-mail. If this is urgent, you can contact my assistant Regina, or I will look forward to responding upon my return next week."

Andrew glanced up at Helen, who was reading over his shoulder. They looked at each other horror-struck. They'd wasted an entire weekend to get a proposal out "ASAP," but they never stopped to figure out what ASAP meant to the bank. And even if the bank president was dazzled by their creativity and fast turnaround upon his return, they sure didn't need to be in such a rush.

When it comes to pace, Millennials seem to know only one speed—fast. They leave the other generations scratching their heads and wondering whether all this instant access to information doesn't have downsides. For example, does checking voice mails and doing an expense report at the same time *really* enhance a person's effectiveness, or does it ruin their ability to concentrate? Does being barraged with nonstop digital, visual, and verbal stimulation augment one's creativity or inhibit one's ability to think? And are digital tools really connecting us to one another or are they actually creating barriers to connections and conversations? Beyond just driving the older generations crazy, what are the advantages of challenging the pace of everything we do, and what are the costs? How do we walk the tricky tightrope of staying open to the new issues Millennials will inevitably raise, while closing the door on the ideas that are just too "out there" to be viable? And how do we engage Millennials effectively in work environments they may perceive as too rigid and slow?

If we want to better understand the need for speed, we first have to slow down and understand how fresh technologies, new workplace norms, and the Millennials themselves are shifting the pace at which we work.

HOW THE PEDAL GOT TO THE METAL

When it comes to pace, Millennials are increasing the rate of speed at which they do things and also the speed at which they expect communication, feedback, and promotions. They've been raised in an amped-up world of information where you don't have to wait until 5:30 p.m. for the news to come on TV. You can access it immediately via cable TV, computer, or PDA. Forget writing a letter to a friend, or even an e-mail. You can text one another instantaneously, or participate in a real-time chat online.

In college, work teams send assignments around electronically, access the library via their school's intranet, and tap into global resources at the touch of a button. And why wait until the next class to find out your marks? They are posted online as soon as the paper has been graded.

The high-speed-chase style that marks Millennials' communication is colliding head-on in the traditional workplace. Recruiters on the front lines run into this all the time. One explained, "I will get a thank-you e-mail from a college student interviewed on campus within five minutes of our meeting. It's as if they were writing the letter on their BlackBerry while we were speaking, and they press 'send' the minute they walk away from my career fair booth!"

In their personal lives Millennials often are the ones setting the pace. It's no wonder they experience caffeine withdrawal when they arrive in the workplace. In the corporate environment change comes slowly. It's costly and complicated to upgrade equipment. Operating systems may be several versions behind, and some types of Web access might be blocked for security reasons or to avoid overloading the server. Millennials accustomed to having a brand-new laptop to use at school will be stunned to find they have to wait a year or two until the company grants them one. Even then it might not be the latest and greatest. And think about software. Once an organization gets everyone up and running and all the data transferred, it's going to take an act of Congress, or maybe even an act of God to change it. The cost of disruption is just too high. Anyone who's ever lived through a changeover of their customer-relationship management software can testify to the ulcer-inducing challenge of surviving it.

That's just on the technology side. What happens when it comes to decision-making processes where "hurry up and wait" is the name of the game? Millennials who have only been held back by the number of bars showing on their cell phones are entering a workplace where decisions work their way through a process so time-consuming it can feel like waiting for a dial-up connection on the Internet.

Some of these differences will be resolved through the simple process of adaptation. Good managers always find ways to be in touch and they will undoubtedly pick up the pace on the most important things. The good news is, in our M-Factor survey, Xers and Boomers were actually slightly more worried about Millennials' frustrations around the need for speed than Millennials themselves. But the generation gap around the speed of work is a big one. To what extent should companies adapt, and to what extent do Millennials just need to slow down and adjust to the ways an organization operates?

CLOCKING MILLENNIALS' NEED FOR SPEED

In today's multigenerational workplace, one of the biggest gaps arises when Millennials are frustrated by the glacial pace of the other generations. Bosses besieged with Millennials seething about the status quo and agitating for change are tempted to revert to the old air raid drills they practiced as children and hide under their desks. The result? Ongoing sniping that sometimes breaks out into all-out war.

No one would argue that the pace of business has increased exponentially in just a few decades. In the short span of a Millennial's life, we've gone from mailing documents, to overnighting them,

MILLENNIALS ON RECORD

"Our generation will leave its mark by being the generation that grew up with things like the Internet but we still can't take it for granted like the next one will. We've gone from 28k to 56k to 128kbs dial-up modems, to DSL, LAN, and fiber optics. We're intertwined with the Web—it influences us, and we influence it—and we're the next in line in terms of shaping the way the world communicates and does business."
— *Dale Till, age 20, Northeastern University student/full-time employee at the Institute for International Urban Development*

to faxing them, to e-mailing them, and now to posting them on a server and accessing them instantly from multiple locations.

Millennials have been presented with a steady stream of tech tools that have allowed them to do everything faster and eliminate the middle man. Why keep driving to Blockbuster when you can have Netflix sent straight to your mailbox? Why change your evening plans to catch your favorite TV show when you have a digital video recorder that allows you to watch it when you want to— without commercials?

The educational system also changed during Millennials' formative years. Suddenly students were allowed to use calculators on math tests. It wasn't important that you showed every single step used in solving the problem, it was just important that you got the right answer. As Roberta Chinsky Matuson put it in an article called *Gen Y Greatness*: "They are ready, willing and able to automate everything in front of them. Don't mistake their ability to use shortcuts as laziness. It's efficiency taken to a whole new level."

When discussing the need for speed, MOR Ashley Strub put it like this: "The way we were taught, we were allowed to be more creative in our solutions. The most important thing to us is efficiency. So in the work we do, we are constantly trying to make things more efficient and faster. We want everything at our fingertips so we can get to the solutions right away." Fast forward to the workplace and that Millennial is chomping at the bit to do the same for you. Or as Matuson says, "If you're willing to learn from them, you too may be able to finish your work in time to attend an early evening yoga class."

For the older generations, making the leap to doing things in new ways feels uncomfortable and often takes a big investment of time up front. "Please," Millennials beg, "can we install the new shared calendar system? You won't believe how much faster you can schedule things!" The Boomer is thinking, "Yes, and it will take me three weeks to learn it!" And the Xer is thinking, "Right, and I'm going to have to go around and train every executive on this floor. It will be a nightmare."

MILLENNIALS ON RECORD

"I wish I could teach the other generations to think about change the way we do. It should not be treated as a threat or an insult to past traditions, but as another step in society's evolution. Our population and culture is far from static, so we need to embrace dynamic ways of thinking in order to catch up with what's already changing, whether we like it or not."

—*Elena Davert, age 18, undergraduate student*

We know Millennials want to help organizations pick up the pace and deal with change, but how fast is fast enough? We can turn around a client project overnight, but should we? Is that really what the client expects? Or, are we putting unnecessary strain on the system, not to mention ourselves? And does it jeopardize quality or make the project more expensive to complete because it's a rush order? According to our M-Factor survey, more than half of Traditionalists, Boomers, and Xers think Millennials are tech savvy but not necessarily in the right areas.

And what about creativity? Focusing on doing things faster can place the wrong emphasis on what's important. Remember the old decision-making quadrant that correlated the *urgency* of a task with its *importance*?

It's easy to focus on the tasks that are both urgent *and* important. (For example: pulling together budget numbers for the senior vice president's board meeting the next day.) It's tempting to focus on the host of tasks that are urgent but not that important (e-mails that require a quick response). Most of us are able to put aside projects that are not urgent and not important (cleaning out the office supply cabinet). But many of us struggle with the projects that may not be urgent but are important and often strategic (like finding ways to infiltrate a new market or developing a new product to fill a niche we don't serve). The bottom line is if we give in to the pressure of speeding everything up, we may cannibalize the most strategic efforts, because they take too much time.

So rather than react blindly to the lure of speed, the generations need to be thoughtful. Here is an opportunity to learn from one another and negotiate the best solutions. Sometimes Millennials will have to understand the established system is on cruise control and the speedometer doesn't need to change! At other times the older generations will need to jump into the passenger's seat, let the Millennials drive, and buckle up for a faster, potentially more efficient ride. Here are some tips for the journey:

• **Set speed limits.** As the pace increases, we have to set new limits. In our experience it is very challenging to move outside one's long-term comfort level, especially if you've been successful with it. One MOR brought up this example: "When my boss wants me to reach out to a client for the first time, he only gives me a phone number. I sometimes feel really uncomfortable calling without knowing them! Plus it's time-consuming because inevitably the person's not at their desk. I would much rather e-mail them and then follow up with a call, but he doesn't give me that option."

You can imagine the boss deliberately not giving the Millennial the e-mail address, because he wants his employee to make a personal connection with the client. He's created a challenge however, because he hasn't explained why this is important or what he wants the Millennial to learn. At the same time, the boss might just be short-sighted. Many clients today find it faster to respond via e-mail rather than wait until they have time for phone calls. If that's the case the boss is slowing everybody down because he prefers to do things the traditional way. We have to talk to each other about why we do things the way we do and be open to changing the pace if it makes sense.

• **Manage the pace.** Just like in the story of the bank proposal being delivered while the president was on vacation, not everything that *can* happen overnight *needs* to happen overnight. You still have to decide the right approach. Teach your staff to *manage* the need for speed. Have them ask clients—whether external customers or the groups you serve internally—when they need something done and what level of completion they are expecting. A Millennial might promise he or she can complete a project the same day only to find out the other department doesn't need it until the end of the month, thus saving resources and preserving sanity.

• **Consider when to drive in the fast lane.** One Millennial was asked to produce a series of mailings to promote a company's new division. Typically, direct mail campaigns took a long time to design, edit, double check, and print. Organizing the database and mailing out the pieces was never a quick process. The Millennial had a knack for video editing and suggested they produce some creative mini-videos, post them on YouTube and e-mail the links out to clients. Not only was the Millennial's idea less costly, it could be completed in half the time and would enable the company to track response rates electronically.

There is no harm in thinking through with Millennials and your team where you could eliminate steps, streamline a process, or use technology to do things more efficiently. In our M-Factor survey, 80 percent of Xers and Boomers said they found Millennials to be well prepared to succeed in the workplace when it comes to creating and innovating. This is your chance to put them to work. Give them any project and ask them what efficiencies they suggest. Millennials will love the opportunity to see if they can make it faster and more streamlined, and it gives you the chance to observe how they work.

Too often, however, Millennials suggest an improvement and it gets so bogged down in policy and procedure they lose heart or give up. One of our MORs who asked for confidentiality made these remarks: "Millennials are always looking for different ways to do things and looking for new solutions. Because we grew up around so much technology, we are a lot less patient. If I identify a problem, I would like to find a solution and have it fixed by tomorrow. I saw a mistake on our Web site that I thought needed an easy fix. I sent a screen shot to my manager and I got a response that they'd have to see how it fit into our timeline and that we might be able to address it in a month or two. I think Millennials wonder why we can't do it now."

You might hit roadblocks when you allow Millennials to try revving up the status quo, but the job of the manager is to clear these out of the way so good ideas can thrive. Remember when electronic airline tickets first became available? Travelers panicked at the thought of not having a paper ticket in hand. Now, unless you're traveling overseas, nobody's worried about it or even wants it. That's because somebody somewhere asked the question, and a manager somewhere gave them the thumbs up to give it a try.

• **Know when to curb your speed.** Sometimes faster isn't better. Rushing to develop a new marketing campaign without studying all the data or hurrying to come up with an architectural design without hearing from all the stakeholders, will cause more harm than good down the road. Other things shouldn't be rushed because there's nothing to be gained by picking up the pace. A company that cleans carpets, for example, can benefit from responding to client phone calls as fast as possible. However, they might not get any benefit from guaranteeing they'll service *every* client's carpets within forty-eight hours. A faster pace is only good if it serves the customer's needs. Whether you are cleaning carpets or scrubbing data, experienced mentors can work with Millennials to analyze the potential gains of speeding up or changing a process.

• **Coach Millennials on how to navigate traffic jams.** We guarantee you, newly hired Millennials eager to hit maximum speed on the road to success have no idea how many roadblocks stand between them and making changes in an organization. There are years of history, territories to defend, Byzantine processes, and of course, resistance to doing something different. When you're new to an organization, it's easy to dismiss these roadblocks as ridiculous, or just a bunch of old fogies with axes to grind and no imagination. What Millennials overlook is that people often have valid reasons to avoid changing the status quo. They may have been burned when it was tried before. Or they are so overloaded with work any change requiring their attention will put them over the edge. Or maybe the change is going to come out of their budget. It's even possible that the current system works well. Without being a complete wet blanket, the older generations need to coach Millennials on the challenges a project presents and help with strategies to overcome them.

Baby Boomer Ventris Gibson helped her Millenial employees work through a touchy situation like this for the Federal Aviation Administration. The FAA noticed a huge shift in the workforce as Gen Xers and Millennials came on board. She was wise enough to acknowledge she didn't know exactly what all of their hot buttons were or what needed to be done to respond, but she knew the issues were important for morale and retention. Ms. Gibson created what she called the "Next Generation Group" made up of Xers and Millennials whose job it is to advise her on ways to help HR evolve and appeal more effectively to their generations. One of the top items on their laundry list was dress code. Operating on a military model of respect, discipline, and professionalism, employees were expected to be "in uniform" (meaning dressed professionally) on the job. In the eyes of many Xers and Millennials, this harkened back to days where people still smoked at their desks. A suit and tie every day of the week? They just didn't understand why they couldn't dress comfortably to do the very demanding work required. At a minimum they wanted "dress down Fridays."

"At first I told them that HR must have a professional presence and cannot be viewed as laid back," Ventris explained. "They seemed OK with that answer, however, there they were at my door a month later asking me to define what I meant by 'professional image.' I realized it didn't matter what I said, because I knew that in another month they would come knocking again. So I told them that if they could make a true business case around this, I would listen." Ventris knew that changing the dress code would be a hard sell. But she wanted to give her committee a chance to try, and rather than be thwarted by institutional roadblocks she wanted them to learn how to maneuver within the system to get things done.

To make their case, the Next Generation Group gathered best practices from the private and public sectors, along with testimonials and loads of data. They even got savvy about how to present the information to Ventris by sending in a Gen Xer who was at director level and had great rapport with her.

"I have to admit," said Ventris "they had done their homework. And the most compelling data they presented for dress down Fridays was that they showed how rarely we get visitors on a Friday!"

So Ventris agreed to try dress down Fridays once per quarter. The Next Generation Group was savvy enough not to complain, but instead accepted their small victory. They waited patiently to prove that even on dress down days they could still be perceived as professional. Their hard work paid off when a few months later Ventris stood up before all seven hundred HR employees and announced, "OK, the horse is dead and I'm getting off. As of next week, every Friday will be dress down and *yes*, you can wear jeans!"

The Next Generation Group wasn't the only one who won; the result for Ventris was a resounding standing ovation!

Teach Millennials how to make the case for change. Will the proposed change save time or money, reduce extra steps, or improve quality? One of the best things the older generations can do to help Millennials manage their need for speed is to show them how to slow down and work around the bumps in the road.

• **Ramp up the feedback.** One of the simplest techniques for engaging Millennials is to pick up the pace of communication. In *When Generations Collide*, we developed a ClashPoint around feedback. A ClashPoint is a topic in the workplace around which the generations are likely to collide, and the magic of a ClashPoint is that no one is right or wrong—the generations simply come at it from different points of view. The ClashPoint around feedback looks like this:

- *Traditionalists* learned feedback happened top-down and on a need-to-know basis. If no one was yelling at you, you were probably doing fine.
- *Boomers*, who were highly competitive, needed to know how they were performing against 80 million others. Feedback was based on a formal performance appraisal, with plenty of documentation for the file.
- *Generation Xers*, who were skeptical about where the company was going and what the future looked like, wanted straightforward, immediate feedback.
- *Millennials*, we predicted, would want instant feedback from a range of sources at the push of a button.

That prediction has come true. Overwhelmingly, Millennials tell us they don't just want feedback from their direct supervisor. How about the rest of the team and the boss's boss, too? And why wait until their next review or even the next team meeting? How about feedback *right now*? Millennials frequently identify lack of clear communication and actionable feedback as one of their biggest frustrations at work. Giving specific, timely input is one of the best ways to keep Millennials focused and committed. It shows you take an interest and helps them stay on track. In a recent Ernst & Young survey, 85 percent of Millennials said their age-group peers want "frequent and candid performance feedback," while only half of the Boomers felt the same way. Likewise companies like IBM have documented an increase in demands for feedback from Millennials.

When we provide fast feedback Millennials feel they are making progress rather than worry that they are stalled or falling behind. Even if the feedback is negative, they can get on track to fix the problem instead of wasting time going down the wrong path. Never fear, these more frequent feedback sessions don't have to be a huge time sink. One manager with an office full of Millennial direct reports told us two ways he solves the problem of long, drawn out feedback conversations. "Don't get me wrong, I love interacting with my young employees, but there aren't enough hours in the day. So here's what I do: If they come into my office I stand and remain standing until the interaction is finished. We don't settle into the comfy chairs, because then it's likely the employee won't get to the point. When they've gotten the information they need, I can usher them out. The other thing I do to speed up my ability to give feedback is to get up and walk around. I stop by each person's desk so that if they need to get my reaction to something they can get it right then and there. If things go on too long, I can excuse myself." Assume Millennials are going to want to spend time with you, but what they want most is your input, and that can be in the form of a few brief comments or even an e-mail.

• **Managers, adjust your driver's seat.** Gen Xers have prided themselves on being the technological whiz kids in organizations, as well as being the skeptics who challenged the status quo and got things done in new ways. To some extent it's going to change as Millennials muscle in on that role. Xers may still be asking the tough questions, but now they're also going to be the ones fielding them. We're already seeing tensions arise as Generation Xers and Millennials collide over who's the most tech-savvy. One MOR commented; "My thought on Xers is they are almost more difficult to work with tech-wise and in terms of generational differences than Baby Boomers. Baby Boomers are more likely to admit they don't know how to use the technology."

Ouch. It's tough to have someone years younger imply they can come up with an idea that's light years faster. On the other hand, Xers have plenty of complaints of their own. "I find Millennials to be extremely unrealistic about what it takes to make technological changes in our organization," commented one Gen X manager. "They are in such a hurry they don't think about how many people will be affected, the costs involved, and the potential for disruption. I would like to see them come to me with a more realistic approach."

For all you Gen Xers feeling bruised on the technology front, let it go and let it work in your favor. Your background will set you up to lead the next tech revolution; you just don't have to *do* all of it.

MULTITASKING: CAN'T LIVE WITH IT, CAN'T LIVE WITHOUT IT

After a recent speech to a group of high-performing salespeople, David was approached by a Baby Boomer who seemed riled up.

"I'm very worried about all this multitasking," she explained.

"Have you run into problems with it at work?" David inquired.

"Actually, it's my son. He thinks it's OK to do his homework while listening to his iPod, chatting on the computer, and even talking on the phone! I've decided the next time I catch him doing all those things while he is doing homework, I'm going to take his phone away!"

"Wow! Your son does have a lot going on at once," David replied. "But tell me something. I'm curious, how are his grades?"

There was a long pause and her eyes got wide.

"He's getting straight A's," she responded. The two of them fell silent as there didn't seem to be much more to say.

The confusion and concern over multitasking has made it one of the most contentious generational topics today. Millennials with a need for speed think it's natural to have instant access to communication 24/7. The other generations don't see it that way. Parents are worried about short attention spans. Teachers are frustrated by having to compete for attention as students text each other in class. Employers are confounded by everything from bad behavior in meetings—like consulting one's BlackBerry while the boss is talking—to lack of productivity during work hours. Even the most basic rules are being tested, such as whether it's OK to wear a headset and listen to music while at your desk.

Wherever you fall on the multitasking debate, you've probably observed that the generations are judging each other pretty harshly—primarily because they've come of age with such different experiences. Baby Boomer Patrick Smith, a commercial real estate developer, explained it this way: "When I was a kid and it was time to do homework, my dad was a hard-liner. You turned the TV off, you turned the music off, you didn't answer the phone, and the room was *quiet* so you could concentrate on your assignments. Knowing how I was as a kid, that was probably a good idea. But children today are doing homework in their rooms, they've got the TV on, the cell phone is ringing, they're probably texting a few friends, carrying on a conversation in a chat room, and listening to music, all at the same time. I don't know how they get their work done."

Mysteriously, most *do* manage to get it done. But why are things so different?

Part of the difference is access. For most Boomers growing up, the household had only one television set and probably a single stereo system in the living room. There were maybe two phones. Parents could tell in a heartbeat if you snuck an eight-track tape into the player or turned on *Bonanza*. Today's communication tools are small, silent, and easily disguised—and they are irresistible. Checking for messages whether on e-mail, cell phone, or Facebook is now as inviting as it used to be to run to the mailbox to see if you had a letter.

When we ask the older generations why they are so concerned about the Millennials and multitasking, responses fall into two categories. One is about politeness. Older people feel if someone is texting while they're talking they're being rude. The other is about effectiveness. They are worried we're raising a whole generation of people who are so focused on speed they will never learn to concentrate, which leads to the even bigger fear that they won't be successful.

The trouble with multitasking. In study after study, researchers have shown that performing multiple tasks at once makes the brain less efficient. Basically, the brain doesn't become proficient at doing multiple tasks, it simply becomes faster at skipping back and forth between them and blocking other information out. So if you are talking on the phone and writing a report with music in the background, your brain is exerting itself to block out the song while it switches rapidly between the conversation and the writing. On simple tasks it probably works fine, although the friend can likely tell you're doing something else while he's talking, and the report won't get done as quickly or as well as it would have if you focused only on that.

On complex tasks, multitasking becomes a bigger problem. The constant switching of the brain makes a person more easily tired, more likely to make mistakes, and more apt to slow down and take longer to complete projects. The reason for this is that similar tasks compete to use the same part of the brain, according to Earl Miller, a Picower professor of neuroscience at M.I.T. "Think about writing an e-mail and talking on the phone at the same time...you cannot focus on one while doing the other. That's because of what's called interference between the two tasks," he explains.

A lab at the University of Michigan uses an MRI scanner to photograph the brain while subjects perform different tasks. Basically, as the subject switches between tasks the brain has to pause to round up the information it possesses about the new task. In other words, according to the *Journal of Experimental Psychology*, when the mind shifts back and forth it actually *slows down*. This shifting back and forth is known as "switchtasking" and there's a high cost to doing this habitually. According to time management expert Dave Crenshaw, these habits cause stress and anxiety to the brain that decrease effectiveness and create other symptoms, such as tiredness, reduced productivity, a shorter attention span, and even physical symptoms such as increased heart rate and nervousness.

The upside of multitasking. However, there are several reasons why speeding things up via multitasking can be effective and perfectly acceptable:

• **Sometimes you can do two (or more) things at once.** If you're getting dressed while participating in an online chat and looking at photos on MySpace, it's likely your brain can switch between operations pretty easily. If there's a slow down in your response to any of these tasks, it wouldn't matter as much as it would if you were flying a jet while trying to listen to the last two minutes of the Super Bowl on your headphones. So, less demanding tasks need less attentiveness and multitasking makes sense.

• **Multitasking fills in the gaps.** "If I'm waiting for a document to print or for something to download, of course I'll be doing three other things," explained one of our MORs. That makes sense, and you're not alone. We all fill those little gaps with other tasks. But some experts argue that's not even multitasking. Instead, it's what's called *layering*, where you add a task that's different in nature on top of a task you're doing in order to save time. Moms do it every day. You don't put a roast in the oven and then stand there for an hour until it's cooked. You pop it in and immediately layer on all the other tasks that can be accomplished while the roast is cooking. The same happens at work. If you're waiting for the meeting to start, you check your e-mail, place a quick call to a co-worker, or order lunch. Multitasking makes total sense in this context.

• **Allow for detours.** From talking to hundreds of Millennials we know that one of the best aspects of multitasking is it makes the workday more fun. "If I'm working on a long, boring project I will check my Facebook page every twenty minutes or so—it's fun and it gives me a little break," admitted one Millennial. Although this causes the brain to do some switching, there's probably a benefit to taking a break from an Excel spreadsheet to check out how your dating life is improving now that you posted your new profile. Everyone's brain needs to change gears now and then. And even if Millennials are blogging about Madonna's divorce or Rihanna's love life, is that so different than relaxing the mind by doing Sudoku?

• **"Boss, I'm so bored."** Face it; a lot of jobs are boring. If multitasking helps liven up the day, why not? Think about an over-the-road truck driver. We'd like to think he or she does nothing for an eight-hour shift but concentrate on the road. In reality, that driver is likely listening to music, chatting on the phone, checking out the GPS, and planning the next three trips. One could argue she is diverting attention away from driving, but one could also argue she is engaging her brain in ways that prevent boredom and fatigue.

So what is the answer to multitasking? The Millennials' need for speed will continue to test the limits of how many different things can be done at one time. Workplaces are going to have to become more flexible to accommodate the various speeds at which people work and to allow people to work in the ways that are most productive for them. Individuals are going to have to become more aware of how their brains function best so they can be effective. Here are some suggestions:

• **Put multitasking on mute.** If you can't tolerate the level of multitasking going on in meetings, say something. Perhaps people need to put down their PDAs and listen to the presenters. Don't forget to coach employees on the behavior that's expected when they are with clients. One national home renovation firm teaches representatives to silence their cell phones while working in the customer's home because hearing them take calls gives clients the impression they aren't tending to business.

• **Turn up the volume on productivity.** If you're managing Millennials, instead of asking yourself, "How can they get anything done with all those interruptions?" just make sure they get something done. You probably can't control the way Tiffani works, but you have a lot to say about her output. Is the project done on time? Is the quality what you expect? If she's late or turning in poor work, you have a legitimate beef and need to coach her on what you expect. That might include advice on ways to be more productive. Millennials are so used to multitasking their way through school, they may need to learn new skills. Here are tips top managers are teaching Millennials:

- **Clump similar tasks together.** If several tasks involve similar skills, like writing something and responding to e-mails, group those together. Then you're not asking your brain to switch around as much.
- **Take mental breaks.** If your brain is tired, that's a good time to have a snack, socialize, go for a walk, or even switch to an unrelated type of task. We had an experience along these lines while writing this book. After a day of discussing, debating, and outlining chapters, we were tired. But around 4:00 p.m. we had a budget meeting to go over a detailed Excel spreadsheet. Needless to say we were dreading it. But a few minutes into the discussion, we both felt peaceful and relieved. The switch from a type of word-related thinking to something involving columns of numbers was actually restful.
- **Prioritize.** Multitasking makes people feel like everything is equally important all the time. Of course that's not true,

but when you are frantically doing five things at once your brain doesn't differentiate. For example, you might be trying to finish up client order forms to get all your sales logged for the month while stressing about the fact you've got forty unanswered e-mails. That can be stressful because it all feels immediate. It's not. Management and sales guru Harvey Mackay, author of *Swim With the Sharks Without Being Eaten Alive*, always emphasizes that the most successful people get the really important things done first. Client orders are the most important because that's how you get paid. And of your forty e-mails, probably only four or five are urgent. Remind yourself what's most important right now, and you'll be less stressed.

- **Be clear on who needs what and when.** As companies have become leaner, reporting relationships have become more complex. A Millennial might report to one boss but have dotted-line responsibilities to two others and be on task forces with three more. This is, in a sense, *relational multitasking*. Every project and every boss is going to seem important. Millennials need help establishing who comes first and how to navigate the politics of these situations. One manager in a large transportation company advises his Millennials to come to him the minute they notice they have competing projects. If the projects are going to overlap, he works with them to make a plan and communicate limitations to others on the project. "Competing priorities are really stressful to young employees, and they have to learn the skills of juggling appropriately or they will either burn out or fail to get ahead in this company."

- **Scope your skills.** If you always write presentations with music blasting, try writing when it's quiet and see what happens. You might just find you think better that way, you get done faster, or you make fewer mistakes. Or, you might find you're an anxious writer, and the music forces you to relax and not be such a perfectionist. Don't assume you know your own mind until you take it for a test drive.

- **Assure the boss it's getting done.** Rather than get annoyed that your boss can't understand how you are drinking a latte while editing photos for the new Web site and doing e-mail...just roll with it. Sometimes all it takes is showing a supervisor that you *are* completing the tasks at hand, even though you don't have a hand to spare. Results speak for themselves.

We've talked about how the need for speed plays out in managing and multitasking, but there's more to it than that. Millennials' impatience is cropping up in how they deal with their careers.

CORPORATE CHUTES AND LADDERS: NAVIGATING TODAY'S CAREER PATHS

Millennial Liz raised her hand at the Monday morning status meeting. It was hard to be heard over all the buzz and excitement. The ad agency had landed its biggest account in years after being considered the underdog in a long proposal process.

Grant, Liz's Boomer boss, called on her.

"I was wondering if you've decided who will be the lead account exec for this client? If not, I want to throw my hat in the ring," Liz proclaimed. She felt confident as she had been on the job for eighteen months already and had been integral to preparing the winning pitch.

The buzz was silenced and an eerie quiet prevailed.

Grant responded uncomfortably. "I haven't decided who the A.E. will be, but I do know we have a great team that together will create one of the best campaigns ever!"

A few people clapped a halfhearted, politically correct response. It was clear the energy of the meeting was not going to recover.

Afterward, Grant called Liz into his office. "Liz, while I sure appreciate your excitement about the new account I think you need to consider who you are up against for the A.E. position. We need someone who has been around the block a few times."

"But I have been around," Liz countered. "I've been here for a year and a half, not to mention that I had two internships during college. It's not like I haven't paid my dues."

Grant could hardly believe his ears. Since when was eighteen months enough time to be considered paying dues?

"Liz, I understand you have been here for over a year but Rodney has been here fourteen years. Not to mention Rita or Barb. They have been in the industry longer than you have been alive. It's only natural that they expect to be considered to lead such a big account. When you asked about getting the job after only being here a year, it was disrespectful to your teammates."

Liz couldn't help but think, Fourteen years? By then who knows where I'll be. If this guy thinks I'm waiting more than a decade to be considered for an A.E. position, he's got another thing coming. Plus, how can it be disrespectful to express that you really want to step up?

"Grant, I understand what you are saying but what can I do to speed that process along? I feel like I'm ready now and I'd like to prove it to you."

"Well, I suppose if you land some new clients, draft several strategic pitches, and really put in your time supporting the senior account executives, you may be able to be fast-tracked and be up for consideration after five years. That would be lightning speed for this company."

Lightning speed? If that was the fast track, Liz knew she was on the fast track out of there.

Millennials are hardwired to want to do almost everything faster and it comes as no surprise to the older generations. What gives Xers and Boomers a bit of a jolt is when the need for speed shows up in their attitudes toward career paths. It seems they want to move onto the next thing as soon as they've mastered the current tasks or sooner. You might say the Xers started it. With the end of lifetime employment and the demise of the unspoken employer/employee contract that gave workers a sense of long-term security, Xers saw no sense in sticking around if they weren't getting ahead. Especially when they felt they had mastered that rung on the ladder and were ready to climb. Companies that couldn't or wouldn't rethink their dues-paying cultures found that Xers would move up the ladder anyway, only it was somewhere else.

For Millennials, not only is the dues-paying dialogue troublesome, it's literally a foreign language. Millennials want to move up the ladder at a clip that makes the older generations' heads spin. "Who cares if it took my boss eight years to reach supervisor level? If I'm qualified why can't I do it now?" In their minds if they can do the work they should be allowed to step up. They are not alone. As the pace of change has increased, all the generations seem to want to advance faster. Eighty-two percent of respondents to the M-Factor survey who said they are *unhappy* in their jobs, believe career paths advance too slowly where they work.

Organizations are between a rock and a hard place. On the one hand, they want to retain top performers and keep them learning and growing. On the other hand, employees tend to be the most valuable when they become competent at a job and then perform that job for a while. A Millennial might say, "If you don't move me when I become capable of doing more, you're wasting my potential." But if you are forever moving an employee just when they achieve competency you are by definition wasting organizational capacity.

At the same time, promotions aren't in unlimited supply in most organizations. They have to be parceled out to the best performers because there aren't enough to go around.

Another challenge is that the generations have different ideas about the speed at which dues should be paid. Many Traditionalists came up the ranks in organizations with very set patterns for how promotions were earned. You served as a bank teller for five years, then supervisor for three years, then manager for another few years, then assistant vice president for two years, and so on. With the expansion of business, nonprofits, and the public sector during the 1960s, seventies, and eighties, Baby Boomers were hired in droves. They were very tuned into hierarchies and understood how long they needed to stay in a certain position before they could get ahead. They also had a large cohort of competitors for that next promotion, making it difficult to accelerate the pace of advancement. Dues paying was important to show you were dedicated. However, Boomers were aggressive about creating opportunities for themselves. If the organization merged, expanded, acquired another company, or spun off a new division, they were quick to seize the chance to break out and move up. Generation Xers came of age during the economic boom of the nineties and the rise of dot-com companies. Xers were willing to pay some dues but expected that career advancement would happen in a shorter time frame. If it didn't, they were willing and able to hop to another job. They also demanded to know how the dues they were paying related to their next career move. It wasn't enough to say, "That's the way the system works" anymore. Gen Xers wanted to know "why" and how they were going to apply what they were learning.

Then along came the Millennials, who, although they won't be as skeptical and anxious as Generation Xers, are impatient to see how they are getting ahead. With Millennials you can't focus on dues paying; it's a foreign language they won't understand even if you talk louder and slower. This generation is accustomed to learning what they need to learn then moving on. The question will be how to manage those expectations and get the most out of Millennials without creating impossible situations for companies.

Maybe the answer is to let Millennials control the pace a bit more. Marie Artim, the assistant vice president of recruiting at the car rental company Enterprise, realized that it's all about how you talk with Millennials about career paths. She explained, "For the

MILLENNIALS ON RECORD

"I think it's all about speed. In communication and thought and how careers should be perceived. We don't linger long and we don't want to linger long."

—*Nathan Hanson, age 28, financial analyst, Target Corporation*

previous generations, we used to highlight that you would work hard and reap the rewards later. We focused on how you can learn from the ground up with lots of opportunities to grow. While this is all still true, we found that with Millennials we had to talk more about career paths being about performance and not tenure. They seem to be interested in speed, and we tell them there is no set timeline and that it is up to them. There may be an average timeline, but we even encourage them to beat it. Most importantly, we really discuss all the tools and feedback they will get along the way."

Empowering Millennials to take a role in the pace and direction of their careers puts the focus more on what they achieve and less on arbitrary timelines, which seems a natural fit for this generation.

How else do Millennials and managers walk the line between the need for speed when it comes to careers and the need to keep employees in positions long enough to develop deep knowledge? Here are some ideas:

• **What you do today, walks and talks tomorrow.** Millennials don't always realize that the skills they are practicing now are leading them toward a more robust career down the road. They may be handling customer complaints or processing claims without realizing this is a way of learning the business from the ground up. Marie Artim of Enterprise has dealt with that issue head on. She explained, "No one comes here thinking they will stay for life, so why beat around the bush? We constantly point out to Millennials what they are learning and how it will make them a smarter business person *anywhere* they go in their career. Of course we would love for them to stay at Enterprise, but that is not always the reality today, so we meet them where they are. We want them knowing they can really trust us because we are being so real about their career paths."

When managers meet with Millennials to discuss job performance, they should be prepared to point out what they are doing that will be helpful in future positions. Better yet, ask Millennials to come to the meeting prepared with a list of all they are learning and a list of what they would like to learn in the future. This puts the onus on them to assess how they are developing in their jobs.

Another challenge with Millennials who are worried there won't be enough career opportunities with an organization is they aren't always clued in as to what the possibilities might be. One CEO of a credit union told us he makes sure Millennials hear about how they can have a robust career path their first day on the job. He hosts a lunch to welcome new hires and at the lunch he asks current employees to stand up if this is not their first career with the credit union. Then he invites them to go around and introduce themselves and list all the jobs they've had during their employment there. He does this, as he put it, "just to show Millennials there is room to grow and give an idea of the career paths."

• **Take the scenic route.** Some jobs are more exciting than others. If you're getting feedback from Millennials saying there isn't enough to do or the work is boring, it's tempting to pigeonhole them as whiners. It takes a bold boss to step up and say, "Maybe they're right and we can do better here." A business manager for a regional theater company took a very straightforward approach to keeping Millennials stimulated at work: "I tell my development staff 'I am going to teach you to be a development person so you can be incredibly marketable whenever you leave here. When you get bored, tell me, and we will shake it up. You can teach someone else how to do it and you can do something else.' The trade off is I spend a lot of time teaching and training instead of doing the new business development stuff I could be doing. But I will have a staff that doesn't turn over in a year and that makes us much stronger as a department."

One way to stretch Millennials' skill-sets is to put them to work as reverse mentors, where they get to teach and coach the other generations. Millennials tend to be natural ambassadors and will relish the chance to share what they know. However, since the "mentees" in such a program will typically be older and higher on the career ladder, they will need to know how everyone is expected to benefit.

Caroline LaViolette, an organization and development analyst, was charged with developing a reverse mentoring pilot program at Lockheed Martin Aeronautics. For this program, mentees were presidents and vice presidents, and mentors were young professionals. Once the pilot program ended, Caroline sent an e-mail survey asking participants to assess their experience. Interestingly, the most positive impact reverse mentoring had on the Traditionalists, Boomers, and Xers who participated was a much better understanding of generational differences. The Millennial "mentors" said they valued getting to know company "celebrities" on a personal level and expanding their personal networks. In some cases mentor feedback led to promotions or lateral moves to other business units. Several Millennials were even chosen for leadership programs. "All in all," Caroline said, "reverse mentoring proved that 'who you know' can be very valuable." Even more valuable was the opportunity to liven up the job experience for Millennials. According to Caroline, "One of the ways people learn best is through challenging work, and the mentors agreed that's what they got out of the experience."

• **Job descriptions: Time to reprogram the GPS.** Automation has changed things, speeding up processes and leaving less and less for humans to do. Yet we don't always revisit job descriptions to reflect how the work has evolved. We're too busy, and who wants to go to the powers that be and tell them your people are underutilized?

But leaving jobs unexamined wastes resources, hurts competitiveness, and creates frustration in workers who want to do more or at least do work that makes sense. A classic example is a department within a rural electric utility that put together its budget for the upcoming year and included salaries for the usual number of meter readers. They failed to reflect that the facility was installing electronic meter reading, rendering the humans obsolete. The sad part is that at the same time the utility was eliminating meter readers, it was experiencing a severe shortage of linemen. If they had recognized the reconfiguring of jobs in time they might have retrained some of the meter readers who were being laid off to become line workers instead.

If you're getting the sense that employees are bored or frustrated in their jobs, it may be time to reexamine the jobs themselves. Reconfiguring responsibilities and rewriting job descriptions can be time-consuming, but if it means you can design roles that will be more stimulating for impatient Millennials, it's worth it. Can you add new tasks from another position to increase variety? Can you cross train employees so they are able to do more than one job? Can you eliminate a position and spread the tasks out to others on the team, perhaps using the savings to provide bonuses or incentives? If you're in a quandary, ask employees for their thoughts on how to liven up the work. Millennials often have suggestions on how to eliminate wasted effort and get more done, faster.

The Gen X regional theater manager decided to lower turnover among Millennials by shaking up the way jobs were assigned. Instead of having one Millennial in charge of advertising, one in charge of public relations, one in charge of mailings, etc., he put the whole team in charge of all the marketing functions, allowing them to choose how the projects got done. While the system may sound chaotic, the Millennials had a ball shifting tasks around and collaborating. Even sticking labels on a mailing is more fun if you're not doing it by yourself and it's not your only job.

- **Consider _parallel_ paths.** As we've interviewed Millennials, we've been surprised at how many of them have such a desire to move fast and multitask they are juggling more than one career at a time. We call these _parallel careers._ A meeting planner for a large national association edits videos on the side. A representative for a small consulting firm builds Web sites in his spare time. This generation is so used to multitasking and leading busy lives, it's not surprising that a single career may not be enough. The question for employers is how can we harness this energy for ourselves? If you're truly interested in keeping a high-potential Millennial, perhaps you can turn that unexplored career desire to your advantage. If you get to know employees' talents, the Millennial who loves to edit videos could be tapped to create video clips for your Web site or the next sales meeting. When it comes to responding to the Millennials' need for speed, sometimes thinking outside the box about job descriptions can be the most motivating choice of all.

- **Shift "career pathing" into high gear.** Many managers have told us they breathed a sigh of relief when the economy recently dipped into recession. They figured a cooling job market would make Millennials less demanding, and it would be easier to stop dealing with turnover and focus on the work at hand. It's true that instead of job hopping, many Millennials are trying to hang on to what they have. In a 2009 survey conducted by Experience, Inc., at the deepest part of the recession, 67 percent of 1,650 young respondents said that in the interest of increasing their job security they planned to hold onto their current job by extending their work hours (33 percent) and taking on more job responsibilities (30 percent). At the same time, however, many high-potential employees continued to feel comfortable making job changes right through the recession. According to an August 2009 _Harvard Business Review_ article, a global poll by Catalyst of high-potential employees at corporations and professional firms found that 20 percent switched companies of their own accord during the downturn and another 35 percent made lateral moves within their organizations. While it's true employees are less likely to leave when the job market is weak, high potential Millennials may already be considering making a move, and they will be even more likely to do so as soon as the job market loosens up again unless companies pay close attention to their career paths. Many organizations are considering whether they can move Millennials into new positions more quickly than they do currently.

One international insurance company required all new hire employees to spend five years working in claims before they could move to other departments. Millennial hires would fall in love with the organization's culture but were unhappy knowing it would be a long time before they could move to something they really loved doing. The company's point of view was that resolving claims satisfactorily for clients was the most important thing they did, so every employee should know how. However, Gen X supervisors on the front lines got tired of losing talented Millennials and lobbied successfully for change. The company recently shortened the term an employee is expected to serve in claims and created new career tracks. One is for those who want to specialize and spend their careers in claims, and the other is for those who want to move into other areas. Employees can grow and advance in either track. The result has been lower turnover and higher engagement.

Another way to build engagement is to pick up the pace of Millennials' career *experiences*.

• **Career rotations: Shifting gears on the fast track.** The fear when you pick up the pace of career pathing is that employees will expect to always move quickly. But sometimes faster movement can create deeper engagement, thus allowing employees to be less frantic about where they are going and helping them settle in for the long haul.

Thomson Reuters realized that one of Millennials' big concerns when choosing a career within their organization was that it wouldn't be the *right* thing. "We found during the recruitment process," explained Rick King, global head of technology and operations, "that Millennials didn't think they knew enough to make a selection.

Rather than lose a great potential employee, we started a program that would help them learn about all the possibilities within the organization, as well as allow our organization to learn more about them." The program is called Graduate Rotation Opportunities West (GROW)—where new hires get to rotate through three different positions for nine months. It is like having three jobs. If they complete all three rotations, they are assured a job offer. "More often than not," explains Rick, "they get multiple offers." In a recent survey, the program proved to be working; 89 percent of GROW participants felt it created a broader understanding of the business, and 83 percent felt it enhanced their skills and technical knowledge. Best of all, retention of those who have gone through the GROW program is at 95 percent.

Rather than simply lobbying for promotions or a faster ride on the career roller coaster, Millennials should talk with bosses and mentors about how to develop the skills needed to get ahead. Sometimes valuable experiences can be gained in the current job that will position them for a strategic career move down the line, if the employee is patient. New hires will need to adapt their time lines from a semester scale to a corporate one, which isn't as clearly delineated and certainly won't be as brief.

The Millennials' need for speed is playing out in how we manage them on a daily basis, how they interact with technology and each other, how they multitask, and how they plot the course of their careers. While it's tempting to get caught up in or frustrated by their continuous game of *Beat the Clock*, by slowing down and understanding the forces at play we can ultimately find ways to manage better.

A week had passed since Grant's agency landed the new client and it was time to announce the team leads. "I've given this one a lot of thought and I think we need a leader with industry experience for this client, which is why Cheri is the perfect person for the job."

Everyone seemed happy, but Millennial Liz's shoulders drooped a little.

"However," Grant continued, "this client is demanding really cutting-edge media ideas and wants fast results. So I have created a new position on this team that I'm calling new media specialist. Liz has in-depth experience and knowledge about online media outlets and social networking that will help the team drive results, not to mention save us loads of time and money."

Following the meeting, Liz walked into Grant's office to thank him for the opportunity.

"I know you won't let us down, Liz. And I think working under someone like Cheri will give you excellent insight into what it takes to be a successful A.E."

Liz left Grant's office and dashed off to talk to Cheri. She had about a million ideas she just had to tell her right now. Cheri—watch out!

part four

we're all in this together

seven

SOCIAL NETWORKING

Hannah's Boomer boss at the automotive magazine needed information on consumer attitudes toward electric cars for presentation at a journalism conference. The deadline was tight. Bradley said, "Dig up whatever you can and summarize it for me by five."

Hannah, a Millennial, was new and wanted to make a good impression. She'd been searching the Web and finding plenty of articles, but that was stuff anybody could read. And some of it was old—articles that had been out six months! She needed help. So Hannah did what any resourceful Millennial would do; she reached out to her network. She changed her status on her Facebook page telling all her "friends" what she was looking for. Then she did a group e-mail to her closest buddies who had jobs in the business world. In case some were stuck in meetings, she sent the same query via text message, figuring they could secretly check their PDAs and get back to her.

Gathering Around the Virtual Water Cooler

Within minutes information was pouring in. A buddy who worked for an energy company forwarded her an internal position paper about the impact of electric vehicles on gas consumption. Another friend e-mailed a PowerPoint presentation on electric cars her boss had presented at a convention. A photographer attached stock photos of the cars for Hannah to use in a slide show. Her boyfriend sent links to YouTube in case she wanted to download any videos. Hannah's college roommate, now a librarian, sent links to articles on her library's intranet with a password Hannah could use to access them. By noon she had plenty to work with, and best of all, she had time. By 3:00 the project was done. She dropped a hard copy on Bradley's desk two hours early. To be safe, she also e-mailed it to him. Then she sent him a text message to make sure he was checking e-mail.

When Bradley saw Hannah's work, he was dazzled. "I wonder how one person put this together so fast? And where did it all come from?" he mused. Mission accomplished!

After Hannah had turned in the report, she checked her iPhone. Lots of people wanted to see how the project was going. The oil company guy texted saying she should keep the position paper under wraps, since he noticed it was marked "Confidential." The photographer e-mailed that he didn't know if the photos he sent were in the public domain or if she'd have to pay to use them. One buddy clarified that the info he forwarded came from Wikipedia so he wasn't sure of the sources.

Hannah thought about Bradley and his presentation. Only minutes before she had felt on top of the world. Now she felt that she, or worse, Bradley, might be in trouble.

If Generation X has been the tech generation, the Millennials are the networked generation. In a handful of years they have altered forever the nature and mechanics of social interaction. This is triggering a storm of generational clashes, both at home and at work. It is also unleashing powerful new options for conducting business that will revolutionize the way we work if the generation gaps can be bridged.

THE GENERATIONS HAVE ALWAYS NETWORKED— SO WHAT'S NEW?

All of us have observed that Millennials have grown up with gadgets and are extremely comfortable with them. "I would feel naked without my cell phone" is a common refrain. But Millennials have gone much deeper than just adapting to technology. They are restructuring their lives and contacts around it, so technologies are becoming tools for conducting complex social interactions.

"I'm in constant contact with my friends and family." "I check my MySpace page every hour or so during the day." "My best conversations happen on Twitter." "My family is closer than ever thanks to my blog." All these are common remarks when discussing social networking with Millennials. While they aren't radical statements, they are very different from how past generations would have described their social exchanges at a similar age. What changed?

For starters, the previous generations were happy just to own a high-tech device—and were all too proud to tote around their "mobile" phones the size of an egg carton. For Millennials, while size still matters, it's not about the devices. As one MOR explained it, "Unlike what the older generations think, it's not really about the tools at all. Other generations look at us and think we are just obsessed with our new toys. But social networking isn't about whether I have an iPhone or a Treo. It's about the applications or the Web sites that enable me to communicate the way that suits me best. The gadgets are just a means of getting there."

We may want to believe this mega-trend will stay safely within the confines of Millennials' social lives, but that's unrealistic. As Millennials infiltrate corporate America, companies will be unable to escape the impact of social networking.

To really grasp the forces that have launched social media, we have to go beyond the gadgets themselves to understand Millennials' unique communication styles. The explosive success of social networking is a blending of two themes:

• **Customization: What's mine is most definitely not yours.** Since Millennials were babies, they have been focused on expressing their own uniqueness. Blame it on a huge population size that made them want to stand out from the crowd, or blame it on Boomer parents who asked Millennials for their opinions on anything and everything. Or blame it on marketers who discovered you could sell more to Millennials if you let them customize what they purchase. They're old pros at designing MySpace pages with their trademark colors or carefully selecting movie quotes to express precisely who they are for their Facebook profile. It is no longer enough to *tell* people what you're all about, you now get to *show* them.

• **Technology: It's not about content, it's about connecting.** For the older generations, the Web was first and foremost a way to access information. Computers were used to process that information, organize it, and store it. As the Millennials came of age, this paradigm shifted. The information was still out there—in fact, it was easier to access than ever. But the real magic of the Internet wasn't about *what* you could find, but about *who* you could find. Navigating in cyberspace was less about locating a destination than about connecting constellations of people. The sites enable users to link up with others around the globe 24/7.

As usage of and dependence on sites like Facebook, MySpace, and Twitter have skyrocketed, generation gaps have widened. In a survey conducted by CareerBuilder.com, nearly half (49 percent) of employers surveyed said the biggest gap in communication styles between workers twenty-nine years old or younger and those older than they are is that Millennial workers communicate more through technology than in person.

While Millennials may be ahead on engaging in social networks, all the generations are logging on and signing in. Throw in a variety of expectations and new rules around how we should communicate, and the generations are bound to collide. Here are the five most common and painful gaps related to social networking we've identified:

GAP #1: THE VIRTUAL WATER COOLER

The first generational clash arises over what people are actually doing on the Web when they're supposed to be writing up that monthly budget report. Fears about everything from online gambling, to epic battles on gaming sites, shopping addiction, violation of company secrets, and much more abound. On each side of the gap are strong generational opinions:

"We were never allowed to waste time like that," commented one Traditionalist bank employee glaring at a Millennial co-worker glued to a computer screen displaying a flashy Web site. "We weren't even allowed to make personal phone calls unless we punched out and went to the break room. Now these people can fritter away time on personal conversations any time of the day!"

"Yeah, right," countered a Millennial. "I do glance at my Facebook page for two minutes every now and then. But how many of them smoke? You don't see anyone criticizing them for taking twenty-minute cigarette breaks four times a day. That's eighty minutes a day they spend standing around outside! Compare that to my ten minutes online in a day."

One of the first things we learned from our MOR interviews was Millennials consider social networking at the office as a kind of "virtual break room." It's like hanging around the water cooler only better. The virtual water cooler lets you touch base with friends and family. You can blow off steam. Or you can recharge your batteries by writing, reading, and exchanging ideas. Who's to say whether it's better to wander around the office or to wander around a cyber world where you feel connected to people and topics focused on your interests?

A Millennial we interviewed who works for a Fortune 500 food company commented: "The other generations wonder how effective we are at the workplace because we are constantly connecting through all these new outlets on the computer. For example, if I need a short break at work, I hop on the Internet and chat. It doesn't mean I'm any less productive. It gives me an outlet to take a breather and get back to my job. But I think other generations might make the wrong assumption."

If you're an overworked Boomer manager staying late and putting in weekend hours to handle your workload, it's natural to wonder whether or not the younger generations are pulling their weight. Are they maximizing time spent on the job or dribbling away hours on personal tasks? With new privacy screens available, an employee can click from watching television reruns on Hulu.com to an official-looking spreadsheet the instant they hear the boss coming down the hall. Millennials counter by saying, "Don't judge me by what you assume I'm doing at my desk. Judge me by what I produce."

In our M-Factor survey, across the board the older generations were twice as likely as Millennials to be "very concerned" that social networking tools could create a big distraction at work. Companies are concerned as well. At this writing, policies run the gamut from free rein to no access at all. Sutter Health adopted a policy that employees could have access to certain social networking sites if they could demonstrate a viable business reason for doing so. One of our clients, a recruiter at Sutter, is able to use LinkedIn because it is related to his job. This policy keeps time-wasting to a minimum and makes employees accountable for the ways in which they use such sites.

Regardless of company policies, the older generations will need to be more open to new approaches for getting work done via social media. Millennials, on the other hand, need to be more aware of how they are perceived. As comfortable as they might be with their own work style, they need to check in with co-workers and supervisors about behaviors that are causing stress. Millennials can lead the way in using social networking to reshape the way business is conducted—as long as they are thoughtful about how they bring the rest of the generations along. Here are some tips:

- **Think before you judge.** If you see Millennial co-workers buried up to their eyeballs in social media, don't assume they are squandering their time on something trivial. They might be getting work done. And even if they are taking a virtual break, is that so bad? We can't answer for you, but we can invite you to think before you judge.
- **Don't assume it's all fun and games.** Social networks started out as just that, places to socialize. But they almost immediately became much more. Those who are adept at using social media are finding ingenious ways to get work done. While a Boomer might not immediately think of hopping on the company intranet to ask for help on a report, it doesn't mean that isn't a valid way to work.
- **Fess up to what's really bothering you.** It's not uncommon to hear from Traditionalists, Boomers, and even Xers that they feel stranded in the slow lane as Millennials hop on new communication vehicles and quickly pass them by. Are you being left out of critical conversations because others have adopted new ways of communicating? Do you feel you are pulling more of the load in your department while others are wasting time? Too often we let discomfort turn into resentment. These issues can be addressed, but only if you fess up.
- **Be willing to bend.** It is not acceptable to opt out with the excuse that you don't "do" social networking. Besides, you might already be using social networking and you just don't know it. Re-

member that online restaurant review you just read? The one with the place to post your own opinions? You may have already engaged in social networking even though you didn't sign on to one of the big sites like Twitter or LinkedIn. Being open and flexible as to how these new tools impact work is part of your job. Likewise if you're a Millennial and your boss is launching a new application for the company that enables work groups to share information, even if you think the site is lame, it's your job to get on it and help out. When the other generations reach across the virtual divide, you should put your hand out, too.

• **Share what you know.** Every generation will soon have favorite ways to engage in social networking, if they don't have them already. If you're madly connecting with friends around the globe and enjoying it, don't keep it to yourself. Why not share your resource with the other generations? It gives them a glimpse into your world, and offers them the gift of a new tool. A lot of Traditionalists and Boomers out there would love to know how to talk screen to screen with the grandkids.

At a conference Lynne and David attended recently, a Boomer executive demonstrated a new app for her iPhone that enabled her to compose a song and send it out around the world so others could listen. Her pride in her song and her delight in sharing it were contagious. We both learned about a new application, but more importantly we learned something about our client.

• **Don't let the real water cooler dry up.** Millennials whose favorite connections happen via social networks shouldn't blow off the old-fashioned networks entirely. The other generations at work want to get to know you, and they will expect to do it their way—at least some of the time. It might seem crazy to a Millennial, but standing up and leaning over a cubicle wall to actually talk to co-workers can earn you a lot of social capital. Millennials should make an effort to sign up for the company softball team, or spend at least one lunch per week in the cafeteria instead of in their own personal cyber café. This will be good for your career and maybe even become a nice part of your social life. If nothing else, it will give your thumbs a rest.

GAP #2: INTIMACY IS BEING REDEFINED

"My goodness I'm frustrated with these Millennials!" exclaimed Bruce, a Traditionalist architect at a large national firm. "I tried to retire last year, but they hired me back full time to be a mentor and coach for the new hires. I'm here all day every day ready to work with them, and what do they do? When they have a question, they shoot me an e-mail! I'm literally sitting twenty feet away, but would you think they'd actually walk across the hall and into my office? It's insulting. Plus, now they tell me they want to add an interactive application on our intranet where they can post design problems and let everyone in the firm contribute solutions. So basically, they'd rather get feedback on a problem from someone they don't know than reach out to me when I'm right here!"

Bruce was so concerned about the Millennials he was supposed to be mentoring, it was almost painful to see. Here was a person with decades of experience being paid a full-time salary to give Millennials the coaching, mentoring, and attention they craved, and he felt he was being blown off. But ask the Millennials and you hear a different side of the story.

"I totally learn from him," commented one young architect. "It's just that I need certain answers and I don't want to waste his time. Rather than go bug him in his office, I e-mail him because it's more respectful of his schedule. He can think through his answer and give it to me at his own pace, and he can provide as much or little detail as he wants. Best of all, everything he says gets documented. Plus, he can refer me to links or other sources on the Web so he doesn't have to teach me everything himself."

We asked the Millennial, "What about the intranet site?"

"Oh, yeah," he responded. "We wanted to share Bruce's ideas with all the new hires around the company and tap into everybody else's input as well. It's virtual mentoring. Plus, because we have so many offices, a networking site like this allows us to get to know co-workers in other locations we'd never meet any other way."

This is clearly a generation gap. Both sides had the best intentions in mind, yet they still managed to get their wires crossed. We've all read newspaper articles about the family that received their phone bill only to learn their Millennial teenager sent 26,000 text messages during the prior month! Many of us have been annoyed by the friend or co-worker who can't take their eyes off their BlackBerry long enough to have a decent conversation (thus the nickname "CrackBerry"). Or, how about the family member who has to be on his or her cell phone even when the family is trying to spend quality time together? Lynne was recently in a movie theater and sat next to a Millennial who was on her cell phone throughout the movie describing each scene to a friend at the other end. It's hard to imagine any redeeming spin one could put on such annoying behavior.

So it's no surprise that the older generations fear Millennials are losing the ability to communicate properly. When asked in the M-Factor survey about etiquette problems at work, Boomers chose "e-mail/text messaging" over every other issue. Because they keep in touch via short text messages or post quick quips on their social networking home pages, Millennials seem less engaged in actual conversation. A worried dad approached us after a speech to an aviation association. He was a pilot who was often away from home and was desperate to stay connected to his teenage kids. "I don't know what to do," he said with a furrowed brow. "I call them all the time and beg them to call me back, and all I get are text messages. Or they tell me to check their MySpace page. I feel completely cut off."

No wonder he feels this way. For Traditionalist families, connectedness happened each evening around the dinner table. Kids were grilled about what they did that day, and parents offered up snippets of wisdom and gabbed about life. When Boomers became parents, dinner together was a harder goal to achieve. Suddenly everyone was engaged in a host of activities. But as long as you could reach out and touch someone via the telephone you could still hear the voice of that loved one and feel you'd connected even if only for a few minutes. For Xers, being connected could happen from almost anywhere—the car, school, or mall. First pagers then cell phones meant friends and family were their constant companions. But Xers actually talked to each other; the difference with Millennials is they now instant message, type, and text in shorthand.

The fear of losing meaningful contact with Millennials is pal-

"WELL, YES, WE COULD READ YOUR BLOG.... OR YOU COULD JUST TELL US ABOUT YOUR SCHOOL DAY."

4/2

pable in our interviews with the older generations. They fear Millennials are engaging in exchanges that are too frequent, too fast, too short, and too shallow. "C me B4 U go" sounds more like a clue to crack the Da Vinci code than a request from your employee to check in before you leave. And if Millennials spend all their free time at work connecting through the Web, what about connecting with the guy or gal in the next office? One Gen X manager commented, "I need our group to feel more like a team—to get to know each other and support each other. I feel like the Millennials are disassociated from the rest of us. If they get a break, they don't join in, they dash to their desktop."

Social interaction at work is evolving at breakneck speed. Traditionalists used to golf together, bonding over an unhurried five or six hours on the links. Boomers went to lunch together or stayed at work late, spending hours discussing company politics and their careers. With Xers the fight for work-life balance meant they wanted to get things done as efficiently as possible during work time, then head for home. Millennials blur the lines completely. They might text message co-workers from a ball game on Saturday just as readily as they post a picture for Grandma on their home page from the office.

The distortion of these boundaries often creates tension at work, but the older generations should consider that this might actually be deepening dialogues and creating new kinds of connections. We said intimacy is being *redefined*, not eliminated. Social media are allowing us to reach across geographical borders to engage people we can't meet face-to-face. They are bridging generational and age differences, departments and levels within organizations, and even ethnic divides. No one can tell your age, the color of your skin, or your country of origin online, unless you choose to share it. This leveling can increase the quality of conversation by removing barriers. Instead of feeling *less* intimate, social networking allows Millennials to achieve more intimacy with others. Boomers and Xers may be scratching their heads when we say

Millennials are achieving more intimacy, when we just said they don't talk face to face, but in the eyes of Millennials, when they can get hourly updates on those they care about, they feel closer than ever. If Millennials are gathering around the virtual water cooler and intimacy is being redefined, instead of being locked out of the cyber dialogue, you may want to log in. Here are some ideas:

- **If you want to connect, say so.** In the opening story, our Traditionalist architect, Bruce, made a painful mistake. He told *us* about the issue he was having with Millennials instead of telling *them*. He could have called all the Millennials into the room or gathered them for a virtual meeting and engaged in a discussion about how to make the mentoring relationship more effective. It's a safe bet the Millennials had no idea they were ticking Bruce off, or more importantly, missing out on critical learning opportunities.
- **Don't get locked in.** We're all short on time, and we are most comfortable with the media we grew up with. It sounds like a stereotype, but we can't tell you how often Traditionalists say they still pine for that face-to-face meeting, Boomers prefer to pick up the phone, Gen Xers would rather hop on e-mail, and Millennials just want to Twitter or blog. For any generation, if you want to connect you might have to vary the way you communicate.

Lynne and David were leading a session at a national conference for United Way staffers not long ago. During the Q&A, a Baby Boomer in the audience turned to a group of Millennials and asked, "If you give or volunteer, how do you like to be thanked?" One Millennial fielded the question by saying, "Just send us a personalized e-mail."

"Don't you want to receive a handwritten note?" the Boomer asked. "It's so much more personal."

"No way," responded the Millennial. "Getting snail mail is so time consuming and boring. I hate coming home from work and having to look in the mailbox and go through all those letters and things. I don't even know what they are. Plus it's all just wasting paper and killing trees."

Thinking outside our own boxes helps us see how the other generations are changing the ways they communicate. Traditionalist grandparents are setting a great example for the rest of us. If they can't visit their kids and grandkids in person, they e-mail them, post pictures on photo sharing Web sites, install a Web cam, and join whatever social networking option the grandchildren will allow them to use. Since 2005, the biggest increase in Internet use has been in the seventy to seventy-five year-old age group. In fact, over half of Americans over sixty-five are now online. This is a testament to the inquisitiveness and adaptability of the group Tom Brokaw called "the Greatest Generation," but it's also a tribute to their willingness to flex for those they love. We all need to be willing to do the same—Millennials included. If your mom would rather hear from you about your trip than read about it on your blog, call her. If your kids prefer to send you text messages, then think about getting a phone with a keyboard so you can text them back. That goes for the workplace, too. If the Millennials want to set up an information sharing site, don't react as if they just suggested setting fire to their desk. Get on board and try something new.

• **Embrace the virtual colleague.** Social networking has enabled Millennials to blur the boundaries between friends and work buddies. This can seem uncomfortable to Gen Xers who have valued their privacy and to Boomers who were told to leave their personal lives at the door. But it can be worthwhile to allow social media to help you get to know those you work with in more personal ways. "If you're on a social networking site with your co-workers, you know a lot more about them than if you just see them at work," commented one Millennial. "I like the fact that I can visit an office in another city and meet up with someone I haven't seen in months and say, 'Hey how's your new baby? I saw the pictures on your Facebook page; she's super cute.' Or, 'I see you did a triathlon for the Leukemia and Lymphoma Society and I did it, too. That's so cool.'"

The same Millennial went on to say she felt she was more connected to co-workers than her Gen X and Boomer colleagues were because she was part of several online business networks. If you haven't tried connecting with work associates via social networking, perhaps it's time to take it for a spin. The benefits are significant. People report feeling more "up to speed" with teammates who work remotely and are often more in the loop on current business issues. In addition, your network can grow significantly when you're not totally dependent on face-to-face or phone contact. "I couldn't believe it," exclaimed one Traditionalist who had recently participated in a chat room with colleagues. "I went to our yearly sales meeting and instead of spending the whole time re-connecting with people, I felt like we were already up to speed."

• **Learn the etiquette.** As the line between personal and work relationships blurs, it's important to pay attention to how the rules are changing. Millennials and managers alike are struggling to define which information posted in cyberspace should be limited to friends and family and what's OK for the world to see—especially the work world. A photo of you on the beach might be just fine to share with an old college roommate but does your new Traditionalist V.P. really need to see you in a thong? (And for sure you don't want to see him in a thong!) The line between friendly "sharing" and socially unacceptable posting is a hazy one. Millennials seem to be much more comfortable revealing information about their personal lives with co-workers than older generations are. "I feel more involved with others at work when they share personal information," explained one Millennial. "It's a form of team building."

On the flip side, a Boomer told us, "This feels like a burden I didn't ask for. I joined a social networking site where I know some of my colleagues hang out. But do I really want to hear the details of a co-worker's honeymoon? And what are my obligations to respond? If they send me a link to their four hundred pictures, does it assume I have to look at them and say something?" David noted that on his last birthday he received over a hundred birthday greetings because his big day was posted on Facebook. "It was great to be acknowledged," he commented, "but now am I supposed to write everybody back?" The expectations are murky at best, and at worst can be downright annoying. So, when engaging in social networking the best idea is to find out if your company has any rules, policies, or procedures that you need to be aware of. And companies will need to take a look at what policies will have to be put in place. At a multinational food company, Millennial employees were fired for sharing trade secrets on a social networking site. They were so comfortable chatting in cyberspace they accidentally referred to information about a new product they shouldn't have. It wasn't a topic that had been discussed much, so they didn't think it was a big deal. But, a policy is a policy, and they violated one so they were out. If the policies had been communicated more clearly, perhaps these employees could have been saved.

Finally, consider when it's best to step away from the computer screen and address an issue in person. In a recent Ernst & Young Survey, 84 percent of Millennial respondents admitted they use technology to avoid difficult conversations at work. There are times (such as conflict situations) when face-to-face is the best choice. Talk with your boss and others on your work team about preferred ways to communicate. Maybe your department really doesn't need that three-hour Monday morning meeting every week because you're effective at staying connected electronically. But perhaps you need another opportunity for in-person conversation. Don't forget there can be tremendous value in letting bosses and co-workers see each other in action up close and personal.

- **Consider your clients.** Even as you grapple with how to manage personal and workplace boundaries around social networking, don't forget about clients. What they learn about you online can negatively affect relationships, or it can strengthen them. We recently attended a get-acquainted meeting with a new Baby Boomer client in a high-level job with a Fortune 500 company. While we had done the usual homework on the client's business objectives and how to make the meeting as helpful and productive as possible, Debra took it a step further. By searching her social networking resources, she found out our client was an alumna of a certain university and was involved with a charity we all knew well. Referring to this connection at an appropriate moment took the conversation to a more personal level. Debra's comment on the meeting was interesting. "I didn't know if I should bring those things up," she explained. "I wanted her to know we had done our homework, but I didn't want her to think I was a stalker! I also didn't know if it was OK for me, a Millennial, to be making small talk about personal matters with someone many levels above me." She was aware that a generational divide existed. She didn't want our Boomer client to feel her privacy had been violated, and she was sensitive to the idea that the client might not be comfortable sharing information about her personal life with the junior member of the team. By being both cautious and polite, Debra made a great first impression.

- **Discover the depths.** Parents who are appalled at the brevity and speed of their kids' text messages fear that meaningful dialogue is going the way of land lines. We disagree. While Sally's tweets about her new office chair aren't exactly Nietzsche, her discussion on another Web site about the certification process for organic farms was eye-opening. The generations need to stop seeing social networking as a frustrating disconnect and realize it might be a profound way of *connecting*. The level of dialogue can be refreshingly deep in cyberspace. But because many members of the older generations aren't online participating, they don't realize that social discourse is alive and well—it's just moved to the virtual living room. Web sites like BrazenCareerist.com host syndicated blogs by Millennial thought leaders around the world where writers post, discuss, and debate issues. Other sites, like CoolPeopleCare.com or MakeMeSustainable.com allow visitors to create movements or communities around social concerns. Members don't just gab, they share their ideas and their lives.

• **Treat yourself.** If you haven't dived wholeheartedly into the world of social networking, indulge yourself. Whatever your favorite activities, topics, or interests might be, they are out there. Whether it is resources you're looking for, or a deep conversation about an issue that plagues you, you'll find it in the social cyberspaces. Let yourself look. Lynne's grandmother was a regional sales manager for *World Book Encyclopedia*. When she was almost ninety, she asked Lynne a question: "What is the World Wide Web, and how does it work?" Her eagerness to understand was impressive, but she also had a concern. Would the encyclopedia itself become obsolete, replaced by online resources?

"Let's say you go to the 'S' volume to look up 'salt mines,'" she explained sadly. "On your way to that page you're going to stumble upon sail planes, sand storms, and sea horses, and a host of other interesting topics that fire your imagination. What happens when we don't do that anymore?"

She died before she got to see that social networking space has become something she would have loved. A place you can explore interests and discover new ideas and even better, you can find people to share them with. Grandma Johnson would have been happy to know Wikipedia has a feature called "Random Article" where the curious can click and be shown an unlimited number of arbitrary entries. So it's really just the vehicle that's changed, not the journey.

GAP #3: THE END OF THE EXPERT AS WE KNOW IT

Millennials will tell you one of the great pleasures of social network-ing is the exposure to a vast array of opinions, or so-called experts. Ask a Boomer how they would have gotten information on buying a new product and they would have gone straight to *Consumer Reports*. Ask a Millennial and they go straight to the consumer. As they see it, why consult a supposed specialist when you can hear from the users themselves? Millennials will tell you there is no single "go to" source anymore. You use your social networks to find a variety of information and make your own judgments.

Social media have enabled the Web to become less a destination and more a dialogue. It is less a library where you find what you need and more like a neighborhood populated by a diverse array of citizens who have opinions, ideas, and information to share. "We don't just go online to look at something," explained a Millennial, "we want to hear what people have to say." That's creating quite a few shifts in how the generations communicate in the work-place.

Millennials have been raised in a world of collaboration. They've worked on teams from grade school to grad school. They are used to sorting and soliciting diverse opinions to make decisions. Why just ask one expert when you can ask everybody? This flies in the face of the Traditionalists' way of seeing the world. They believed in authority figures and trusted them to give the best advice. A classic example is what we're seeing play out in health care. Traditionalist doctors, used to being the last word (and only word) when it came to diagnosing a patient now have to deal with clients who have diagnosed themselves because after all, they have WebMD.com! Boomers believed in brands. If you bought a brand-name product you got a good result. Generation Xers had seen so many market-ing campaigns deceive, they believed authority figures lied. Because they trusted only themselves, they did their own homework on what to buy.

Now say hello to the Millennials, who believe anyone can be an expert if they have something to say. A great example is Wikipedia, the web-based, multilingual encyclopedia mentioned earlier that is written and edited by thousands of users. Rather than rely on "expert" contributors, Wikipedia users write and edit content for public access on topics where they have passion and expertise, thereby enjoying the role of creator, not just consumer. Is the information sometimes questionable? Absolutely. Sources like Wikipedia may not be 100 percent accurate, but often it's interesting and to the point. And it's become reliable enough that as of 2009 it was attracting around 65 million visitors monthly. While previous generations trusted Betty Crocker to tell them the best way to feed their families, now young consumers aren't just *finding* experts by hopping on social sites, they are *becoming* experts by posting their own tricks of the trade. Physicians are learning not to dismiss patients' own medical research on diagnoses, but instead are saying, "I'm glad you're so engaged in your health, let's talk about it."

Of course there are downsides to this. Professors gripe that Millennials who are researching term papers on the Web will cite Norah Jones as often as the Dow Jones. The fear isn't that they are expanding their horizons, it's that those horizons don't have reputable sources. The gaps being caused by "the end of the expert" must be addressed for businesses to protect their own credibility and for Millennials to succeed in their careers. Here are some tips:

• **Be careful who you call an "expert."** Consider Hannah and the presentation on electric cars she put together for her boss, Bradley . . .

Hannah was just about to leave work when her phone rang. It was Bradley. "How did your presentation go?" she asked nervously.

"Well," he replied, sounding cautious, "from what I could tell, they really liked it. However, they did want to know where we got the information on the impact of electric cars on gas consumption. A lot of them are up to speed on the research and hadn't seen those stats. Didn't you say an expert from an energy company helped?"

"Ahh," Hannah replied nervously, "it was actually an old college friend of mine who got that information from a confidential report."

"What am I suppose to tell them?" her boss demanded, raising his voice. Hannah didn't have an answer.

The danger of the wide range of sources available on the Web and via social networks is that it can be very tough to assess their credibility. It may not cause a big brouhaha if you don't have all your facts correct on whether Lindsay Lohan spent an extra night in rehab, but untrustworthy experts can definitely get you into trouble on the job. If you're assigning a project to Millennials, make sure you discuss what sources you consider credible. Explain why certain authorities will carry more weight within your organization. Make a deal that if they want to cite sources outside the accepted list, they must provide a rationale for why these "experts" should be trusted.

At the same time, stay open-minded. When given an assignment, Millennials are likely to reach out to sources of information the other generations may not have considered. They are adept at using social networks to link in peers, customers, users, researchers, opinion leaders, and a host of others whose ideas might be valuable, and would be hard to reach via any other type of forum.

• **Privacy please.** Putting information out into cyberspace may be a no-brainer for Millennials, but the other generations won't be so quick to hit the send or post button. While you might be dying to see if members of your social network can help you prepare for a huge sales pitch, it might not be appropriate to let the world know you're going after that piece of business. Understanding the boundaries around privacy is crucial. Coach Millennials not just on which things are confidential, but specifically on what can and can't be discussed in open forums. When the Web was invented, companies had hours of discussions about who would be given access and how to control it. This is the same thing again, and it will get resolved. As we travel into new territories you will need to explore new policies and procedures, then adjust along the way. For example, you might explain to Millennials that they absolutely cannot reveal the name of a new client in the travel industry, but it's OK to ask those in their networks what they think of a certain travel experience or destination. The key is in being very specific about what "privacy" and "confidentiality" mean when moving into cyberspace.

GAP #4: PEDOPHILES, PORN, PLAGIARISM, AND POP-UPS

We've talked about the shift to gathering around the virtual water cooler, the redefinition of intimacy via cyberspace, and the end of the expert as we know it. But travel any new road, earthly or virtual, and you have to be alert for the dangers that might arise. (Well, maybe not pop-ups.) The World Wide Web is no different. It's like a map of the globe, with some roads less traveled than others. We can't opt to stay home just because we're nervous about what's out there. For parents, help is available. Web sites like the Barking Robot offer social networking tips to help parents and educators understand and confront the tough issues. The more interactive technology becomes, the greater the danger of trade secrets being leaked, of proprietary information being shared inappropriately, of time being wasted on nonwork-related distractions, and of work cultures being watered down by a lack of privacy and professionalism.

Unfortunately, Millennials often seem oblivious to the threat. This was reflected in our M-Factor survey. Boomers and Xers were twice as concerned about social networking tools creating security or privacy issues at work as their Millennial counterparts.

A classic example of trying to control access and impressions is the way recruiters are now using social networking sites to find out about candidates they are considering hiring. For a time, Millennials would post just about anything on social sites and could assume it wouldn't hurt their chances of finding a great job. This was partly because they were naive about the impact poor choices could have on their careers. "That was just college; it doesn't reflect how I would be as an employee!" It was also partly because the older generations weren't really paying attention. At some point, the other generations caught up with the technology. Maybe it was because savvy Millennials became the recruiters and suddenly companies knew exactly where to look to dig up every bit of intelligence they could about future recruits. The tables were turned, and hiring managers could glean all sorts of tidbits on topics they weren't allowed to ask about in interviews—things like drug and alcohol use, memberships in organizations or affinity groups, attitudes and opinions, morals, even intangibles like character. In ways, it's a dream come true for recruiters—the ability to evaluate a candidate's private life in ways they never could before.

Image control presents issues for organizations just as it does for individuals. Companies have spent millions of dollars and billions of person hours carefully crafting and controlling perceptions of their brands. But it's almost impossible to control the ways copyrights, logos, or brands are depicted in cyberspace.

The challenge deepens when we consider that information doesn't vaporize in cyberspace the way we once thought it would. It used to be that you could send something like a photo or an angry e-mail and assume it would eventually disappear or get deleted. Not true anymore. Major legal cases have hinged on recovering supposedly deleted incriminating e-mails from laptops. Careers have been ruined over sexually explicit messages sent from married politicians to underage interns. Employees have been embarrassed by inappropriate videos, photos, diaries, or even comments that got into the wrong hands. And once such things go viral, it's impossible to go invisible. According to the M-Factor survey, more than 70 percent of Boomers and Xers agreed personal behavior on social networking sites would influence their decisions to hire or promote someone.

In 2009, Facebook avoided lawsuits and curtailed outrage from loyal users for an attempted change in policies on user-generated content. The implication of the impending change was that photos of your new baby or an old résumé would be retained permanently by the site even if you removed them. Besides basic privacy issues, concern was raised about what could happen if Facebook was bought by another, less ethical company that would have rights over the content. Thanks to the advocacy group Electronic Privacy Information Center (EPIC) and 88,000 vocal Facebook members, the company retained its original terms of service, and a formal complaint was never filed. But the groups feel they still have a big job ahead of them—staying involved and trying to convince Facebook to rewrite their terms in English so users can understand them better.

While the benefits of social networking applications are huge, there are risks aplenty. Pedophiles, porn, plagiarism, and pop-ups may get the most press, but they are just the tip of the iceberg. Now more than ever it is important that the generations get on the same page when it comes to exploring this brave new world. You need to:

• **Understand the risks.** If you're a leader or manager and you aren't up on the threats posed to your organization by misuse of social networking tools, ask someone from IT for a tutorial. Have them show you the kinds of sites involved, how they are used appropriately, and where problems arise. One of the biggest challenges for the business world is that it's often the younger generations who are creating and using the new sites and applications, then the older generations are supposed to come up with the strategies to police them. That's hard to do when you're always a few steps behind. You may want to consider inviting one of your savviest Millennials in on those strategy meetings.

Another advantage of diving in and understanding this topic is that you may find risks you imagined aren't really a big deal—or could even be an advantage. One CEO was furious when he heard an employee had posted all of their archived television commercials online until he realized the commercials were averaging 30,000 hits per day. While the cost of posting them was small, the free publicity was priceless.

• **Learn the rules.** What if you are "friended" by your boss on a social networking site? Is there a smooth way to ignore him or her on the grounds of privacy? Do you change the way you use the site? Give up and go back to using e-mail? Or as one Millennial put it, "Help! My boss and my mom are both on Facebook now; I don't know what to do!" In our MOR interviews, many Millennials told us they want control over who is part of their work and personal networks and they resolve this by creating two separate accounts— one for personal and one for professional.

MILLENNIALS ON RECORD

"I use Facebook but I don't like to use it for work. I'm on LinkedIn, which to me is more professional. My Facebook account is to keep in touch with my friends and family."

—*Samantha Fogliano, age 25, senior account executive, Surge Worldwide Healthcare Communications*

Meghan Bromert, another MOR, put it this way: "Blurring the line between your professional life and your personal life can be dangerous. There could be ramifications, especially with photos." Another Millennial summed it up this way: "I just don't put anything up there that I don't want the world to see."

Even if you tightly control the images and events that play out on your own social networking page, you have little control over what others post. It's nerve-wracking to get pinged with a message saying, "so-and-so just posted a picture of you," especially if that person was with you at your college roommate's bachelor party. It's also time-consuming to get comments or images removed if you don't like them. There are resources to help you play the game right and stay out of trouble. The *Dummies* books recently added *Facebook for Dummies* to the series of titles. If you're too embarrassed to carry it around, any Millennial will tell you to just download it to your Kindle.

GAP #5: GOING BEYOND MYSPACE TO THE WORKPLACE

Baby Boomer Theresa was V.P. of Operations and covered plants and sales offices in thirteen states. Many of her employees had never even met her. Theresa arrived early Monday morning, entered the company's intranet site, and immediately started work on her LeaderBlog for that week. Then she checked the interactive part of the page where employees could pose questions to her. There were four questions from Millennial new hires. She was still amazed at what young employees would ask her right there for all the company to see. She would never have dreamed of talking to a top executive that way. Deep breath.

Now onto the employee newsletter portion of her company's site, where a live chat was in progress with people discussing the delay in the completion of a new East Coast plant. She joined the chat to give her perspective. Then it was time to click into her Monday morning Web cast. Viewers could log on from anywhere and watch the short broadcast featuring herself and two other top leaders in the company.

Theresa sighed. She didn't mind the exposure, but she hated the little camera pointed right at her face. It was tough enough to master all the new technologies, but a good hair day, too? She had a few minutes after the Web cast to visit a private social networking site for women leaders in manufacturing.

Ping! A little box showing an e-mail popped up in the bottom corner of her screen. Theresa's daughter had posted new pictures of the baby on Picasa. That would be a nice break later in the day. "Eight a.m.," she mused, "and all is well."

American industry is nothing if not adaptive. Who would have thought even a few years ago that leaders like Theresa could be doing everything from blogging to computer broadcasting as part of their everyday routine? As soon as social networks started reshaping the ways the generations interacted with one another in everyday life, businesses started finding ways to connect and cash in. Most often these were experiments to see how products could be marketed, but very quickly the new social media have become rich opportunities for the generations to reach across the workplace divide and link up in new ways. Here are some examples:

• **The CEO blog.** It used to be the CEO's space was in a cushy chair behind a rosewood desk the size of an aircraft carrier's deck. Today the CEO's place is in cyberspace; the top dog has started to blog. Companies as diverse as JetBlue Airways, Marriott International, Pitney Bowes, and Sun Microsystems feature CEO blogs that enable the highest level executives to speak informally and directly to the entire workforce, as well as to customers and shareholders. For Boomers and Traditionalists, this is a huge shift. It used to be few had access to the top floor, let alone a private audience with the high commander. Along came the Millennials, and now the walls are tumbling down. We got a hint of this when we interviewed leaders at the time Millennials first entered the work scene. One Boomer top leader commented:

"I was sitting in my office going over a report to the board, I looked up, and there's a Millennial intern gaping at me. He couldn't have been more than nineteen, but he looked twelve! I wondered how he got past Margaret, my secretary, and what he wanted. Well, he

just wanted to introduce himself and tell me how much he was
enjoying his internship with the company. Shook my hand and that
was it. I mean, I've always had an open-door policy. But that was
the first time somebody that young actually came through it!"

Millennials, more than any other generation, are boundary-less
when it comes to hierarchies. They've been mentored, coached, and
led by elders who respected and cared about them. Nothing's going
to stop them from reaching out with that same sense of familiarity
when it comes to the workplace.

One of the biggest complaints new Millennials had when they
went to work at Thomson Reuters was that they didn't see how their
jobs aligned with the mission of the company. "We wanted to get
them closer to the company's goals," said Rick King, global head of
technology and operations, "but we also wanted them to get closer
to their leaders." So Rick decided to start an internal blog. "At first
I wasn't sure if there would be much traction, but I knew the Millennials loved to consume information electronically. For me, it was
a way to try to 'meet' five thousand employees who worked for me.
My goal was to instill confidence. I couldn't believe how it took off
and how many employees were reading and responding to my blog
posts." But the popularity alone wasn't the biggest surprise. "What
also shocked me," he explained, "was that they were as interested in
my personal stories as they were in the company strategy. New hires
I've never met came up to me in the halls to talk about my dogs,
my hobbies, and even give me condolences when my grandmother
died at one hundred and eight years old. I realized that they want to
know about the leader first, then all of the strategic stuff. We truly
believe this increases engagement, as it instills more confidence in
who is at the helm."

Social networks provide just the right blend of immediacy and
accessibility to enable Millennial employees to connect with role
models and mentors around the company. They are a perk for those
who need to reach Millennials as well. Leaders can comment in real

time on issues and get in front of an entire audience, not just the chosen few who attend top meetings. Better yet, they can reveal their personalities, and they can start dialogues. Many of the blogs also have options for employees to post questions or engage in a conversation around a particular topic.

But beware: Millennials are pros at this and can sniff out a pretender faster than they can text a message. If you're the leader, keep your comments as honest as possible. Gen Xers in particular are going to tune you out the minute they hear that classic Boomer political-speak they've come to distrust. You know, phrases like "area of opportunity" or "we're not behind, we're just off course." Don't couch your messages in double-talk. And don't talk down to the generations. You may feel several lifetimes older than your employee base, but you don't need to let on. Remarks like, "You kids probably don't remember this, but . . ." are a real turn off. If you're struggling to stay in touch with the generations and unsure of what they are interested in, ask.

We mentioned earlier that U.S. Bank organized an advisory board of high-potential Millennials called the "Dynamic Dozen." One purpose of this group was to help upper level executives get the touch, feel, and pulse of this very different generation. Mac McCullough, who is in charge of the Dynamic Dozen, quickly noticed the value Millennials place on technology that best supports collaborative work. Mac's team established a networking Web site that provides a forum for Dynamic Dozen members to share their ideas with their sponsors, with U.S. Bank senior leaders, and with each other. The site, US Place, keeps the team up-to-date on weekly news items and updates related to projects currently in review; it gives them critical administrative tools such as a calendar and a library of reference materials; and, most importantly, it allows the Dynamic Dozen to share their feedback on projects brought before them and capture ideas around potential improvements or future projects.

"We have found that, while each member of our Dynamic Dozen team brings a unique perspective in terms of business line or experience," commented Mac, "their shared experience as members of the Millennial generation definitely informs the nature of their comments and suggestions." In one illustrative example, when presented with a marketing concept currently under consideration, a Dynamic Dozen team member took it upon herself to research similar tools already in the marketplace. She then posted a brief on the pros and cons of current offerings—as well as her views on how U.S. Bank would be uniquely positioned to improve on these tools—on the US Place site, soliciting feedback from her Dynamic Dozen colleagues. The resulting online conversation provided the necessary input from the Millennials' perspective and of equal value, a real-time example of how effective the collaborative model can be for both the Dynamic Dozen and the project sponsors.

• **Post and host.** It's fine to share book reviews and travel tips, but eventually most of us can't resist connecting around careers. Social network pages are being unleashed as "go-to" destinations when Millennials are looking for work. Why?

- **The reach is so much greater than the network of any one person.** You can put the word out through dozens of friends, and their friends and their friends' friends.
- **They are more customized.** Job candidates can post not just their résumés, but samples of their writing, videos they've made, blogs they've written, and a host of other information that tells a more complete story about who they are and what they've accomplished.
- **Information can be targeted.** Millennials don't have to send out random appeals to the universe. They can focus their efforts, for instance by letting various networks know the specific type of position they prefer or the dream company they want to work in.

- **They move faster than conventional networks.** Boomers
  used to mail out résumés and wait days, weeks, or months
  to hear back, always wondering where that precious package
  had ended up. For Xers it was a little better. With e-mail
  they could check back more easily. And if the recruiter
  felt like it, he or she could shoot back a quick reply to say
  they'd received it or that all the positions had been filled. A
  Millennial might put out a query asking if anyone knows
  of openings in marketing in a high-tech company in New
  England and receive a response within hours—not days or
  weeks.

All these advantages don't mean it's easy to find a job, but they
certainly provide more options for conducting searches, and they
give the searcher a feeling of being able to put their best foot forward and showcase their capabilities more fully.

Companies are also enjoying the benefits of social networking when it comes to finding talent. They can put out information
about their organizations more easily, more affordably, and in more
compelling formats. "We used to rely entirely on placing ads in the
newspapers," explained one recruiter. "We still do that, but it's expensive and inefficient, and it doesn't really reflect who we are. Now
with the Web we can do so much more. We can add pictures, post
jobs, and accept résumés. The challenge is that we still have to rely
on candidates finding our site. Now with social networking, candidates not only find us easier, but pages on sites like Facebook and
MySpace can do a more complete job of telling our organization's
story." Sites might include a blog written by new hires, an online
chat forum with recruiters, or a place to ask questions and get them
answered. LinkedIn, for example, has become a tremendous tool
both for finding work and finding candidates. Job seekers can post
résumés that go way beyond the traditional paper kind. LinkedIn
allows people to post additional information like blogs, personal interests, special projects, and other information that gives employers

a deeper picture of who they are and what they have to offer. The pressure is on to keep these sites growing and improving.

Beyond the page itself, recruiters are getting savvy at using the networks to their advantage. They are creating affinity groups that can help in finding diverse employees or people with certain specialties. For example, job search engines such as naacp.monster. com are entirely focused on recruiting diverse candidates. Social media also make it simpler to find the most desirable candidates of all—those who are currently employed—by using contacts to reach them, or by letting them know what's available. A benefit of LinkedIn is that all recommendations posted are public. This encourages those referring a candidate to be honest, since they will be held accountable,

Whether you're an employer or an employee, make sure you aren't just posting for posting's sake. It won't be enough to just check the box. As one Millennial put it, "It's like at the beginning just having a Web site was cutting edge. But now, you need to have a really cool Web site for it to have an impact." The same applies here.

And be sure to ask for a second opinion. You may think your appeal will knock the socks off recruiters, but make sure you ask a few people from other generations if they agree. The same goes for organizations. Don't let a team of only Boomers define what your company's social network recruiting strategy is going to be. They know how they got to be successful, but they may have no idea what will work in these new environments. If you haven't got at least one Millennial on the recruiting team you're probably in trouble.

We talked about employees gathering around the virtual water cooler, how they are redefining intimacy in new forms of social connectedness, the end of the expert as we know it, the fears that arise around the scary aspects of operating in the cyber world (pedophiles, porn, plagiarism, and pop-ups), and ways employers are using tools like CEO blogs and MySpace in the workplace. Social networking will continue to open up pathways to do business differently, and Millennials will continue exploring them. Rather than see only the risks, we'll do better if we take a tip from the Millennials and go along for the ride.

It was midday on Friday and Hannah was working on projects for her Boomer boss Bradley. They had recovered from the embarrassing electric car presentation she'd researched and had since had numerous discussions about the best ways to use social networks in the workplace.

Hannah peeked out into the waiting room. She couldn't believe how many applicants were waiting to be interviewed, especially since Bradley had just announced the new position a couple of days earlier.

She poked her head into Bradley's office.

"Wow!" she commented, "I can't believe how many applicants you already have."

"I know," he beamed, "and all of them have journalism experience as well as experience covering the automotive industry—even with electric cars! I never thought we would find so many who fall into the exact niche I'm looking for."

Hannah smiled and asked, "So social networking paid off for you this time?"

Bradley smiled. "Ever since we got on the same page it's been a great tool. You've figured out how to use your social networks for research without getting us sued or getting me fired. And I learned how to use social media to find great job candidates. I owe you one."

eight

COLLABORATION

Bonnie walked into the living room to find her daughter Rachel video chatting on her computer. Papers were spread out on the couch, the dog was licking up remnants of nachos on the floor, and there was now a salsa stain on the wool throw she had gotten for Christmas.

Bonnie didn't want to complain as she loved having her daughter home for spring break. But she also knew Rachel was graduating in six weeks, and if she didn't figure out her future plans, the living room would never look like the Pottery Barn catalogue again.

Rachel was laughing happily until she noticed her mom staring. "Listen, I've got to go. My mom needs me. Say 'hi' to Abbie, Mom," Rachel turned her computer toward her mom so she could wave to her friend. Then Bonnie heard Abbie respond, "I love what you wrote for the essay and I'll noodle on the closing. I still need your help on my thesis statement; I think it's a mess. Talk to you later."

Rachel gave a thumbs up and logged off. She turned to her mom, "What's up? Sorry about the mess. I'll clean it up."

Bonnie was over the mess and had moved on to something else that was far more disturbing.

"Are you working on your grad school application?" she asked tensely.

"Yeah. I'm almost done," replied Rachel. "I'm just putting the finishing touches on the essay."

Bonnie paused. Not sure how to broach the topic. "I couldn't help but overhear Abbie say she would noodle on the closing."

"It's just not where I want it yet, and Abbie is really good at clever endings."

Bonnie plopped herself down on the couch next to her daughter and let out a heavy sigh. "Isn't Abbie applying to the same graduate schools you are?"

"Yeah."

"Well, you know how competitive it is to get in, especially with so many more applying in this economy. Do you really think it's a smart idea to be sharing your essay with Abbie?"

"You've got to be kidding, Mom," Rachel responded. "Abbie is helping me. She writes for her college newspaper. She is so much better at getting things down to eight hundred words than I am. Let's face it, you and Dad are in science; writing has never been your thing."

Just then Rachel's computer dinged and she immediately started to read something. She let out a squeal. Two seconds later, the video chat rang and Rachel answered. It was Abbie. "I knew you could do it. I loved how you inserted the quote."

The girls continued to gab as Bonnie got up from the couch and walked away. She knew more than her conversation was over, so was her way of thinking.

Traditionalists established their reputations as *contributors*, serving the greater good of the institution and doing whatever needed to be done. Boomers have been the *competitors*, pushing themselves to stand out from that crowd of 80 million and driving organizations to become bigger and better. Xers are the *controllers*. Believing they could rely solely on themselves, they have drawn on their individual talents and entrepreneurial skills to invent and achieve.

Millennials will be the great *collaborators*. This is a generation weaned on cooperation at home and teamwork in school that did most everything—including attending prom—in groups. They see their parents and peers as colleagues, not rivals. And they've developed an ease with social media that will allow them to collaborate with anyone, from their neighborhoods to the Netherlands. Millennials are bringing these skills and qualities with them to the workplace and in doing so are pushing the boundaries of how the generations work together and how we manage them.

When we interviewed Millennials for this book the concept of collaboration surfaced over and over again. They see themselves as skilled collaborators and we see them that way, too. Eighty-two percent of respondents in the M-Factor survey said that Millennials were somewhat prepared to very well prepared when it came to collaborating at work. Millennials are already telling us they are frustrated by other generations that don't seem to want to partner on projects to the extent they do. In fact, we see an explosive gap on the horizon as independent Xers—who are accustomed to controlling their assignments and working independently—struggle to manage collaborative Millennials comfortable sharing just about everything. The Baby Boomers will also grapple with how to manage Millennials who are more comfortable deferring to the team than showcasing their own abilities and accomplishments. Leaders and work groups will have to establish how much collaboration is desirable, and to what extent individual initiative should be rewarded.

Like a magnet, Millennials are exerting a pull toward collaboration at work through four distinct trends we describe here as: Work as a Team Sport, Leaders as Collaborators, Extreme Office Make-over, and Knowledge Transfer—the New Collaboration Frontier. While these trends present great opportunities for discovering new ways to work and to lead, they will also create clashes. In this chapter we explain the trends on the horizon and how you can manage and work with them.

1) WORK AS A TEAM SPORT

Millennial Zach was excited to start his new job as the manager of IT for a midsize law firm. He knew the firm needed to tackle everything from updating their intranet communication strategy to recruiting on the Web. He was up to the challenge. The problem was, on his first day he realized he was the only one up for it. When he tried to talk with the partners about his ideas for everything from hardware to software, he was brushed off. When he tried to get on the agenda for the firm retreat, he found out he wasn't even invited. Zach knew the firm was supportive of the IT strategy, but he hadn't realized they didn't want to be part of the process. As one managing partner explained, "We all have huge caseloads and don't have time to get involved with that stuff."

Zach knew the process wasn't going to be any fun if he had to go it alone. He missed the daily tech talks he had in trade school. As tempting as it was to log on and post his résumé, it had taken him a while to find such a great job and he didn't want to give up. So, he logged on to try another option. He set out to find his own network of IT professionals in the law field. By lunch time, he had read numerous blogs written by fellow technology managers around the world who shared how they too were lone sailors in their firms, many of whom admitted going it alone wasn't such a bad thing, as they had more freedom than anyone else in the office!

Zach found a group that hosted weekly Web casts in which they took turns presenting case studies and best practices. He also found a group of techies who met once a month right in his own city to go bowling. Throughout the day, Zach signed up for everything from bowling to blogs. He even launched his own blog and sent the link around to the different networks he had discovered. He was thrilled that by the end of the day he already had a couple dozen subscribers. He was even more thrilled that he was no longer sailing alone; he was now part of a crew.

While every generation has possessed teamwork skills, Millennials will take them to a whole new level. As they transition from the "team" of home and family and the teams they worked on in school, sports, and social activities, they will expect to form new bonds at work. The worst thing you can do to Millennials is isolate them. One Generation Xer who manages Millennials in a Fortune 500 insurance company noted: "We are known for having robust training, but now we're falling short with Millennials because we put people in a training room for six months and isolate them from our corporation's true culture. Millennials can't stand that. They love the training program and being with the other new hires, but they are miserable being cut off from the larger group."

This can seem foreign to Xers who often came from divorced households or families with two working parents. Many came home to an empty house after school, organized their own activities, and learned to operate independently. If they got fed up with imaginary friends or actors on ABC's After School Specials, they connected with other Xers who were operating independently as well. As newly hired employees, Xers used their skills as solo survivors to take the load off overworked Boomers and get the job done. When getting an assignment, the Gen X style was: "Boss, you tell me the parameters and expectations for the project. Then I'll go away. (And hopefully, *you'll* go away, too.) I'll report back when the project is done." Although this style initially made Baby Boomers nervous, they came to rely on Gen Xers to grab a project and run with it.

Skip ahead and here comes a whole new generation for whom

independence isn't efficient, it's a hindrance to getting things done. While Xers saw independence as strength, Millennials see collaboration as power. In fact, our research tells us Millennials decide if they're staying in a new culture based on whether or not they feel connected. Select Minds Research found that 28 percent of workers age twenty to twenty-nine reported leaving a job because they felt disconnected from the organization.

"Connectedness" for Millennials comes chiefly from the opportunity to collaborate with their peers. This is not unusual. In fact, in our M-Factor survey every generation said they found their own generation the easiest to work with. It's the extent to which Millennials seek out one another that is striking. They will walk into your workplace and immediately start searching for buddies. If they are the only Millennial on the team they can feel isolated or worse, unmotivated to stay. They form bonds rapidly and become disenchanted if it doesn't happen quickly enough. After all, they can meet someone in a coffee shop and immediately connect as "colleagues" on LinkedIn. Within seconds they know where that friend attended school, what political party they associate with, and where they went for their last holiday. Why should they struggle with connectedness in their own workplace? Select Minds Research also found that 20 percent of Millennials had quit a job because of poor relationships with co-workers. Clearly this generation will vote with their feet if they don't think they fit.

This is one reason Millennials are attracted to affinity groups, or what are sometimes called ERGs (employee resource groups)— cohorts formed around a variety of affinity points such as ethnicity (African American or Latino groups), a special interest (women engineers or green architects), or even age (young leaders groups). According to Select Minds, nearly half of Millennials rated the availability of support/networking programs for employees with common interests as a "very important" factor in their decision to join and/or remain with an employer.

When it comes to collaboration, Millennials are reaching beyond their peers, their affinity groups, and the other generations at work to find "teammates." They are able to connect and convene with virtual teams across cyberspace and around the globe. The upside of this is a true expansion of access to information. They are more aware than the rest of us that sometimes the best resource isn't in the building or even in the same ZIP code. And they don't disband these teams when they move or change jobs. As a result, Millennials amass an interconnected network of contacts who will remain linked throughout their lifetimes. Dan Rasmus, director of Work Vision for the Microsoft Information worker group has dubbed these "supernetworks" and says that as Millennials progress through their careers they're going to bring that supernetwork with them wherever they go: "They will also bring with them an erasure of boundaries and a collective intelligence that is worldwide and not necessarily owned by a company." The result is that Millennials are structuring teams in ways most of us have never considered, and the new access to skills and ideas will be advantageous for everyone.

Since we've been talking about the way Millennials see work as a team sport, here are tips for capitalizing on their desire to collaborate:

• **Put Millennials together on teams.** If you want to make the Millennial work experience more fun, create teams for them. They will bond by blowing off steam together and providing support for one another when the going gets tough. Even better, by putting their creative minds together, they can push one another to come up with ingenious solutions. And with their superior team skills, they are likely to be highly efficient. *TIME* magazine featured an article about a moving company called Gentle Giant that once hired an entire athletic team as movers so friends could work together. Besides finding students who were actually in shape enough to lift the furniture, they also got a whole team of employees who would collaborate well, could probably handle their own scheduling, and would already know how to work through conflicts effectively.

This teaming of Millennials can save the boss time. If Millennials are bouncing their ideas off one another, they won't be quite as quick to bounce into the Boomer's office every time they want to share a new thought. One manager gave his Millennials this directive: Whenever they hit a roadblock in their project they were to brainstorm possible solutions with their peers and come up with the three best options *before* coming to him. "That trained them to work on the problem together rather than run to me immediately," he explained. "It exercised their problem-solving skills and forced them to evaluate the best solutions before presenting them. I have to say it also trained me to stop trying to solve everything. It taught me to push the problems back to them and count on their abilities to come up with ideas. As a Boomer, it's too easy to make yourself responsible for everything that goes wrong. The Millennials got coaching from me eventually, but not until they did some legwork first."

While Millennials may be ahead of the curve in networking at work, the other generations can help them develop their networks outside the office. Many Boomers built their Rolodexes by picking up the phone, attending business lunches, exchanging business cards, joining associations and clubs, and attending industry conventions. Xers' networks are more about individuals—people they met in college and in the various jobs they've held who stay connected over time and form support networks to exchange favors and business leads.

For Millennials, a lot of networking will take place in cyberspace. But they also need to learn the value (and the process) of connecting face-to-face. From Rotary to the Advertising Federation, networking opportunities abound in every community. Such organizations provide contacts, sales leads, mentoring, learning opportunities, and chances to get involved with civic projects—all of which will benefit the Millennials and your business. But Millennials might never be exposed to these groups without your help. And in fact, in many instances these organizations are shrinking because they have failed to engage the younger generations. If you facilitate connections, you're not only helping groups that are the cornerstones of your community, you are passing along in-person networking skills to the next generation. For many in your community and many of your customers, face time is still important, and mentors can show Millennials how it's done.

• **Manage the generational mix.** Having been coached all their lives, Millennials are a generation in search of mentors, and creating teams that mix the generations is a great way to help them find them. Joanna Linsley, a research analyst at Robert W. Baird & Co., described the challenges of joining a highly competitive financial firm and being assigned to a department where she was one of a small group of professional women. She was hungry for feedback as well as for coaching from accomplished women in all areas of the firm. She told us, "Completely selfishly I wanted more networking. Any time I had a review with my boss he'd say 'you need to meet this person, or look at this woman's success story.' It was great advice, but I wanted to find an easy way to connect with other women at Baird. I wanted to make it worthwhile for them, and I didn't want to be pestering. I wanted to see these women in person so introductions could be made, conversations could be started, and I wouldn't be intimidated."

In a classic example of perceiving work as a team sport, Joanna came up with an ingenious solution. She went to a trusted mentor and asked what he thought of their firm creating a networking event for all the generations of women who work there. He thought it was a great idea and helped her sell it to the right decision makers, including Leslie Dixon, the chief human resources officer at Baird. While Baird had previously held a similar event for women and planned to host another in the future, Joanna's suggestion got the ball rolling. Leslie not only supported the idea, she put Joanna (at age twenty-three) on the planning committee. The result was the hugely successful Connecting with Women at Baird event, which brought generations of professional women from all over the company together to socialize, network, and learn. Baird didn't stop there, though. It is now creating an employee resource group for women in the firm with a special focus on helping female new hires get the mentoring and support they need to succeed in a traditionally male environment.

Joanna wasn't finished collaborating, however. Eager to keep learning, she asked Leslie Dixon for feedback on her performance as a member of the event planning team. Even though they don't have a formal boss-employee relationship—they aren't even in the same department—Joanna felt, "I have complete respect for her, and I need more opportunities for feedback, so I am trying to find ways to get it. I knew I had so much to learn from her so why not ask?" As Joanna demonstrates so ably, Millennials thrive on access to the other generations, and mixing them in teams is a great way to accomplish this.

Another example of mixing the generations on teams occurred at Liberty Diversified International, where the CEO, Mike Fiterman, is a classic entrepreneur with forward-thinking ideas. When he needed a method to get new ideas off the ground, LDI assembled "B.A.T.s," which stands for Business Action Teams. These are made up of employees from all the different divisions at all levels. Best of all, teams include every generation. The company learned quickly that Millennials loved being on the teams and were willing to dive in and take on big roles. Where Boomers and Xers might have assumed those with more seniority would take the lead on projects, Millennials didn't hesitate to volunteer. When it came time to deliver findings to the company's executive team, Millennials were right there presenting the data. Mike Fiterman commented, "It was wonderful to get such a well-rounded perspective. Had it not been for these teams, we wouldn't be on the cutting edge of creating new green and sustainable products." Clearly the company benefits from the teams, but so do the Millennials who have the opportunity to work side by side with experienced employees in a setting that allows them to feel their voice is heard. The exposure for them has been fantastic. In fact, one Millennial that served on a B.A.T. got recognized not just for leadership skills, but for his ability to speak Chinese. The result? At the ripe age of twenty-four, he is now serving as a team leader in the company's Taiwan office.

• **Update your definition of diversity.** Collaborative Millennials tell us they see access to diversity as a way to enrich the team experience. The more perspectives, the better. And they don't see diversity as being limited to just age, gender, ethnicity, country of origin, or religion. To them the definition is much broader.

MILLENNIALS ON RECORD

"For our generation, diversity isn't so much about making sure we have equal parts of all religions and all races. The most important thing is having diversity of thought and diversity of mind-set."

—*Elena Davert, age 18, undergraduate student*

Millennials will continue to stretch and expand the meaning of diversity. They have been exposed to it all their lives via television, the Web, day care, school, and travel abroad. As schools have become more accessible, Millennial children have had the opportunity to attend classes with students who look different from one another or are differently abled. Shows like *Sesame Street* portrayed a diverse group of friends and put forth a message of acceptance and understanding. Millennials themselves are very diverse. At last count, 38 percent of Millennial teens in the United States are nonwhite, compared to just 27 percent of Baby Boomers when they were that age. Due to immigration, Millennials have become familiar with a far wider range of racial and ethnic backgrounds than their older counterparts and are tuned into the many distinctions diversity can bring. According to a recent Pew Trust survey on diversity, Millennials are also the generation most likely to be accepting of gay coworkers and the most likely to be supportive of gay marriages.

What's important, though, is Millennials have moved beyond

accepting diversity to *embracing* the benefits of a diverse team. This is the generation that is accustomed to calling India for tech support and recently had the history-making choice between a woman and an African American man for the Democratic presidential nominee. Now they are also taking diversity to the next step and expanding the way it's defined.

MILLENNIALS ON RECORD

"Diversity means *everything*—religion, race, ethnicity, gender, age, politics, and sexual orientation—an international perspective as well as a domestic one. It's different thought processes and diverse communication styles. If we cannot be open and embrace diversity, we limit our learning and progress, and we start asking irritably, 'Why isn't our business competitive?'"

—*Nikki Schmidt, age 29, manager of business programs, The Conflict Center*

When asked why he chose to join a particular company, one Millennial designer in a high-tech firm responded, "It was the most diverse place I visited. They had people from different countries speaking different languages, they had all the generations, they had people who came from different companies with new ways of doing things, and they even had people who knew different operating systems!"

When it comes to collaborating on teams, the Millennials' appreciation of diversity includes everything from thinking styles to personality types to skill-sets. This will only make the team experience—and output—richer. When forming teams you can expect Millennials to think outside the inclusion box and look for new ways to collaborate with people who have a variety of perspectives.

MILLENNIALS ON RECORD

"I don't necessarily define diversity along racial lines. While it's important, it's only part of it. Diversity for me is really different viewpoints. Certain organizations might have people who have the same thoughts and no one questions anyone. That isn't diversity no matter what their racial mix might be."

—*Steve Mell, age 25, electrical engineer, Century Engineering Inc.*

• **Learn from Millennials how to break up and make up.** Economic turmoil, cost-saving efforts, competitive pressures, and the need for specific types of talent have meant that teams these days are composed of more than just permanent, full-time employees. We frequently see players on the team who appear to be wearing somebody else's jersey. Today's contributors might be part-timers, returning retirees, freelancers, temps, or outside contractors—or they may be rotating through from another department. Whereas in the past, those who weren't full-time were not considered full-on members, the teams of tomorrow will need the wisdom of all these players. Millennials have the skills to put together diverse teams and make them tick.

While Boomers still have nightmares of being picked last in gym class and Gen Xers escaped the problem of collaborating by starting a company in the garage, Millennials figured out that in order to collaborate they had to bring together and disband teams efficiently. How do they do it?

• **They know how to say "Hi."** Millennials learned from school projects and in extracurricular activities to form teams rapidly, create functional relationships, and tackle the job at hand. It's a good idea when new teammates of any generation come on board to help them get acquainted. Maybe there's an ice breaker your team can use to find out about each person as well as what talents and skills they bring to the team. Let them showcase their expertise a bit. It's guaranteed that independent Xers will dread these "games," but they'll also get on board when they realize communication barriers are coming down.

One of our Millennial clients who managed a retail store used the questionnaire included here as a way for new teammates to get to know one another. This can be used to get to know new members on a team. You can use their answers to make the team run more smoothly as well as to craft small rewards or celebrations down the road.

NEW TEAMMATE QUESTIONNAIRE

- Identify one of your heroes and what you admire about them.
- Name an event that shaped you during your formative years.
- What's the best class you ever took and why?
- What is something that would surprise us about you?
- What is something you're really proud of besides your family?
- What's one of your best skills on a team?
- What's one thing we should make sure you're not in charge of?
- How can we help you be successful on this team?
- Favorite song or performer?
- When is your birthday?

What else do Millennials do to get to know their teams?

- **They mix the personal and the professional.** Picture a Millennial hanging around in a conference room full of strangers waiting for the new team's kickoff meeting to start. Chances are they won't be handing out business cards and asking people their titles or whether their level is a G–9. They're more likely to call out, "Did anyone here watch

American Idol last night?" Let the bonding begin. Millennials tend to draw fewer lines between the personal and the professional, which allows them to create connections quickly.

- **They know how to say "Good-bye."** Millennials know how to let go when projects end. Even as they wave farewell, though, Millennials never really say good-bye. They are merely adding teammates to their supernetworks, knowing they will undoubtedly encounter these team members down the road and until then, they can stay in touch electronically.
- **They admit what they don't know.** Millennials are comfortable looking around the table and saying, "OK, we need someone on budget. Who's good with numbers?" Millennials are so accustomed to trying to make their teams efficient they don't seem bothered by putting their weaknesses front and center. It's hard to imagine a Boomer saying, "I stink at financial reports. Ted, can you handle it?" We can learn a lot from Millennials' willingness to divvy up tasks based on skills, not politics or hierarchy. They are also comfortable saying, "I want to learn that," and opting for an assignment that will expand their capabilities.
- **They know how to delegate—maybe too well.** Because Millennials are accustomed to handing off work to the most logical person, they are good delegators. It makes total sense to them that the person with the best skills should handle a particular task. This creates interesting generational clashes. Millennials have been known to take a project their boss handed off to them and happily hand it over to someone else, not understanding that the boss meant for *them* to do it. If someone else can do it better, why shouldn't they pass it along? They've also been known to question their bosses on why they're being given "grunt work" when they think another project would tap into their talents more fully.

This doesn't go over well with Gen Xers, who are eager to hand over the lower level tasks, or with Boomers, who feel the best way to learn a job is from the ground up. But we shouldn't overlook Millennials' ability to parcel out work in an efficient manner. When you delegate to Millennials, talk to them about what you expect them to learn and why the job is important for them to do. If you don't want them to hand it off, make sure they know it. One final note on delegation. For you Boomers who have piles of paper all over your office and to-do lists longer than the phone book, this new generation might just be what you need, so you can start delegating the load before it becomes too heavy to carry.

Given Millennials' expert touch at making work a team sport, it's easy to overlook their weaknesses, but here are two blind spots to keep in mind when managing them.

• **Teach Millennials not to run from a fight.** Because they've done so much collaborating in teams, Millennials often are great cheerleaders and not so great when a teammate drops the ball. One anonymous MOR described his experience this way: "In college when we had problems with team members, we usually just worked around them and got the project done rather than get bogged down with conflicts. I always figured it would even out—maybe next time I'd be the weak link because I didn't have the skills, or I was too overloaded with work—so we just covered for each other. Usually at the end there was an evaluation of teammates so you could give them the negatives there." While that's a great way to keep things moving smoothly, it doesn't always fly in the workplace. If you're on teams with Millennials you can ask team members to discuss how you will evaluate performance and deal with the rough spots. A good way to propose this in a team setting is to say, "Let's talk about what's working and what's not working."

At Enterprise Rent-A-Car, teamwork and collaboration are more than just buzzwords. Each branch is set up in teams of five to six employees. For an employee to be eligible for promotion, they need to be able to show how they have worked in a team. They are judged on who else they have mentored and on who has been promoted before them and how they helped make that happen. Even if an individual employee has delivered stellar customer service, the whole branch needs to score above the company's average Enterprise Service Quality index, or ESQi, before that person can be promoted. As Marie Artim, the assistant V.P. of recruiting at Enterprise, put it, "It's not enough for you to have done a good job, you have to have helped the whole team succeed." To make this happen, one thing they do weekly is what they call "The Vote." They sit down and discuss who is doing a good job and who is struggling. Unlike the TV show *Survivor*, where those who are underperforming are voted off, the dialogues focus on what the team can do to help.

You can put your own version of the ESQi to work. Identify the problems and let the team brainstorm possible solutions. That way you are focusing on the work that needs to be done instead of on the individual, and you're helping Millennials get their sea legs when it comes to how they'll be evaluated. Don't be surprised if Millennials take less-than-stellar reviews pretty hard; they are used to gold stars, trophies, and praise. You may want to ease into negative feedback or offer it privately the first time. If Millennials persist in denying accountability or making excuses, have a mentor take them aside to discuss the situation and help them get up to speed. Another option is to have peers give them feedback. This sometimes hits home more resoundingly than the same message delivered by someone from a different generation.

• **Don't let Millennials hide behind the team.** Millennials we interviewed felt conflicted about when and how to showcase their own accomplishments when working as part of a team. One MOR who joined a Fortune 500 company commented: "My boss would say things like, 'I know it was a group effort but you really should send out the project summary yourself because it shows you were the project leader and that our department led the way.' I felt uncomfortable with that—like I was backstabbing my teammates to get the credit."

Another Millennial put it this way: "The work should speak for itself. Why should I have to kiss up to that person or send recap e-mails saying all the things I've been doing when in reality, it was a big group effort?"

This presents an interesting generational conflict. Millennials see work as a team sport, so they often balk at the idea of one individual standing out. Managers need to be willing to reward employees for a team's successful performance. Millennials, on the other hand, must recognize that bosses need to know how the individuals operate on the team so they can evaluate skills, talents, and weak spots. If Millennials hide behind the team, it's harder for the manager to fully understand an individual's contribution and more difficult to personalize the way an employee is managed.

As important as teams are to Millennials' views of collaboration, that's not the whole story. They go the next step and extend collaboration to the way they want to be led. Which brings us to our next trend . . .

2) MILLENNIALS SEE LEADERS AS COLLABORATORS (WITH DECISION-MAKING POWER)

Manage a Millennial and you'll be straddling a fine line. They like and respect decisive leaders who have a strong vision and can drive toward the goal. Millennials appreciate their leaders' wisdom and want to learn from them. In a 2008 Robert Half survey, Millennial respondents chose "working with a manager I can respect and learn from" as one of the most important aspects of the work environment. But they also want to collaborate with leaders on the vision and to have a say in how they will get there. This is not meant to be disrespectful. When they offer to engage with managers or leaders, they aren't trying to take over; they're trying to help out. Millennials feel a sense of responsibility toward the team and a strong desire to be a part of how it is run—even if they're on the bottom rung of the ladder.

There are times when top-down, command-and-control leadership is absolutely what's needed. But on a day-to-day basis Millennials are looking for a more collaborative leadership style in which the team gets to have a say. This can be a stretch for the other generations. Boomers and Xers have been accustomed to a style in which a lot of the thinking and creating is done individually; that input is then brought to the group for discussion and decisions. This is a more individualistic process, and it can be adversarial if the purpose of the group is to pick apart ideas or choose one over the other. One MOR commented: "We seem to be much more group-based and not as individualized. For example, in our department, the older generations want things to be 'mine.' The Millennials don't care— we just want it to work. And if that means working together, we don't mind sharing credit and ownership." We learned of a great example of this from a client, a training facilitator for a multinational chemical company . . .

One of our most popular team-building programs featured a hands-on activity in which squads were expected to transfer "toxic waste" from a small bucket to a large bucket where it could be safely "neutralized" within a specific time frame. Participants could only use the equipment provided to them. If the transfer was not made within the specific time period, the waste would blow up and destroy the world. The company had success with this exercise in the past, especially with Boomers whose competitive drive made the exercise all the more engaging. However, when facilitators rolled it out for Millennials, they saw a drastic difference.

For starters, teams were required to select a leader and quickly map out their strategy. Observers were shocked at how fast Millennials could choose a leader compared to the past, when Boomers would spend time jockeying for the position. When the teams moved on to mapping out strategies, again they couldn't believe how collaborative the Millennials were. Previously, Boomers' egos would play into the strategy as they tried to make sure their ideas were not just heard, but incorporated. With Millennials, they found that different ideas were put on the table rapidly, but it didn't matter whose was chosen. The Millennials had no problem walking away from their own ideas if the team was more excited about someone else's. "I was amazed at watching the Millennials," commented the manager who conducted the activity. "They were focused on accomplishing the task from a collaborative mind-set. I was so used to Boomers having a harder time letting go of their own ideas." The most stunning difference was in the amount of time it took. The facilitators had allocated an hour for the activity in the past. The Millennials were done in fifteen minutes!

The ability to flex roles on a team leads to more flexible relationships with leaders, because the authority doesn't have to be absolute, it can be a give and take. One MOR summed up her generation's desire to collaborate with leadership like this: "For Millennials, it's all about a two-way street with the manager. If the manager can give feedback, they should be able to receive it from us, too. If they can come up with ideas, they should listen to mine." That two-way street can feel like the highway to hell if you're short on time or not excited about input from someone who's been on the job only four months. If your voice was never heard when you were a twenty-something, it can feel unfair or out of line when they start speaking up. Here are tips to pave the way for a more collaborative relationship between leaders and Millennials:

• **Let Millennials know it doesn't always take a village.** Millennials need to know they have permission to freely offer ideas, and then when collaboration time is over, they need to go along with the decisions being made. Be clear which things *they* get to decide and which things *you* get to decide. As we talked about in the chapter on meaning, this generation will want to take on projects they can run with. But they need to understand their leaders have every right to make the big calls.

- **Have an open door policy, but get a lock.** Millennials love a management style where they can pop in and talk about things any time. They've had 24/7 access to their parents and they'd like to have it with you. They are going to want to pick your brain, ask your advice, pitch an idea, or just goof around as a way of getting to know you better. It makes sense to do what professors do—have office hours. Create times when people know they can pop in, and block out time when you can't be disturbed. For the times when you *do* lock the door, don't worry that the Millennials are just milling around waiting for you to open up. While it may seem that working independently and collaborating are opposing work styles, Millennials seems to do well at both. We were pleased to learn from our M-Factor survey that respondents felt Millennials were equally strong in both areas—over 84 percent said Millennials were prepared for both independent work and collaborating.

- **Collaborate with the new kids on the block.** Collaboration doesn't work so well if you're the only one doing it. Beware: As you bring Millennials into the fold you will have to spend a fair amount of time coaching the other generations on how to work with them. In our MOR interviews, dozens of Millennials expressed dismay that the older generations didn't seem to want to collaborate with them. They were appreciative that the more experienced people were willing to mentor and teach them (top-down activities) but disappointed that the older generations didn't seem as comfortable being on an equal footing (brainstorming, arguing, or knocking ideas around). The generation that may need the most encouragement is surprisingly Gen Xers. Sparks are bound to fly when their independent style that relishes "me time" to work on projects bumps up against a generation that wants plenty of "we time."

As a leader you can model a willingness to engage in discussion and debate with Millennials. You can call on them in meetings and give them permission to speak up. You can point out to the group when a Millennial has a great idea or has proposed something that just won't fly. The more you make this a standard operating procedure, the more Traditionalists, Boomers, and Xers will adapt to a collaborative leadership style. Or as one MOR put it, "I want a leader who will treat us just like any other employee, show us respect, include us in team meetings and team decisions regardless of tenure, and make us feel like we are part of the group from day one."

- **Collaborate with the longtime residents, too.** We just talked about what the other generations can do for Millennials; let's flip that around. The frank head-to-head style Millennials use with one another might not work as well with the rest of the generations on the team. Although Millennials have treated their parents as peers, their more experienced generations of co-workers may not appreciate being treated as equals. Leaders can make a huge difference in the way teams function by coaching Millennials on how to collaborate effectively with those who are years or even decades older. Here are some simple behaviors you can coach Millennials on to help them be more effective:

  - **Don't pass up the past.** It helps when Millennials acknowledge that they are new to the team and they respect what has gone before: "I am so inspired by the success you've had with this project over the last eight years, and I am excited to be part of developing the next version of it." (FYI—It's not kissing up, it's called respect.)
  - **Give a nod.** Millennials can show respect for someone from another generation by publicly acknowledging their wisdom: "One thing I learned from Frank is we have to protect our brand so if we rename the product, I suggest we keep the name similar to the rest of the product line."
  - **Be willing to build it (and they will come).** To counter their reputation as the entitled generation, Millennials need to show they have a good work ethic. They can volunteer for duties that will support the project before jumping in with

suggestions for how to do things better. As they prove their
ability to get things done, people will be much more willing
to listen.

- **You can embrace diversity and still offend.** If you haven't
picked up on this fact yet, the Millennials are young. When
this book is released, the oldest won't have hit their thirtieth birthdays yet, and some can still count their age on their
fingers. Millennials may love diversity but they aren't im-
mune to offending others and can be blind to differences
that exist. We heard a story recently of a Millennial summer
intern who was discussing his experience with a Traditionalist executive. At the end of the interview the exec asked him
how the company could attract more Millennials. The intern
looked right at him and said, "Well, it would help if there
were fewer old people here." Painful, and yet it's a teachable
moment.

    Even within our own walls, we have run into diversity
faux pas. In a discussion around diversity and how to address
it, Lynne reminded Debra of the importance in organizations
of addressing gender inequalities. After listening for a while,
Debra finally sighed and asked, "Aren't we past that issue already?" Lynne could hardly believe it. While she was genu-
inely happy that Debra had had many opportunities in her
career, she also wanted her to be aware she was a beneficiary
of battles fought by women who came before her. Sometimes
being immersed in diversity means that Millennials are blind
to the different roads older generations have traveled and the
price they have paid. A young peace activist could easily insult
a Vietnam veteran's patriotism. Or a grandchild could offend
his grandfather by not removing his hat at a baseball game
when the national anthem is played.

The Millennials' more relaxed, accepting approach to diversity
could make other generations believe they don't appreciate how far

we have come and further cement their label as the entitled generation. Rather than get mad, start talking. No one likes to hear,
"Back in *my* day, people appreciated these things." But just because
Millennials may not know the advances your company has made in
terms of inclusion doesn't mean they aren't willing to listen. Which
brings us to another critical function of the collaborative leader.
That is:

- **Stick up for the generations.** Sometimes we need leaders
to break up the roadblocks between team members. So when you
hear, "That Judith is so set in her ways!" or "That Riley is too full
of opinions," it's your job to correct the impressions. You set the
tone by saying, "I agree with you that Judith is defending the status
quo, but she's been very successful with that product line and she
has every reason to defend it," or, "Sure Riley is pretty cocky, but if
you listen to what he has to say, I think you'll realize he's got some
great ideas."

- **For every job that must be done, there should be an ele-
ment of fun.** Part of building a culture of collaboration is having fun
together. Too often Boomer leaders worry if they're having fun with
employees they are wasting time, and Xers worry about looking like
they lack authority. Millennials tell us they can be more productive
at work if they're allowed to have a little fun along the way. This
generation was raised on learning through play, starting with Mister
Rogers and continuing right on up through college. Part of how
they are going to want to learn in the workplace will be through
"playing" together. Many corporate training programs now involve
learning games, simulations, and competitions to engage emotion
and creativity in the learning process. Of course, this doesn't mean
you need to wear a clown suit or turn your mission statement into a
rap song to get the Millennials' attention (although it couldn't hurt).
They are simply looking for a working environment where they can
enjoy the people they work with while getting things done. And
fun is not just good for Millennials. Boomers who've been doing
a job for thirty years might be ready to kick up their heels a little.

Our M-Factor survey revealed that while Millennials were leading the way, 98 percent of all the generations said that having fun at the workplace was important to them, too.

If we asked you to name some fun places to work, it's likely the big four accounting firms would not be the first places that come to mind. Yet, when we interviewed Manny Fernandez, KPMG's national managing partner–University Relations and Recruiting, he immediately brought up the importance of fun in the workplace. In fact, *fun* is one of the three cornerstones of their recruiting value proposition for Millennials and yes, we are still talking about an accounting firm.

"I ran our audit business in Denver for several years, and during that time the Sarbanes-Oxley Act of 2002 came in and our people were in huge demand from other firms and companies," Manny explained. "We had to identify our competitive advantage." KPMG has studied ways to connect with the Millennial generation. Their philosophy is to focus on three key themes that are important to Millennials— global opportunities, building leaders, and—you guessed it—having fun in the workplace. As Manny explains it, "fun" is a lot more than just parties. A big piece of it is being part of a team. "We've always had an open door style. We naturally work in teams on projects, so it's easy to incorporate Millennials. Today's young employees aren't afraid to walk into a partner's office and introduce themselves. Our partners understand that this kind of access and openness is what makes us a great place to work." In 2009, KPMG won the prestigious Catalyst Award for its "Great Place to Build a Career" initiative. While the Catalyst Award honors exceptional initiatives that support and advance women in business, the focus on being a great place to build a career has benefitted Millennials overall.

Another way to have "fun" at KPMG is in giving back. The company recently hosted a series of spring-break trips for recruits and new hires so they could give back by building houses for Habitat for Humanity. That's not just a nice thing to do, of course. KPMG made the business case for leaders showing that creating a more fun, collaborative environment reduced turnover. As Manny explains, "Five years ago turnover was five to ten points higher than it is today. Aspects of the workplace like creating a fun environment are big differentiators."

So we've talked about how teams will change with the arrival of Millennials and how leaders will be asked to lead in new collaborative ways. You've got collaboration nailed, right? Not quite. While we couldn't be more thrilled to see so many Millennials hungry to learn from the older generations, we are gravely concerned that these lessons will never be taught if all the wisdom walks out the door before Millennials are able to absorb it. The challenge here is brain drain. As millions of veteran employees get ready to exit and millions of fresh-faced Millennials are ushered in, collaborating on the transfer of knowledge will be critical to an organization's success. And Millennials are uniquely suited to play a big role.

3) KNOWLEDGE TRANSFER—THE NEW COLLABORATION FRONTIER

Patricia's Traditionalist boss, Hugh, took her aside one day.

"Listen Patricia," he explained, "we need you to start setting aside time to mentor the new hires in your department."

"Oh, I'm very active in our Mentorium Program," she answered quickly, "In fact, I'm hosting the . . ."

"That's not what I'm talking about," Hugh interrupted. "It's all that knowledge you have up here." He tapped the side of his temple. "At last week's board meeting, we realized that over 40 percent of our workforce is eligible to retire in the next six years. If we don't get you and your Baby Boomer colleagues to start teaching what you know, this organization could be very vulnerable. I will be rolling out a formal program in the coming months but for now I need people to step up and start sharing!"

Patricia didn't answer. Her lips were pursed so tightly it would have taken a crow bar to pry them open.

"Is there a problem?" Hugh queried, breaking the silence.

"No," Patricia lied.

"OK then, I'll be in touch with next steps but in the meantime, start thinking about how you are going to share all of that." He stopped talking and pointed to his forehead.

Patricia stalked out of the office wishing he had accidentally poked his eye out. The company was in the middle of layoffs and she was convinced she was being fired. Why else would he suddenly care that she hadn't trained others on all the stuff she knew? After twenty-seven years it came down to this!

As a diligent Boomer, over the following weeks Patricia grudgingly assembled a robust presentation highlighting many of the intricacies of her job. She scheduled a meeting with her department and even cc'd Hugh on the invite.

On the day of the presentation, Patricia was caught off guard. Not more than fifteen minutes into her grand overview, she caught a few of the Xers and Millennials looking at their watches. She couldn't believe they weren't paying attention to her historical time line of the department's evolution. She had dug up stats dating back to before the company even had computers! The biggest insult came ninety minutes later when she finished and asked if there were any questions. Not one hand went in the air and after a long silence, the room cleared as though there had been a bomb scare.

As she closed down her laptop and gathered her materials, she thought to herself, "Well, I tried to share my knowledge but they just aren't interested."

With millions of Baby Boomers heading toward retirement, a potential knowledge crisis looms on the horizon. Decades of experience and wisdom will head for the exits unless organizations think now about ways to gather, document, and share it. At the same time we have close to 80 million Millennials accelerating up the on-ramp. Caught in the middle will be a smaller cadre of Gen Xers desperately trying to grasp the knowledge of the departing Boomers while straining to get the new hires up to speed.

A knowledge traffic jam is fast approaching, yet few companies are revved up to deal with it. The M-Factor survey revealed that while one in three respondents felt *they* are good about sharing information with other generations, only one in eight strongly felt the *other generations* are good at sharing knowledge with them. Where is the disconnect? These numbers aren't good, and higher turnover rates, a recent increase in layoffs, and increased worker mobility all compound the problem. It is incredible how frequently talented employees move on, move up, or move out without making sure their most critical knowledge has been captured for those who remain. A recent survey by our research partner, the Institute for Corporate Productivity (i4cp), found that companies that do a good job of knowledge retention show a direct correlation with higher market performance. When done well, the benefits of knowledge retention are great. Better solutions can be generated if all the generations are sharing information. Costly mistakes can be avoided when new hires can find out what happened before they came on board. New employees can get up to speed more quickly when others avoid "hazing" and are willing to share information. Given the benefits you would imagine organizations would be rushing to get on the knowledge transfer bandwagon. However, the same study by i4cp found that over 60 percent of respondents indicated they have no formal knowledge retention programs under way at all!

This lack of planning is made worse by generational roadblocks that prevent knowledge sharing. The good news is we believe the generations are more than capable of tackling the issues, and collaborative Millennials will play a big role. This is a generation that enjoys learning from elders and is happy to be mentored by them. At the same time, they will throw out the old idea that knowledge has to flow from the top down and will fight for systems to allow information to be shared in all directions. They will be willing to ask why things are being done in certain ways, and they will push to get rid of outmoded methods. They will use technology to reinvent the way information is stored and accessed. And they will take an active role in collaborating with the other generations to spread knowledge around.

When we speak with clients about how to get the generations collaborating around knowledge, they usually want to do it but don't know where to start. We like to break the process down into three big questions to consider. These are:

- Is your culture ready or not?
- What gives you a stomachache?
- Is anyone talking about it?

We know that knowledge transfer isn't exactly top of mind when you think about exciting projects. In fact one of our Millennials commented, "Maybe people would like it more if it didn't have such a boring name." But we believe if you explore these three questions, you will save your organization an invaluable amount of time and money, you'll learn a lot and enrich your career, and you'll bridge countless generation gaps along the way.

Question #1: Is Your Culture Ready or Not?

Every generation plays an important role in knowledge transfer and the more willing they are to participate, the more the organization will benefit. Whether you lead a company, manage a team, or are an individual contributor you are responsible for enabling the sharing of information. But, most employees seem to think there is an official office of knowledge transfer someplace else that will take care of it. Few companies have created cultures in which sharing knowledge is everybody's job. Too often the older generations are threatened thinking if they share too much, they lose power and possibly jeopardize their future. The younger generations don't want to do things "the same old way" and would rather start from scratch.

With the influx of the Millennials we are seeing a huge opportunity. As natural collaborators they appear to be less concerned with who owns the information and more interested in how they can get their hands on it and share it. They want to soak up the know-how they need so they can operate faster and more efficiently. Unfortunately, generation gaps get in the way:

- **It's not my job.** In survey after survey, when asked about pressing concerns, CEOs say they are worried about brain drain. When we interview people, however, it's tough to find anyone who is actually reviewed, rated, or rewarded based on their ability to transfer knowledge. In fact, in the 2009 i4cp survey, almost 50 percent of respondents said "lack of accountability" was a significant factor in preventing implementation of effective knowledge retention practices. When asked to what extent the organization measured the effectiveness of knowledge retention efforts, 89 percent of respondents said to a "small extent" or "not at all." Imagine how much more willing Millennials would be to seek out role models and actually listen to their input if they knew they were being evaluated on it.

- **We don't have time.** If knowledge transfer isn't built into job descriptions and people aren't held accountable for it, guess what gets done first—transferring knowledge or your daily responsibilities? Let's face it, there is little motivation to find the time. Sure, some experienced workers are natural coaches and mentors. They know instinctively that if an interesting issue is being discussed they should invite their mentees into the room. But for knowledge transfer to be successful we have to build it into the regular workday and make it part of the job.

- **Learning is not a one-way street.** The business world today is fighting the old knowledge pyramid. This was based on the idea that the people who have been around the longest have the most knowledge and should pass it downward to the younger generations who should soak it up. For many types of knowledge this still holds true. But other knowledge can percolate up from the bottom when Millennials are hired, and this can be uncomfortable. Boomers, who pride themselves on being good at everything, tell us they feel like idiots learning from someone who looks young enough to be the babysitter. And many Gen Xers hate the feeling of not being the hippest and most techno-savvy people in the place anymore. Exacerbating these hang ups, both Xers and Boomers tell us Millennials aren't the best listeners. "I got partway into my explanation of how to do something," explained a Baby Boomer supervisor, "and the Millennial was sighing and looking longingly out the office door. It doesn't exactly make you want to teach someone."

Millennials, on the other hand, say they feel uncomfortable only taking in knowledge. "We would feel better if knowledge went both ways," explained one MOR.

The 3M Company has developed a mentoring program that pairs one high-level director with eight to ten Millennial new hires from outside their reporting structure. The directors, who are typically Boomers, teach Millennials those unwritten rules within 3M's culture and the Boomers "get to hear on a regular basis the thought process of the new employees," according to the director of workforce diversity, Ann Marie Gaus. "When the director goes back to his or her own team, they can be more sensitive to how this young generation thinks."

We've outlined the issue and the potential barriers to watch out for. Never fear, we've come up with solutions to help you get started engaging collaborative Millennials in beating brain drain:

• **Make it part of the job.** Organizations can engage Millennials in the collaborative side of teaching, learning, and documenting knowledge as soon as they start work. One aerospace firm assigned newly hired engineers to do a series of interviews with retiring senior engineers about landmark inventions and capture them on videotape. These videos were added to the company archives and can be accessed by anyone. The company engaged the Millennials in gathering knowledge, they used a fresh means of gathering information that could be posted to the intranet, and they recognized the importance of capturing senior engineers' insights before they walked out the door. But what makes the exercise so successful is the expectation behind it. Senior people were *expected* to do the interviews before they left the company. Junior engineers were *assigned* the job of capturing knowledge.

Air Products and Chemicals, Inc., knew that with the retirement of many engineers, they could potentially lose valuable knowledge. To be proactive, one process they implemented was what they called "Two in a Box." It's simple and of short duration for learning critical knowledge related to the job. They partner Traditionalists or Boomers with Gen X or Millennial employees to teach them about their jobs. Beyond assuring that wisdom and knowledge don't walk out the door, the program is having an unexpected impact. According to Joe Lamack, Global Career Development Program manager, "We're finding we have a better chance of retaining those who have the information *as well as* those who are receiving it, as they both realize the value and importance of sharing the knowledge."

What else can you do to make sure your culture is ready to handle knowledge transfer?

• **Don't threaten the veterans.** Or as David DeLong puts it, "make sure older workers feel the love." DeLong, the author of *Lost Knowledge: Confronting the Threat of an Aging Workforce*, suggests we reassure Traditionalists and Boomers who have knowledge to share that they aren't working themselves out of a job. "Veterans will only teach Millennials if they are convinced it's in their best interest to do so. My research shows fear of losing one's value by sharing expertise is an almost universal emotion in organizations today." DeLong offers Boston Scientific as an example of a company that had to combat this response in a plant with a history of layoffs when it needed expert machinists approaching retirement to train Millennial apprentices. The machinists' manager conducted an ongoing communication campaign making it clear repeatedly that the firm's only concern was passing on their critical skills before they left. DeLong advises, "Experienced employees need to feel they are not undermining their own value when being asked to teach others what they know."

That's fine for the older generations but what about the younger ones? We know the concept of brain drain isn't a real knee-slapper these days, and Millennials know it, too. Knowledge sharing isn't likely to happen unless we can find some engaging ways to do it. The key thought here is:

• **Knowledge transfer doesn't have to be boring.** Who's to say it can't be fun to share knowledge? If any generation will know how to turn collaborating into something fun, it's the Millennials. How about a contest? One sales organization took the whole team on a retreat to celebrate a successful year. The first night, while hanging out around the campfire, a new Millennial hire suggested they go around and each tell a story about a triumph they've had with a client as well as their biggest blunder. The Boomers and Xers were content just chugging their Coronas but went along with it anyway. The stories varied. Some were practical, some painful, and some were hilarious. But at the end of the night every salesperson, from the most seasoned to the newest hire, could agree that the stories weren't just fun, they were extremely enlightening.

We've talked about ways to create a culture that supports the sharing of knowledge and engages Millennials in the process. Next we need to think about the information itself. How do you even find out what you need to transfer? One of the best ways to get at this is to find the experts in your office and ask them our second question.

Question #2: What Gives You a Stomachache?

In working with companies that were struggling with brain drain, we tried an experiment. We took retiring Traditionalists and Baby

Boomers aside and asked them a simple question: "When you think about leaving, what gives you a stomachache?" To date, not a single person has hesitated to tell us what would worry them the most should they not show up for work one day.

- A Traditionalist operations worker for a large university campus: "We have ancient heating and cooling systems in some of our dorms. When they fail, I hate to think how anybody else would get them back online!"
- A senior Boomer sales rep: "I've been on this one client account for sixteen years. I know every single person in their purchasing department, and I know all about their budgets so I can be very strategic about pricing."
- A Gen X medical administrator: "I do all the insurance claims for three doctors; I don't honestly think they could file claims if I wasn't here."
- A Millennial associate: "This is a small company and I am the only person who keeps our Web site up-to-date. If I left they wouldn't even know how to upload my boss's weekly blog."

Savvy organizations are realizing that any generation can walk out the door with valuable knowledge. Here are steps you can take to engage the generations in creating a safety net:

- **Who needs to know what?** Don't assume only the most senior people have the most important knowledge. Identify what ideas, procedures, or practices are most critical to your success and make sure that knowledge is being put into the hands of those who need it most. That might be a Millennial. UPS understands that the relationships customers have isn't with the executives at Big Brown, it's with the folks who come through the front door of their businesses every day. When a new driver is set to take over the route of an experienced driver, he or she spends days covering that route with the existing driver getting to know the customers at each stop. UPS knows if they hand off these relationships properly, their business will flourish.

As Millennials enter your organization they will be scanning the environment for clues as to what is valued most in your culture and how to get the knowledge they need to succeed in it. That means you have to be very clear with them what knowledge is most important, why, and how to get it. You also need to be honest and . . .

• **Acknowledge what's *not* worth sharing.** Obviously not everything is important to pass along. In fact, some knowledge deserves to be dead and buried. The arrival of a fresh-faced generation is a great time to shake things up and dismantle the old structures and practices that don't work anymore. Because Millennials are problem-solvers, they will be thrilled to be assigned to find new ways of doing things. To get started, ask yourself and your team to what extent transferring knowledge to the next generation will be a spark and to what extent it will be a wet blanket. Make it OK for outgoing employees to identify practices that might be ready for the landfill. Assign them to make a list of things they would retool if they were coming in to take over this job. Be prepared for pushback. An employee who's been in the job awhile isn't going to relish admitting some aspects of it are obsolete. Praise them for being honest. For example, if an outgoing accounting supervisor tells you the new Millennial hire should take a look at why duplicate accounting records are being kept, don't say "You moron, why didn't you eliminate a lot of these yourself?" Instead, thank the person for bringing these "opportunities" to your attention and ask for more. Then let the Millennials know what things you'd like to see changed when the transition takes place.

• **Ask Millennials what *they* need to know.** Too many Boomers and Xers trying to be responsible about knowledge transfer will spend hours diagramming processes and listing procedures that need to be taught to new Millennial hires. That's fine, but don't forget to ask existing Millennials what it is they wished they had been taught when they came on board and what type of knowledge would help them do their jobs better going forward.

OK, so we've considered the culture and the knowledge itself, but that knowledge won't be shared until the generations start communicating. So far, so good. The Millennials are eager to collaborate, and the Boomers and Xers have plenty of wisdom they'd like to share, so how hard can it be? Harder than you think. Read on.

Question #3: Is Anyone Talking About It?

Generational resistance to knowledge sharing is alive and well. If you're a Traditionalist trying to educate the other generations about your company's past, the last thing you want to hear is that things will change the minute you walk out the door. If you're a Baby Boomer worried about keeping your job during an economic slowdown, the last thing you want to do is share your most valued wisdom with a bunch of upstarts who earn less and could potentially get promoted into your job. If you're a high-potential Gen Xer trying to make your mark, why would you want to step up to the next position if it meant you had to do the job the exact same way the guy did it before you? If you're a Millennial in your first professional job, this is when you want to showcase the fresh ideas you brought with you from school. It goes against the grain to do things the old way even if others think you need to learn it.

These generational attitudes are perfectly reasonable. We have to work through them if we ever hope to get the knowledge train rolling.

In a financial downturn, organizations get a break—sort of. Their best and brightest people are less likely to retire or change jobs, so it buys more time to kick knowledge sharing into high gear. However, if companies undergo layoffs they have to deal with a sudden and unforeseen loss of knowledge that can be quite damaging. And unfortunately during tough times employees become more paranoid about their jobs so they are less likely to communicate about it. Unless you can create a basis of trust among the generations, sharing what they know is never going to happen. We've been talking in this chapter about the importance of collaboration to Millennials, and this is a golden opportunity to put it into action.

• **Make knowledge sharing relevant for Millennials.** "I have a lot to teach but the Millennials just don't want to listen!" is a refrain we hear frequently from the other generations. Often the problem is we don't give them a *reason* to listen. Put information into the context of their future careers or the important skills they need to learn to get ahead. Experienced employees are repositories for decades of organizational memory. But much of it is stuff Millennials will never need to know. Why waste their time and attention span describing a former competitor that is now defunct? If you're managing or mentoring Millennials, practice self-editing. By avoiding long stories that have no relevance for the Millennials you work with, you are training them to listen when you do speak up.

Another key to fostering intergenerational dialogue is to . . .

• **Mine for silver.** It probably isn't a huge leap to imagine that most of your Traditionalists aren't hangin' with the newbies or posting comments on their Facebook wall. Yet you need people with experience to coach and train the newcomers. We recently heard a classic example of mining for silver to bridge generation gaps:

After more than thirty years of service, a highly valued employee at General Mills was up for retirement. Joe Rossini had seen so much in his years at the company and everyone he encountered was blown away by not only the breadth of his experience but the depth of his knowledge as well. He knew absolutely everything there was to know about the world of coupons. He remembered everything, from which Cheerios coupons had dropped in what newspapers in the mid-1980s to which Hamburger Helper photo drove the highest redemption rate. Talk about a loss for the company!

Rather than letting Joe simply walk out the door never to be seen or heard from again, General Mills figured out a way to keep him involved by having him help train their employees—new and old. Rossini University was born! The honored retiree now comes in for two half-day training sessions, Rossini University for new hires and Rossini Grad School for experienced employees. Joe takes employees through a basic "101 class," imparting at least a portion of the wisdom he acquired over the years and a more advanced class for experienced marketers. One Rossini Grad School student said, "He just has so much knowledge from all those years of experience. There is no way I could get access to that kind of information if it wasn't from him." A new hire university student told us, "I have heard so much about him that it was fun to finally see who he was and experience his style." And nothing gets the generations collaborating together like student T-shirts for all the participants!

In 2003 Procter & Gamble and Eli Lilly joined forces to form YourEncore, creating a pool of retired veteran scientists and engineers with specific expertise each company could call upon for temporary help. *Human Resources Executive* magazine reported in 2008 that YourEncore now boasts over twenty-eight member companies and a pool of several thousand experienced employees who can be hired for projects on an ad hoc basis. While this is a great solution for organizations experiencing brain drain that find themselves understaffed, it is also a fantastic way to provide seasoned role models and mentors who can help get the younger generations up to speed.

• **Put all hands on deck.** Knowledge retention happens best when all the generations are included, especially newly hired Millennials. If they start knowledge sharing habits early, they'll continue them throughout their careers. We found an outstanding example of this at energy giant Conoco-Phillips. The company had undergone twelve acquisitions in eleven years. They carried on operations all over the world. They faced a multitude of challenges in solving complex issues extracting oil from the ground in a variety of settings. Reinventing the wheel or repeating mistakes would be vastly expensive in such a system. But how could they share information and answers across the globe between petroleum engineers and geo-chemists who barely knew one another? As Dan Ranta, director of knowledge sharing, explained: "There was a dearth of trusted relationships. With petroleum engineers these take time to build. We wanted to shorten that time frame and get right to problem solving." The company pioneered a program that created Networks of Excellence (NOEs), formed around specific technical questions or problems. An issue is posted online as an open discussion item and anyone interested in working on the problem is invited to join. Questions are submitted from all over, and everyone who's part of the NOE can see them and comment or provide an answer. The monetary value of the problem is locked in, so participants understand the ultimate value of what they are working on. The NOE remains active until a satisfactory solution is found. The open discussion item is then "closed" and made part of the company's archives. Ranta started with a single NOE and can currently boast over 120 active networks. One ingredient that makes the process so powerful is that new generations are invited to participate right from the get-go. "We indoctrinate all new employees coming in," explained Ranta, "so participation in solving and sharing across boundaries becomes part of the culture."

Imagine the value of this process to a Millennial. They are encouraged to use their collaboration skills and allowed to participate in solving important problems. They develop networks throughout the organization. They learn from the wisdom of participants of all ages.

For many organizations one of the toughest problems in passing on knowledge is documentation. We suggest you:

• **Say good-bye to the 3-ring binder.** If Traditionalists had a procedural question they would historically head for the bookshelf with the rows of 3-ring binders. Now with the arrival of the Millennials and the explosion of technology, knowledge capture can happen right on an iPhone or BlackBerry.

Unfortunately, the generations are not in sync when it comes to choosing the best alternatives. Lockheed Martin Aeronautics noticed a generation gap when they asked soon-to-retire Boomers to pass on their expertise to younger workers. According to the *Wall Street Journal,* "The Boomers preferred PowerPoint presentations, while the younger workers favored more interactive learning methods." With so many options available you might want to put Millennials to work coming up with new processes and then mentoring others.

Darrell Burrell, training program specialist with the U.S. Nuclear Regulatory Commission, reported that his department recently acquired a communities of practice software program from Tomoye. He explained, "I run the Nuclear Safety Professional Development Program, and what the Millennials are doing with the software is capturing data that will help others coming into the organization be prepared for rotations. If you spend time in a nuclear plant in Pittsburgh, for example, you can post information for your co-workers about how things work there, where to stay, where to eat, etc., so future employees can get the information instantaneously. It can be a blog, but you can also upload documents, photos, videos, or whatever you need. The Millennials love it because, as they say: 'I don't have to ask all these people; I can just go to the site and find what I need.'" So far, the older generations aren't using it, but it's a starting place that's working so well for the Millennials it's bound to catch on.

Are you ready? What gives you a stomachache? Is anyone talking about it? These are the three questions to keep in mind when you're considering how to tap into the Millennials' desire to collaborate and stem brain drain by engaging them in knowledge transfer.

A few days after Patricia's presentation, Hugh asked her to repeat it for another department

"Great," Patricia thought resentfully. "I'll go out after twenty-seven years with the reputation for being the person who bored the younger generations to death." As she started in on her presentation she saw the same disinterested looks as before. She paused and looked out at all the youthful faces.

"There's a reason I am telling you this," she intoned. "In a few years, many of my peers and I will be gone and the mantle will pass to you. You need to understand the business strategy and our competitive strengths to survive. If you are very good at it, you will be the ones to take the company to the next level.

"There's a lot to learn," Patricia continued. "Some of it is on our server, but a lot of it is here in my head." She paused, and turned off her computer slide presentation. "You tell me. What do you want to know?"

There was a stunned silence then hands slowly started to rise. How did she move up through the ranks? Where could young employees find out more about how her department had toppled their biggest competitor? Was there any way a Millennial could get on the newly formed team to work on documenting best practices?

She fielded questions for over an hour and left the room a little breathless. Somehow Patricia had warmed up to the idea of sharing. Better yet, the younger generations were interested in learning. Telling them why it was important had done the trick. Along with asking what they wanted to know.

Just then Hugh came down the hall.

"Patricia!" he said smiling. "I'm sorry I couldn't make it. But I wanted to congratulate you. Everyone is buzzing about knowledge transfer and I have two Millennials who just told me they want to work for you! Maybe we will be able to get our arms around brain drain after all."

Patricia just smiled. She had gone from not caring about knowledge sharing to wondering how she could make it more exciting the next time.

We've covered the ways Millennials collaborate through teams, through new ways of interacting with leaders, and through the process of knowledge transfer. But there's one piece we haven't talked about yet, and that's where all this collaborating is supposed to happen. Many organizations opening the door to Millennials are about to undergo...

4) THE EXTREME OFFICE MAKEOVER

As collaborative Millennials flood into the U.S. workforce, now is a good time to take a look at the physical side of managing. Other than the addition of cubicles and a reduction in cigarette smoke, most office setups haven't evolved since the 1950s—unless you count *Successories* posters that ironically showcase concepts like "collaboration." Millennials are pushing for workspaces that are fun and creative and offer some amenities. They prefer flexible configurations that allow for different kinds of work and collaboration.

At Liberty Diversified International (LDI), they have a robust internship program. With the new generation of Millennials coming on board, the company discovered they were not excited about living and working in a cubicle. It was too quiet and way too lonely. Ann Miller, LDI's corporate culture specialist, commented, "While this was foreign to us Xers, we listened to their request and took down the cubicle walls. We couldn't believe how excited they all were to have their desks pushed together into one big pod. But what really surprised the other generations was how they worked. Managers would report to me that every time they walked by the pod they all seemed to be talking to each other. The managers couldn't figure out if they were working or not; it looked like all they were doing was socializing."

As the internship period rolled on, supervisors were pleasantly surprised to find that the work not only got done, but deadlines were met ahead of time and the results were stellar! Ann Miller pointed out, "The way they worked was so different. Most Boomers in our organization will go to the cafeteria for a fifteen-minute break at the same time every day. They do a crossword, eat a snack, socialize a little, and head back to their desks. I rarely, if ever, see a Millennial in the cafeteria. They like an office setup where they can bring the break room to their pod. We are getting amazing results by recognizing they are going to work in a completely different way."

It used to be that "flexible work arrangements" referred to alterative work hours or being wired up to work from home. Now Millennials are coming into the workplace with very different ideas about what flexibility means. "This is my office," one Millennial told us, holding out his BlackBerry. "This is *my* office," said another Millennial, pointing to his car. A Millennial recruiter laughed, "I'd have to say LinkedIn is my office."

We shake our heads at these notions, but talking to Millennials about where and how they like to work is a real eye-opener. Too often the older generations are so worried about protecting the status of the corner office and maintaining productivity they're not exactly open to new options. But a generation that has come of age operating out of Starbucks is bound to have some new ideas about what kind of spaces work best. Because of their desire to collaborate and their comfort level with working from anywhere, Millennials are challenging the way offices look and how they are arranged.

MILLENNIALS ON RECORD

"For the older generations, the status of the office meant a lot. We are perfectly fine putting a laptop in our bag, and our car becomes our workplace. We don't really strive for that window office."

—Syed Zaidi, age 26, ERS senior consultant, Deloitte and Touche, LLP

Our first reaction as we interviewed Millennials and the managers who employ them was that the office space of the future sounded chaotic and potentially expensive. When we got down to the nitty-gritty we realized the trends Millennials are ushering in are often practical, affordable, and much-appreciated by the other genera-

"You don't get an office. You get cargo pants."

tions. As you read, think about how you might be able to flex your notions of "office space."

Is Your Work Space Working?

Earlier generations believed you'd get a lot more work done at work if there were fewer distractions. Offices were silent, doors were closed, carpets had thick pads to prevent unwanted noise. Businesses looked professional. Dark paneling and plain walls made it appear you were serious about what you were doing. Conference rooms were like prison interrogation centers—little color or comfort and certainly nothing to stimulate the imagination. Get ready for a generation that likes to be inspired by the place where they sit down and plug in.

Yet few offices actually are inspiring for the collaborative new kids on the block. We recently visited the headquarters of a large multinational company and were met by the Baby Boomer who would escort us for a visit with the CEO. We stepped into a paneled private elevator that purred as it lifted us toward the thirtieth floor. Our escort explained apologetically that he didn't know if he'd be allowed to take us all the way to the CEO's office, since he was only a C–14, but that he would leave us at the desk of Rosa, the executive assistant. Sure enough, Rosa greeted us, took our coats, served us coffee on a little tray, and dismissed our C–14 as if he were the delivery boy. Then we glided down a long hall to the inner chambers. The CEO's office was large enough to house a family of twelve. Located far from the workforce below, it was hardly a setup that would encourage collaboration.

For Traditionalists and Boomers who were climbing the ladder of success, the high–up corner office seemed close to heaven. It was the Gen Xers who pushed the workplace to become less formal, opting for casual dress and more flexible styles of working and communicating. Now along come the Millennials who are going to push work*space* even further. What are the trends when it comes to creating spaces that foster teamwork and collaboration?

• **Putting play space in the workplace.** We talked earlier about teams having fun, but what about the actual physical space? Millennials don't need a piñata hanging from the ceiling, but they like spaces that inspire innovation and encourage a sense of play. Whether it's the paint, the décor, the furniture choices, or expressions of individual creativity, Millennials like to work in spaces that feel comfortable, loose, and fun. At Pixar in Emeryville, California, a lot of the animators decided early on that they didn't want to work in drab cubicles. So instead, the company found "groovy" little cottages that they bought for them. Walking through the animation department is like walking through a neighborhood for dwarves along "streets" of little houses, each with an address on the door.

- **Decent digs.** Millennials judge employers on the quality and look of the workspace. Their college dorm rooms were adorned with fridges, flat screen TVs, and sound setups that looked like recording studios. They appreciate such features as ergonomic chairs and good lighting. According to Trex Morris, America's director of real estate services for Ernst & Young, the new AT&T offices in Atlanta feature bright colors, sofas, lounge chairs, and a bar and stools "that might seem more appropriate in a social setting than a Fortune 500 office." Millennials, who mix their work lives with their personal lives 24/7 want the office to be as comfortable as home.

- **Brag about the neighborhood.** Location can be a big factor in recruiting Millennials. According to Rebecca Ryan, author of *Live First, Work Second*, three out of four Americans under twenty-eight say that where they live is as important or more important than where they work. If you're not located in a lifestyle hot spot— what research firm Knoll, Inc., calls "neighborhoods that offer lots of amenities and things to do during breaks and after work such as restaurants, bars, shops, and other places where other young, talented people are likely to be."— you may have to create new opportunities in your community.

Robert W. Baird & Co., the financial firm headquartered in Milwaukee, is one such company. While a great city, Milwaukee doesn't usually top the "Sexiest Cities to Work In" lists. However Baird has still managed to be named one of *Fortune Magazine*'s "100 Best Companies to Work For" the last six consecutive years. What have they done? Worked on how to make their community more of a "destination" for Millennials. Corporate recruiter Dana Ernst explained that Baird has been very involved in a citywide organization called FUEL Milwaukee, recognized as the largest professional network of its kind. FUEL specializes in helping companies recruit, engage, and retain talent, while offering employees everything from social events at local restaurants to business networking opportunities like a "CEOs in Conversation" program at a local performing arts center. Young hires new to Milwaukee can become instantly connected with both the community and their peers, creating a comfort level that makes them want to stay.

Decatur, Illinois, another less-than-obvious career destination, started a similar group as an offshoot of their Chamber of Commerce. Dubbed the 501 Club because social events commence promptly at 5:01 p.m., the group met such a big need it grew from thirty members to over fifteen hundred in just two years. Sponsored by leading employers like ADM, Budweiser, Caterpillar, and Decatur Memorial Hospital, the organization is free to members and has greatly increased the sense of community among the area's young professionals.

Flex Your Space

Think about the image of a classic, successful Traditionalist workspace. The entire place was built around the idea of *permanence*. Our parents and grandparents survived the Great Depression and wanted clients to be impressed with their substance and dependability. They wanted employees to gaze longingly at the spacious corner office down the hall and aspire to earn a place in it.

Flash forward to the workplace of today and permanence is becoming a thing of the past. Millennials are less interested in having a great office than in having cool tools to work with. They don't just want a single nice space to work in; they prefer a variety of styles and modes of working. Millennials want options built into the physical space that make it easy to access and engage with colleagues. A Millennial might spend an hour in the boss's office collaborating across the desk, then move to the lounge to spread out in easy chairs with laptops to pour over a project with peers. Just to break things up, they might schedule an afternoon brainstorming session over snacks in the cafeteria and finish up alone at the local bookstore café replying to e-mails.

Employees are searching for more places to gather and collaborate. Unfortunately, too many workplaces were designed with the idea that conference rooms are like condiments, a nice accent but not something you need too much of. "Great," you're thinking. "We just remodeled the office a few years ago, now we're supposed to spend more money?" But flexible spaces don't have to be expensive. Simple additions like conference chairs on wheels that can be moved around as needed or small tables that can be pulled apart or pushed together depending on the size of the group can increase the amount of usable meeting space. Conference room equipment can be designed to be more flexible, too. Why be tied to a formal projection screen if you can paint the walls a light color and project anywhere?

Consider whether you can get more use out of existing spaces. Many companies have cafeterias, patios, and auditoriums that stand empty much of the day. Often these can be easily converted to be more user-friendly... or just plain used.

The global furniture company Steelcase has studied the impact of generational differences on office design for years. They suggest that offices be separated into different "zones" that support various types of work, including quiet space for creativity and private conversations, and flexible "noisy" spaces for collaboration. That fits for Millennials, whose college libraries are often divided along the same lines. It does more than just facilitate productivity; it enables learning. According to Bruce Simoneaux, applied research consultant for Steelcase, "We've heard from younger workers that the number one way a new hire learns is from overhearing conversations of veterans on the staff. But what happens too often is companies put older, more experienced workers in enclosed offices and not only don't younger people hear their conversations, they're intimidated by these private offices and feel cut off from those people." Flexible space design allows the generations more access to one another— and more opportunities to collaborate, not just with peers but with mentors and leaders as well.

Creating spaces that allow employees to work in different ways is good for the other generations, too. We've all experienced the desire to step out of the office for a breath of fresh air, a chat, or a stroll down the hall. New options for the physical workplace will re-invigorate productivity. Here are some ideas for enhancing collaboration via your physical space:

- **Space for every generation.** Not everyone appreciates the same things. A nice desk might be important to a Baby Boomer, whereas a fast, new, and smaller laptop might be nirvana for a Gen Xer. Before you invest in improvements, survey employees on what's important. That way you get the biggest bang for your buck, and you don't waste money on initiatives that won't be appreciated.
- **Space for privacy.** Some tasks require deep concentration and some conversations between workers need to be kept confidential. Consider the Steelcase idea of zones. One zone is "a mobile work surface allowing colleagues to partner and collaborate. A lounge space creates the second zone, supporting casual interactions and private coaching. And the third zone is one where information and materials can remain confidential."
- **Space for the veterans.** Disassembling old-style office spaces can be disruptive to established employees. They may associate their current office with status and will resent having this perk removed if the objectives of a reconfigured space aren't introduced carefully. Consider letting people keep their private offices, but add small conference tables and chairs within their offices for casual meetings. Instead of taking something away, you're adding options. Talk to them about how open spaces encourage mentoring and urge them to try it out. Ron Gallo, manager of Global Portfolio Optimization for Chevron, noticed Millennials are not alone in readily accepting an open, collaborative environment. "Younger workers not long ago were in college working out in the open: they sat at Starbucks, worked on a laptop, talked on a cell phone, and drank coffee, all at the same time. So, in general they're more accepting of an open

environment. But we've got older folks that prefer the new open workspaces, too." In Houston corporate headquarters, with a mix of open workstations, private offices, and group spaces, "individuals can mentor without distracting others," says Gallo. "It's a collaborative environment that realizes people collaborate in different ways."

• **Space for Mother Earth.** The M-Factor survey showed that while 88 percent of Millennials feel environmental awareness is at least somewhat important when considering joining an organization, only 20 percent thought their company did a good job addressing it. Your space can be one of your most powerful recruiting tools. Millennials will notice small touches that make quality of life better in the workplace and for the planet. These might include "green" amenities such as opportunities to recycle, air filtration or windows that open, access to outdoor spaces for walks or lunch, workout rooms, places to store bicycles, healthy foods in the cafeteria, and choices of low-impact materials in items like carpets or paint.

Universities are leading the way in these efforts, often propelled by Millennial students. Clarke College recently hosted a water project in which, for one week, students and faculty discontinued buying bottled water and coffee and then donated the money they saved to a world water conservation effort.

If you're new to these efforts invite Millennials to lead the charge; they'll have lots of ideas and will feel good about your commitment to taking the right steps.

• **Space that's safe.** Millennials were raised hearing Amber Alerts broadcast on radio and TV and watching around-the-clock coverage of devastating school shootings such as at Columbine. They wore security bracelets at day care to prevent abduction and were hand walked to the bus stop by protective parents. While you might not give it a second thought, Millennials are conscious about workplace safety. One manager for a national retail chain that hires mostly Millennials told us how embarrassed he was when an interviewee for a job in a mall asked him what employees were supposed to do in case of a bomb

threat. "I don't know, run!?" was his flustered reply. Since 9/11, most organizations have had to be pretty knowledgeable about safety procedures, but make sure recruiters and supervisors are apprised of yours.

Collaboration. Only when you look beneath the surface do you realize what a powerful trend it is and how it is playing out in the lives of Millennials. From their desire to work in teams, to their vision of a new, more participative form of leadership, to their eagerness to contribute to the transfer of knowledge, and finally to their push to redesign the spaces in which we work, Millennials will continue to press for new and profound ways to leave their stamp on the workplace, and ideally, leave it a better place than it was when they came in.

Bonnie pushed her way into the house hauling a heavy bag of groceries. Peals of laughter erupted from the living room and she peered in to see her daughter, Rachel, and seven or eight college-age kids flopped on various pieces of furniture with laptops.

"Hi, Mom!" Rachel called out. "We're working on prep for our GRE exam. Everybody here is applying to grad school."

Bonnie remembered her strong negative reaction to Rachel working with her friend on the application essays for grad schools. Studying for the entrance exam like this was even more foreign. Some of the kids appeared to be lying down, a few wore iPods, and the noise level was significant as they laughed and gabbed. Rather than bore the group with a description of her own studying days that would have started with, "In my day...," Bonnie mused to herself how her own studying had been anything but social. The last thing she would have done was collaborate with potential competitors who would be applying to the same schools. In her day, the focus was on learning from the "expert," Mr. Stanley Kaplan and the GRE study guides he provided for a hefty fee. Now the "experts" included everyone in the room, along with the sources they could find on the Web, and all their social networking buddies working toward the same exam. Knowledge transfer would have been top-down, from the manual or instructors straight to her brain. Now this group had information flowing in from all directions, ranging from tutors to online study groups to e-mails from older friends who had taken the exam the year before.

Even the "space" had changed. Bonnie remembered sitting bolt upright under fluorescent lights in an uncomfortable kiosk at the library—something Rachel and her friends would equate to a holding cell. It was a miserable way to learn and although the hardness of the chair did keep her awake, Bonnie realized that she would have been so much happier draped over a BarcaLounger studying with her peers. These students looked relaxed and cozy as they pored over resources and compared notes. Sun came through the picture window as Rachel passed around a tray of snacks. "A few months ago I would have thought this was totally the wrong way to prepare for an exam," Bonnie acknowledged to herself. "Now I kind of wish I had collaborated like this."

And thinking of the benefits of collaboration, Bonnie realized happily she now had a team of eight to help her carry in the rest of the groceries.

CONCLUSION

Ready or not, Traditionalists, Boomers, and Xers, here they come! We've identified who the Millennials are and explored the seven trends that define the M-Factor: the role of the parents, entitlement, meaning, their great expectations, their need for speed, social networking, and collaboration. We have attempted to reveal the world of work through the eyes of a whole new generation arriving in the workplace while reflecting on the points of view of others already on board. And we have alerted the business world to how to manage the forces that will be at play in reshaping everything from how the generations work together to how workspaces are designed. Now it's up to you.

Are you willing to make room for Mom and Dad and make sense of entitlement? Are you ready to embrace the Millennials' search for meaning and manage their expectations? Are you braced for their need for speed? Are you prepared to explore the Millennials' desires

Unleashing the M-Factor in Your Organization

to collaborate? And are you set to discover the world of social net-working?

These are big challenges, and yet it's often the small ones that make or break a connection at work. The real questions might be: Are you willing to be the person who puts a stop to the negative chatter circling the office about the new Millennial hires? Are you able to put ego aside and consider that the newest generation might just have the best ideas? Are you receptive to learning from someone younger than you are, and to letting them learn from you? The arrival of a new generation in the workplace presents an opportunity to examine how we do things and perhaps test out a few new approaches that will make us even better.

Make no bones about it, Millennials have a huge role to play, too. They can set a tone of respect and willingness to listen in their new work situations. They can study the natives and learn to navigate a foreign culture with sensitivity. And maybe, once in a while, they can consider that things have been done a certain way in the past for good reasons. This will help them choose their battles wisely.

The good news is, if all the generations are ready and willing, the timing is perfect for getting workplaces all over the world to start out on the right foot and take advantage of this golden opportunity. One of our favorite findings in the M-Factor survey was that 65 percent of all respondents were excited or optimistic about the Millennials entering the workforce. The other 35 percent might need a little convincing.

In our trainer certification program, we kick off the first day with an activity that we call the Influences Icebreaker. We give participants a list of historical events that occurred during each generation's formative years and ask them to circle the ones that influenced them the most. Answers range from The Beatles and Vietnam to Britney Spears and the Oklahoma City bombing. We have found people love sharing their stories about where they were when they first glimpsed O. J. Simpson in his white Bronco or when they first watched MTV. But then we take the exercise a step further and ask participants to share how those events shaped who they are at work today. This is where we have gotten some of our richest and most memorable insights. We have heard from Traditionalists who were children during the Great Depression and how it influenced them to be loyal to employers and to Buy American. We've heard Boomers share their memories of Dr. King and the Civil Rights movement and how that still makes them believe positive change is possible. We've heard Xers talk about watching the Space Shuttle Challenger explode and how it taught them that even the most revered institutions aren't perfect. And we have heard Millennials describe where they were and what they felt on 9/11 and how the scenes of people helping one another influenced their belief that by working together we can make a difference. These dialogues are powerful and we never fail to see lightbulbs go off above people's heads as they listen to generations other than their own explain where they came from and why they see the world the way they do.

The reason these bursts of insight shine so brightly is they are personal. We think about someone from another generation with whom we've been colliding and suddenly we understand *why*. The "aha" moment is priceless! But too often at work, by the time the lightbulb goes on, a lot of damage has already been done. On the organizational level, great recruits get passed over, career paths are blocked, morale is damaged, and communication is stalled. On the personal level, confidence is damaged and trust is broken—all because we could only see through our own generational lens. Or because our motive was to prove who was right or wrong, better or worse.

The magic is to go back to the Influences Icebreaker and understand that each generation is shaped by different events and conditions that result in unique ways of looking at the world. And by seeing where the generations are coming from, we can move beyond accepting our differences, to a more powerful place where we embrace them and use them to our strategic advantage.

It's a message we hope you will continue to champion in your own organizations and personal lives, and we thank all of our dedicated clients, trainers, and partners who have helped to spread the message throughout corporate America.

In championing the generations we realize we have our work cut out for us—even *beyond* the Millennials. Lately at speeches and in interviews we've been asked more and more often, "What is the name of the generation that comes after the Millennials?" A part of us wants to answer by saying, "Wait a minute, we need to learn about the events and conditions that shape a generation before we can know who they are! The generation that comes after the Millennials is barely out of diapers. We don't know yet what will shape them but we invite you to be part of the process of getting to know yet another fascinating group of young people.

We've come to realize it's not about labeling the next generation; it's about being excited and eager to find out who they are and what makes them unique. While writing this book, David and his wife, Sharon, had a new baby girl, Sadie, and Lynne became a grandmother (although as a classic Boomer, she isn't sure yet if she'll be going by the name "Grandma"). We will watch with eager anticipation to see what this next generation will be like and how they leave their mark on the world.

How compelling it is to think that David's new baby and Lynne's grandchild will be part of a generation that benefits from a big dose of the Traditionalists' loyalty and patriotism, and will be influenced by the optimism and idealism that made Baby Boomers strive to change the world. Think what they will learn from the Generations Xers' entrepreneurial spirit and belief in balance, and from the Millennials' can-do attitude, passion to collaborate, and willingness to have fun along the way. With all these gifts, no doubt they will be able to achieve anything.

acknowledgments

More than anything else, we both feel fortunate to have been each other's friend, mentor, collaborator, and business partner for so many years. Few writers have the luxury of knowing that no matter what happens someone always has your back. Writing another book together and sharing this generational journey has been a gift.

Allan Grosh, you have been there day after day to support us and cheer us on. Your wisdom, leadership, and strategic vision are irreplaceable, and only surpassed by your patience and kindness. Thank you for believing in us, and for being a mensch.

Nancy Peterson, you came on board eight years ago and have been a dedicated, smart, and steady influence ever since. With your galaxy of skills you make our work lives easier and our work product that much better. For that we and our clients are forever grateful. Kel Gratke, whether we are on the road or in the next room, you keep the business running smoothly. We appreciate it, and our families do, too. Debra Fiterman, you made our book and our ideas better from the day you walked into our office and started shaking things up. Thank you for presenting us with new generation gaps and being willing to bridge them so beautifully. Seth Mattison, we love how you fight to be the voice of your generation. We have no doubt you will do Millennials proud as you share our insights across the country. Linda McDonald, there is no one better to have in our corner than you. You've been a feisty and caring advocate and a great friend since Day One.

Millennials on Record (MORs), while statistics help us legitimize our work, it is your voices that allow us to go beyond the numbers to the hearts and minds of a generation. Thank you for your perspectives and for opening our eyes to so many valuable lessons. Institute for Corporate Productivity (i4cp), one of the greatest challenges as authors is to prove what you believe to be true. Thank you for being the best and most professional research partner we could have asked for. Clients and certified trainers, if it weren't for you, we couldn't do what we do. While we can shed light on where the gaps are, it is all of you who have to do the heavy lifting in building the bridges. Thank you for partnering with us and for sharing the best practices that will benefit so many of our readers.

Linda Fiterman and John Rappell, just when we were feeling flat and didn't have an ounce of innovation left, you jumped in to spark the flames. Your creativity is priceless. Mark Chimsky, you are a kind man with loads of perspective on what makes authors tick and what makes books work.

Our agents Sandy Dijkstra and Jill Marsal, you continue to have the right piece of advice at the right moment. You have been tremendous help in giving this project focus and we thank you and your crew for being such insightful advisors and friends.

Matt Inman, how lucky we are to have an editor who can view the world through a Millennial's eyes and see into the written word like an old soul. Your thoughtful suggestions and wise edits have made this project a pleasure from the get-go. We feel honored to have collaborated with you.

Pat and Herb Lancaster, and Tom and Liba Stillman, as much as this book is about a new generation stirring things up, you remind us on a daily basis about the importance of respecting and learning from the generations that have gone before us. We love you. Marty Stillman, your advice has never been more on target, or more appreciated.

Friends of the generations, whether you're sharing links and blogs, or cool generational stories and stats, we have always appreciated your passion for this topic and willingness to make sure we cover it all. Please don't ever stop.

ACKNOWLEDGING MILLENNIALS ON RECORD

Our heartfelt thanks to Debra Fiterman, who interviewed our "MORs" for this book. You've been an advocate and true champion for your generation.

We are also grateful to all of the MORs who agreed to be interviewed. Whether we were able to use your name or you were required to remain anonymous, your insights and honesty added much to our understanding. Your voices speak throughout the book.

Carolyn A.
Stephanie Bononi
Andrew Boots
Meghan Bromert
Evelyn C.
Jenny D.
Elena Davert
Graton E.
Chad Fiala
Samantha Fogliano
Samantha Fryer
Archana G.
Bobbie Godbey
Greta Hanson
Nathan Hanson
Mindy Hsu
Vinnika J.
Ava Jackson

Kate Jakubas
George L.
Jonathon M.
Steve Mell
Michelle Minter
Ben Neeme
Luke Norman
Joel O.
Katy Peterson
Ryan R.
Daunielle Rasmussen
Kristin Richards
Julie Rinaldo
Rachel Rosen
Ashley Strub
Hayley S.
Michael S.
Nikki Schmidt

Tom Serres
Jack Schoonover
Julie Strand
Kate Thomas
Dale Till
Jenna Tucker
Kheang Ven
Jessica W.
Ian Winbrock
Tyson Wooters
Syed Zaid

notes

CHAPTER 2: PARENTING

20   *Traditionalists, aka "the World War II generation" . . . "were mature beyond their years in their twenties"*: Tom Brokaw, *The Greatest Generation*, (Random House, New York, 1998), p. 34.

21   *"marriage was a commitment and divorce was not an option"*: ibid., p. 231.

21   *"a time when excess not deprivation, was the rule"*: ibid., p. 65.

22   *earning them the flattering new name "Black Hawks!"*: Kay Randall, "Mom Needs an 'A': Hovering, hyper-involved parents the topic of landmark study." The University of Texas at Austin. Web. August 2008.

22   *"helicopter parenting appears to cross racial and ethnic lines, as well as socioeconomic status"*: Sharon Jayson, "Helicopter parents cross all age, social lines," *USA Today*, April 3, 2007.

24   *"the most over-managed generation of children"*: Tom Brokaw, *Boom! Voices of the Sixties* (Random House, New York, 2007), p. 577.

26   *A recent online poll by Experience, Inc.*: Business Wire. "Helicopter Parents: 25% of Parents are Overly Involved, Say College Students; Experience, Inc. Polls College Students about Parental Involvement." All Business. January 2006. Web. August 2009.

26   *over half of parents surveyed were "much more" involved with their children*: College Parents of America, "Survey of Current College Parent Experiences: Overview of Results." Web/pdf. March 30, 2006.

27   *parents were involved the "right amount"*: Kathy Wyer, "Most college freshmen like close parental involvement, survey says." *UCLA Today*, Faculty and Staff News, January 24, 2008.

27   *students who reported high levels of contact with their parents*: Elia Powers, "Involved Parents, Satisfied Students." Inside Higher Ed. November 2007. Web. June 2009.

27   *43 percent of Latino students*: Wyer, "Most college freshman like close parental involvement . . ."

29   *one in four Millennial workers consults his or her parents when making employment decisions*: "What Millennial Workers Want: How to Attract and Retain Gen Y Employees," Robert Half International and Yahoo! Hot Jobs, 2007.

30   *parents actively promoted their son or daughter for a position*: "Company recruit-
      ers see a rising level of parental involvement in collegiate job searches,"
      Michigan State University, *MSU News*, April 24, 2007.

30   *moved back home with their parents after graduation*: "2008 College Gradu-
      ates Moving Back Home in Larger Numbers." CollegeGrad.com Press
      Release, July 22, 2009.

35   *teens who wanted a job but couldn't find one*: Catherine Rampell, "Teenage
      Unemployment Rate Reaches Record High," *The New York Times*, Sep-
      tember 5, 2009, p. 1.

47   *a third of parents communicate with their college-age kids one or more times a day*:
      College Parents of America 2006 survey results.

CHAPTER 3: ENTITLEMENT

52   *The U.S. unemployment rate in 2000*: "Labor Force Statistics from the Cur-
      rent Population Survey." United States Department of Labor, Bureau of
      Labor Statistics Web site. Data extracted August 7, 2009.

53   *51 percent of 2007 grads left campus with a job in hand*: "Fewer Grads Have
      Jobs, More Headed to Grad School," National Association of Colleges
      and Employers (NACE) 2009 Student Survey findings reported in "Spot-
      light Online" at www.naceweb.org, May 13, 2009.

53   *companies surveyed were planning to hire 22 percent fewer grads*: Laura Fitz-
      patrick, "Job Forecast for College Seniors: Grimmer Than Ever," *TIME*
      magazine, March 4, 2009.

54   *U.S. unemployment rate reached 9.5 percent in June*: Bureau of Labor statistics,
      August 2009.

54   *likely to look for new jobs as soon as the downturn reversed*: "54% of Workers
      Have Aspirations to Leave Job When Recession Ends," *American Work-
      place Insights Survey*. Adecco Group North America, June 25, 2009.

54   *many industries were offering deferred start dates*: "You're hired—next year:
      The recession is changing the way American firms recruit people." *The
      Economist*, April 30, 2009.

57   *"This country has always needed a base population of cocky entrepreneurs"*: Jake
      Halpern, "The New Me Generation," *The Boston Globe*, September 30,
      2007.

58   *students took the Narcissistic Personality Inventory (NPI) between 1982 and
      2006*: "Narcissistic and Entitled to Everything!: Does Gen Y Have Too
      Much Self-Esteem?" Aspen Education Group report on the Narcissistic
      Personality Inventory of students 1982–2006, March 2007.

59   *"praise teams"*: "Employment—Being Babied: Young workers being handled
      with care, but at what cost?" *The Topeka Capital-Journal*, June 17, 2007.

59   *a box of Kleenex in my office*: Sharon Jayson, "Yep, life'll burst that self-esteem bubble." *USA Today*, February 15, 2005.

61   *"They're told they are special"*: Frank Lee, "Millennials: coming to an office near you," *St. Cloud Times*, World/Nation Section, p. 1A, July 8, 2007.

62   *students surveyed said that they expected Bs just for attending lectures*: Max Roosevelt, "Student Expectations Seen as Causing Grade Disputes," *The New York Times*, February 18, 2009.

63   *If someone goes to every class*: ibid.

65   *Children's Memorial Hospital...struggling with turnover*: Diana Halfer, Elaine Graf, and Christine Sullivan, "The organizational impact of a new graduate pediatric nurse mentoring program," *Nursing Economics*, July/August 2008.

67   *Millennials who said they were unhappy at work*: In *Plugged In: The Generation Y Guide to Thriving at Work* by Tamara Erickson; source is noted as Wilner and Singleton, *The Quarterlife Crisis: The N-Gen Transition to Adulthood*, nGenera, February 6, 2007.

CHAPTER 4: MEANING

86   *"Millennials will choose workplaces and employers"*: "Is Your Firm Ready for the Millennials?" Emory University: Knowledge@Emory online business journal, March 8, 2006.

87   *51 percent of young workers...were prepared to accept a lower wage*: "Around the Globe the Desire for Meaningful Work Triumphs Over Pay, Promotion, and Job Choices," *Kelly Global Workforce Index* findings release. Kelly Services, February 25, 2009.

87   *"The majority of the thousands of twenty-somethings I've interviewed"*: Christine Hassler, "Generation Y: Keeping Them Happy With Less Pay, More Perks," *The Huffington Post*, September 16, 2008.

90   *the number of working mothers*: Allyson Sherman Grossman, "More than half of all children have working mothers," *Monthly Labor Review: Special Labor Force Reports—Summaries*, February 1982.

90   *percentage of families living in suburbs*: Morley Winograd and Michael D. Hais, *Millennial Makeover: MySpace, YouTube, and the Future of American Politics* (Rutgers University Press, New Jersey, 2008), p. 69.

90   *amount of time Generation X children spent with significant adult role models*: ibid., p. 70.

91   *At its peak the rate*: David Crary, AP National Writer, "U.S. Divorce Rate Lowest Since 1970," SFGate.com, May 10, 2007.

92   *the art of* inspiring a shared vision *between leaders*: James M. Kouzes and Barry Z. Posner, *The Leadership Challenge*, 4th edition (Jossey-Bass, San Francisco, 2007).

96   *incoming freshmen had volunteered*: Don Tapscott, *Grown Up Digital: How the Net Generation is changing your world* (McGraw Hill, New York, 2009), p. 277.

100   *"Businesses need to think like nonprofits*: Craig and Marc Kielburger, *Me to We: Finding Meaning in a Material World* (Fireside), 2008.

111   *Millennials feel more engaged*: Bruce Tulgan, *Not Everyone Gets a Trophy: How to Manage Generation Y* (San Francisco: Jossey-Bass, 2009) pp. 77–78.

CHAPTER 5: GREAT EXPECTATIONS

144   *The U.S. high school dropout rate*: Gary Fields, "The High School Dropout's Economic Ripple Effect," *The Wall Street Journal*, October 21, 2008.

145   *Abbott Northwestern started their own training center*: "About Train to Work: Overview," Project for Pride in Living. Web. Accessed July 1, 2009.

CHAPTER 6: THE NEED FOR SPEED

163   *"They are ready, willing and able to automate"*: Roberta Chinsky Matuson, "Gen Y Greatness," *Pink* magazine. Web. Accessed August 14, 2009.

164   *"If you're willing to learn from them"*: ibid.

171   *Millennials said their age-group peers want "frequent and candid performance feedback"*: Brittany Hite, "Employers Rethink How They Give Feedback," *The Wall Street Journal*, October 13, 2008.

174   *"Think about writing an e-mail and talking on the phone at the same time"*: Jon Hamilton, "Think You're Multitasking? Think Again," NPR online, October 2, 2008.

175   *when the mind shifts back and forth it actually slows down*: Joshua S. Rubenstein, David E. Meyer, and Jeffrey E. Evans, "Executive Control of Cognitive Processes in Task Switching," *Journal of Experimental Psychology: Human Perception and Performance*, Vol. 27, No. 4, 763–797, 2001.

175   *these habits cause stress and anxiety to the brain*: Dave Crenshaw, *The Myth of Multitasking: How "Doing It All" Gets Nothing Done*, (Jossey-Bass, 2008).

187   *at the deepest part of the recession*: Judy London, "Gen Y, Which Will Rule the Global Workforce Tomorrow, Takes Lumps Today," Institute for Corporate Productivity (i4cp), *TrendWatcher* report 456, April 24, 2009.

187   *a global poll by Catalyst of high-potential employees*: "High-Potentials Still Job-Hopping," Harvard Business Publishing *The Daily Stat*. Web. August 18, 2009. (Source: "High Potentials in the Downturn: Sharing the Pain?")

CHAPTER 7: SOCIAL NETWORKING

196 *the biggest gap in communication styles*: Anthony Balderrama, "Generation Y: Too Demanding at Work," CareerBuilder.com, December 26, 2007.

206 *biggest increase in Internet use*: Sydney Jones and Susannah Fox, "Generations Online in 2009," Pew Internet and American Life Project report, January 28, 2009.

208 *they use technology to avoid difficult conversations*: "The generation gap: the real story at Ernst & Young," Ernst & Young generations study findings, 2008.

212 *Wikipedia may not be 100 percent accurate*: "Wikipedia: About," Wikipedia, the free encyclopedia at http://en.wikipedia.org, 2009.

214 *social networking tips to help parents and educators*: Derek Baird, "Social Networking Tips for Parents and Educators," Barking Robot. Web. January 2009.

216 *Facebook avoided lawsuits*: J. R. Raphael, "Facebook's Privacy Flap: What Really Went Down, and What's Next," *PC World*, February 18, 2009.

218 *Dummies books recently added*: Carolyn Abram and Leah Pearlman, *Facebook for Dummies* (Wiley Publishing, Inc., Hoboken, NJ, 2008).

219 *Companies . . . feature CEO blogs*: Jeanne C. Meister, "Learning for the Google Generation," *Chief Learning Officer*, April 2008.

CHAPTER 8: COLLABORATION

231 *leaving a job because they felt disconnected*: Diane Pardee, Amanda Watkins and Jason Chupick," 'Connection' and 'Collaboration' Drive Career Choices for Generation Y Workers, SelectMinds Study Finds," Business Wire, February 7, 2007

231 *20 percent of Millennials had already left a job*: ibid.

231 *availability of support/networking programs for employees*: ibid.

232 *"They will also bring with them"*: Diane K. Danielson, "Welcome to the Matrix: There are 76 million reasons to update your office for Gen Y," *PINK* magazine, August–September 2006.

232 *TIME magazine had an article about a moving company called Gentle Giant*: Penelope Trunk, "What Gen Y Really Wants," *TIME* magazine, July 5, 2007.

236 *At last count, 38 percent of Millennial teens in the United States are nonwhite*:, "Gen Y and the Future of Mall Retailing," Jones Lang LaSalle IP, Inc., 2002.

236 *most likely to be accepting of gay co-workers*: "How Young People View Their Lives, Futures and Politics: A Portrait of 'Generation Next'," a survey

conducted in association with: The Generation Next Initiative and Documentary produced by McNeil/Lehrer Productions, The Pew Research Center, January 2007.

243   *"working with a manager I can respect and learn from"*: "A new generation in the workforce," *Survey Generation Y*, Robert Half, 2007.

253   *companies that do a good job of knowledge retention*: "Lack of Knowledge Retention: The Hidden Cost of Corporate Downsizing," Study: Despite Correlation with Positive Market Performance, Most Companies Fail to Retain Knowledge When Workers Leave, Institute for Corporate Productivity (i4cp), February 2009.

253   *no formal knowledge-retention programs underway*: ibid.

255   *implementation of effective knowledge-retention practices*: ibid.

258   *"not undermining their own value"*: David W. DeLong, *Lost Knowledge: Confronting the Threat of an Aging Workforce* (Oxford University Press, Oxford, New York, 2004), p. 69.

263   *YourEncore now boasts over twenty-eight member companies*: Marilyn Dickey, "The Brain Drain," Human Resources Executive Online, (LRP Publications) April 2008.

265   *Boomers preferred PowerPoint presentations*: Erin White, "Age is as Age Does: Making the Generation Gap Work for You," *The Wall Street Journal*, June 30, 2008.

265   *software program from Tomoye*: Tomoye EECO, Tomoye Community Software, Tomoye Corporation, 2009.

270   *animators decided early on that they didn't want to work in drab cubicles*: "The Incredibles at Pixar," *Ain't It Cool News*, Ain't It Cool, Inc., by Harry Kowles, March 2005.

271   *new AT&T offices in Atlanta*: "Seeing Eye to Eye with Generation Y: CoreNet Global Members Share Ideas for Productivity in the Multigenerational Work Place," CoreNet Global Atlanta Chapter newsletter, Fall 2008.

271   *where they live is as important*: Rebecca Ryan, *Live First, Work Second: Getting Inside the Head of the Next Generation*, Next Generation Consulting, 2007, p. 12.

271   *"neighborhoods that offer lots of amenities"*: "Supporting Generation Y at Work: Implications for Business," Knoll, Inc., 2008.

273   *They suggest that offices be separated into different "zones"*: "Think Fast: Leveraging your most valuable assets," a Steelcase 360 article, 2007, p. 3.

273   *"the number one way a new hire learns"*: ibid.

274   *"a mobile work surface"*: ibid.

274   *"Younger workers not long ago"*: ibid.

275   *"individuals can mentor without distracting others"*: ibid., p. 4.

index

Winning the war for talent, engaging a multigenerational workforce, becoming an employer of choice, attracting (and keeping) Millennials, beating brain drain, getting the most out of every employee... These are topics that keep our clients up at night.

If you're searching for actionable, entertaining, well-researched insights on how to manage generation gaps, look no further. We have the solutions you need. Our experience with top companies gives us the background to provide you not only with information, but with ideas and answers.

Keynote Speeches

•

Workshops

•

Training

•

Trainer Certification

•

Diagnostic Tools

•

Corporate Entertainment

BridgeWorks

SOLVING THE GENERATIONAL PUZZLE

• • •

www.generations.com